Praise for Brian Leaf's *Top 50 Skills* Series

 W9-CKP-873

Top 50 Skills for a Top Score: SAT Math

"What a surprise, what a relief! An SAT guide that actually meets you where you are, talks to you with wit and compassion, and clears away the panic of test-taking. And, the writing is first-rate too. Bravo Brian Leaf."

Rebecca Pepper Sinkler, former Editor, *The New York Times Book Review*

"I enjoyed the informal writing style, and the flash cards for math are brilliant! Students are used to stacks of vocabulary words in preparation for the verbal portion of the test, why not drills on flash cards for the math section?"

Denise Brown-Allen, Ed.D., Upper School Director, The Pingry School

"If everyone starts using Brian's secrets and strategies, The College Board and ETS are going to have to rewrite the SAT!!"

Max Shelton, George Washington University, Class of 2012

Top 50 Skills for a Top Score: SAT Critical Reading and Writing

"Brian Leaf has hacked off the head of America's high school boogie man—the dreaded SAT. He clearly lays out how the test works, accessible preparation strategies, and how to maximize one's score. Any college applicant can benefit from his thoughtful and well-researched advice."

Joie Jager-Hyman, former Assistant Director of Admissions, Dartmouth College, author of *Fat Envelope Frenzy: One Year, Five Promising Students and the Pursuit of the Ivy League Prize*

"A long time ago, in an era far, far away, I took the SAT—and I can remember the pressure and anxiety of it like it was yesterday. Lucky for you modern-day seniors, Brian Leaf has written the SAT guide to end all SAT guides. He thoroughly demystifies the test and lays out the 50 skills you need to max out your score. Better yet, Mr. Leaf writes with such humor, wit, and unpretentious expertise that you'll find yourself reading this book just for fun. I did. It almost—almost—even made me want to take the SAT again."

Sora Song, Senior Editor, *Time Magazine*

"What's more scary than facing SATs? Or more boring than prepping for them? For a student swinging wildly between angst and ennui, the solution is Brian Leaf's *Top 50 Skills for a Top Score: SAT Critical Reading and Writing*. Leaf, himself a genius at connecting with teenagers, meets students at their level, and spikes every drill with common sense and comedy. I especially loved the Superbad Vocabulary section—not your usual stuffy approach to language deficit disorder. Guaranteed to relax and engage the most reluctant (or panicked) student."

Rebecca Pepper Sinkler, former Editor, *The New York Times Book Review*

Top 50 Skills for a Top Score: ACT Math

"Anyone even thinking of taking the ACT needs this short but targeted guide to the math section. You simply can't afford not to spend the time reading his laser sharp drills that break down every type of problem on the ACT, show the math behind each type, and then provide drill sections based on that skill set. Even poor math students can learn to recognize all the types of math on the ACT and learn the ropes enough to get most of the easy and medium questions right every time. Mr. Leaf's guide is even entertaining as he gives the skill sets names like "Green Circle, Black Diamond" to make it feel like you are skiing rather than slogging through lessons. If you want a short but concise guide to the ACT with every trick and mathematical explanation necessary to get a perfect score, this is the book for you. You may even actually LEARN real math in the process as Mr. Leaf's love of the subject shines through so you don't just feel you are learning for a test."

Dr. Michele Hernandez, author of the bestselling books *A is for Admission*, *The Middle School Years*, **and** *Acing the College Application*

"Brian Leaf knows how to talk with students and in his book, *Top 50 Skills for a Top Score: ACT Math*, you can hear his voice loud and clear. Students who follow Brian's "Mantras" and work through the practice questions will gain confidence in their work, as well as improve their ACT scores."

Barbara Anastos, former Director, Monmouth Academy

"Feels like you have an insider divulging secrets from behind the walls of the ACT! At times going so far as to circumvent the math skills themselves, Brian gives practical tips and tricks specifically designed to outwit the ACT's formula, and he does it all with a sense of humor and fun. Nice job!"

Danica McKellar, actress (*The Wonder Years***,** ***West Wing***) and mathematician and author of** *New York Times* **bestsellers** *Math Doesn't Suck* **and** *Kiss My Math*

Top 50 Skills for a Top Score: ACT English, Reading, and Science

"This book is a good read even if you *don't* have to take the ACT."

Edward Fiske, author of the bestselling college guide, the *Fiske Guide to Colleges*

"The **specific** skills needed for the ACT, confidence building, stress-management, how to avoid careless errors . . . this book has it covered!"

Laura Frey, Director of College Counseling, Vermont Academy
Former President, New England Association for College Admission Counseling

McGraw-Hill's Top 50 Skills for a Top Score:
SAT Critical Reading and Writing

Brian Leaf, M.A.

New York | Chicago | San Francisco | Lisbon | London | Madrid |
Mexico City | Milan | New Delhi | San Juan Seoul |
Singapore | Sydney | Toronto

The McGraw·Hill Companies

Library of Congress Cataloging-in-Publication Data

Leaf, Brian.
    McGraw-Hill's top 50 skills for a top score: SAT critical reading and
writing Brian Leaf.
        p. cm.
    "Over 400 SAT questions; 150 SAT Vocabulary Flashcards; Bonus Section:
Writing The Perfect 12 Essay; Superbad Vocabulary: Watch Movies and
Learn New SAT Vocab."
    Includes bibliographical references and index.
    ISBN-13: 978-0-07-161395-8 (alk. paper)
    ISBN-10: 0-07-161395-1 (alk. paper)
    1.   SAT (Educational test)—Study guides. 2.   Universities and
colleges—Examinations—Study guides. 3.   English language—Composition
and exercises—Examinations—Study guides. 4.
Reading—Examinations—Study guides.   I. Title. II. Title: Top fifty for
a top score SAT critical reading and writing.
    LB2353.57.L43 2008
    378.1'662—dc22

                                                           2008051613

Copyright © 2010 by Brian Leaf. All rights reserved. Printed in the United
States of America. Except as permitted under the United States Copyright Act
of 1976, no part of this publication may be reproduced or distributed in any
form or by any means, or stored in a database or retrieval system, without the
prior written permission of the Publisher.

    6 7 8 9   QDB/QDB   0 1 4 3

ISBN: 978-0-07-161395-8
MHID: 0-07-161395-1

Printed and Bound by Quad/Graphics/Dubuque

McGraw-Hill books are available at special quantity discounts to use as
premiums and sales promotions, or for use in corporate training programs.
To contact a representative please e-mail us at bulksales@mcgraw-hill.com.

Contents

How to Use This Book vi
Easy, Medium, Hard, and Guessing vii
About Brian Leaf, M.A. viii
Acknowledgments ix

Pretest 1

Top 50 Skills

Sentence Completion
Skill 1   Don't Be Such a <u>Blank</u> 14
Skill 2   This Suit Is NOT Black 16
Skill 3   Positive, Negative, or Neither 18
Skill 4   SAT Crashers Rule #4: 20
            Process of Elimination
Skill 5   Two Blanks 22
Skill 6   Vocab I: Compliment or Insult 24
Skill 7   Vocab II: Superbad Vocabulary 26
Skill 8   Vocab III: Deodorant and 30
            Spanish Class
Skill 9   Vocab IV: Splitting Words 32
Skill 10   Couples Counseling 34
Skill 11   How to Be a Sentence 36
            Completion Master

Reading Comprehension
Skill 12   Italics 40
Skill 13   The SAT Reading Meditation 42
Skill 14   "Plethora" Most Nearly Means 44
Skill 15   Direct Info 46
Skill 16   What Are You Trying to "Suggest"? .. 48
Skill 17   ASS of U and ME 50
Skill 18   Some Attitude 52
Skill 19   Two Passages 54
Skill 20   Main Idea 56
Skill 21   Gretchen Is "Such" a Good Friend .. 58
Skill 22   Parallel 62
            Special Section: How to Read 64
Skill 23   How to Be a Reading Ninja 66
            Alternate Nostril Breathing and 70
            Meditation

Writing Multiple-Choice
Skill 24   Subject/Verb Agreement 72
Skill 25   Subject/Verb Agreement Tricks 74

Skill 26   Pronoun Clarity and Agreement 76
Skill 27   Correct Transition Word 78
Skill 28   Brave, Honest, and Relaxed 80
Skill 29   Comparison 82
Skill 30   Correct Preposition 84
Skill 31   Adverbs End in "ly" 86
Skill 32   I vs. Me 88
Skill 33   A Few More Rules 90
Skill 34   Direct, to the Point, Not Redundant .. 92
Skill 35   Misplaced Phrases 94
Skill 36   Jedi Master Yoda 96
Skill 37   Editing Paragraphs 98
Skill 38   How to Think Like a 100
            Grammar Genius

Essay
Skill 39   Brainstorm 106
Skill 40   Brain Freeze Help 108
Skill 41   Outline 110
Skill 42   Write Your Intro 112
Skill 43   Transition Sentences 114
Skill 44   Body Paragraph I 116
Skill 45   Body Paragraph II 118
Skill 46   Conclusion 120
Skill 47   Other Stuff That Matters 122
Skill 48   Proofread 124
Skill 49   How to Be a Writing Monster 126
Skill 50   Brian's Friday Night Spiel: 130
            Recommendations for the Days
            Preceding the Test

Bonus Skill: Writing The Perfect 12 Essay 132
Easy, Medium, Hard, and Guessing Revisited .. 136
Now What? 137
Posttest 138
Solutions 148
Vocabulary Flash Cards

How to Use This Book

It's simple. The questions that will appear on your SAT are predictable, and in this book, I will teach you exactly what you need to know. I will introduce each topic and follow it with drills. After each set of drills, check your answers. Read and reread the solutions until they make sense. They are designed to simulate one-on-one tutoring, as if I'm sitting right there with you. Reread the solutions until you could teach them to a friend. In fact, do that! My students call it "learning to channel their inner Brian Leaf." There is no better way to learn and master a concept than to teach it!

Any new concept or question type that you master will be worth 10 or more points toward your SAT score. That's the plan; it is that simple.

This book is filled with SAT Reading/Writing Mantras. They tell you what to do and when to do it. This is the stuff that Paula, who got perfect 800s, does automatically. The Mantras teach you how to think like her.

"Sounds good, but the SAT is tricky," you say. It is, but we know their tricks. Imagine a football team that has great plays, but only a few of them. We would watch films and study those plays. No matter how tricky they were, we would learn them, expect them, and beat them. SAT prep works the same way. You will learn the strategies, expect the SAT's tricks, and raise your score. Now, go learn and rack up the points!

Easy, Medium, Hard, and Guessing

The SAT is not graded like an English test at school. If you got only half the questions right on your sophomore year English final, that'd be a big fat F. On the SAT, half the questions right is about a 500, the average score for students across the country. If you got 75% of the questions right, that'd be a C in school, but almost a 600 on the SAT, the average score for admission to schools like Goucher and University of Vermont. And 89% correct, which is a B+ in school, is a beautiful 700 on the SAT, and about the average for students who got into Georgetown, U.C. Berkeley, Emory, and Wesleyan.

Use the above info to determine how many questions you need to answer on the SAT. The sentence completion and writing questions are organized in order of difficulty, from easiest to hardest. (The reading comprehension questions are not.) If you want half correct, or 70% correct, don't rush through the easies just to get to the hard ones. In school you might need to finish tests to do well; here you do not. You need to get to the very hardest questions only if you are shooting for 700+.

In this book, the drills that follow sentence completion and writing skills are also arranged easiest to hardest. Knowing the level of difficulty of a question is important. The easy questions are worth just as much as the hard ones. So don't rush and risk a careless error just to reach the hard questions. If a question seems hard, take another look for what you are missing. Ask yourself, "Which Skill can I use? What is the easy way to do this question?" After you complete this book, you will know!

Guessing? Don't randomly guess. But if you are unsure of a question, sometimes you can get it right by the process of elimination. When you can confidently eliminate at least one answer choice, take an educated guess. If you get it right, you gain four times as much as you lose if it's wrong. So educated guesses pay off. Of course, when you have completed this book, you'll rarely need to guess!

About Brian Leaf, M.A.

Six, maybe seven, people in the world know the SAT like Brian Leaf. Most are under surveillance in Princeton, NJ. Brian alone is left to bring you this book.

Brian has seen the SAT from every angle, even teaching yoga to the test makers at ETS Corporation. You are about to find out what Brian learned from them while they slept in deep relaxation.

Brian is the author of McGraw-Hill's *Top 50 Skills* SAT and ACT test-prep series. He is also the author of *Defining Twilight: Vocabulary Workbook for Unlocking the SAT, ACT, GED, and SSAT* (Wiley, 2009). Brian is Director of the *New Leaf Learning Center* in Western Massachusetts. He teaches SAT, PSAT, and ACT prep to thousands of students from throughout the United States. (For more information, visit his website www.BrianLeaf.com.) Brian also works with the Georgetown University Office of Undergraduate Admissions as an Alumni Interviewer.

Acknowledgments

Special thanks to all the students of New Leaf Learning Center for allowing me to find this book. Thanks to my agent Linda Roghaar and my editor at McGraw-Hill, Anya Kozorez. Thanks to Pam Weber-Leaf for great editing tips, Julie Leaf for sentence completion material, Zach Nelson for sage marketing advice, Ian Curtis for assiduous proofreading, Kyle Rodd for his encyclopedic vocabulary, Manny and Susan Leaf for everything, and of course, thanks most of all to Gwen and Noah for time, love, support, and, in the case of Noah, hexagon finding and rejuvenating watermelon sandwiches.

Thanks also to the following individuals who generously allowed me to use their work as reading passages: The Coen Brothers (Skills 18 and 21), Emma Sakson (Pretest), Kyle Tucker (Writing the Perfect 12 Essay), David Rice (Pretest, Posttest III, Skill 15), Ian Curtis (Skills 17 and 23, Writing the Perfect 12 Essay), Colette Husemoller (Skill 14, How to Read, Skill 20, Posttest III), Noah Dirks (Skill 37), Alex Milne (Essay Skills, Posttest I), Manpriya Samra (Skill 13: Drill 2), and Danielle Keith (Posttest II).

Pretest

This pretest contains questions that correspond to our 50 Skills. Take the test, and then check your answers in the 50 Skill sections that follow.

> Each sentence below has one or two blanks, each blank indicating that something has been omitted. Beneath each sentence are five sets of words labeled A through E. Choose the word or set of words that, when inserted in the sentence, best fits the meaning of the sentence as a whole.

① Ryan's oral presentation on skiing was _____, full of liveliness and zeal.

  Ⓐ verbose

  Ⓑ inaudible

  Ⓒ animated

  Ⓓ hesitant

  Ⓔ lackluster

② Though occasionally he is on time, nine days out of ten, Jimmy arrives _____.

  Ⓐ early

  Ⓑ tardy

  Ⓒ promptly

  Ⓓ rationally

  Ⓔ convincingly

③ Even at age two, Amrita moved with a _____ gait, gracefully handling hills, rocks, and uneven terrain.

  Ⓐ rational

  Ⓑ rocky

  Ⓒ mediocre

  Ⓓ difficult

  Ⓔ smooth

④ A scientist must stay alert; sometimes new technologies emerge from _____ instead of from planned experiments.

  Ⓐ collaboration

  Ⓑ persistence

  Ⓒ accidents

  Ⓓ forecasts

  Ⓔ laziness

⑤ The mindfulness program was designed to teach patients in remission from major depression to _____ awareness of their thoughts, feelings, and sensations in a nonjudgmental and _____ way.

  Ⓐ cultivate . . nonreactive

  Ⓑ lose . . unbiased

  Ⓒ reduce . . safe

  Ⓓ build . . lavish

  Ⓔ grow . . deleterious

⑥ Fans of the TV show *The OC* argue that critics who decry the show as _____ have not understood its deeper meaning and social significance.

  Ⓐ insightful

  Ⓑ profound

  Ⓒ alleviating

  Ⓓ vapid

  Ⓔ lucid

7 The primary purpose of the study was to find _____ proof; Salazar wanted to demonstrate that the findings of the original investigation were indisputable.

Ⓐ incontrovertible

Ⓑ terminable

Ⓒ supple

Ⓓ imminent

Ⓔ pertinent

8 Nita observed the deep connections that existed between the members of the band, and yearned for that kind of _____ in her life.

Ⓐ treacle

Ⓑ fellowship

Ⓒ facile

Ⓓ requiem

Ⓔ alleviation

9 Certain types of cats are _____, and never leave the ground, while others climb trees to stalk prey.

Ⓐ philanthropic

Ⓑ phobic

Ⓒ sympathetic

Ⓓ terrestrial

Ⓔ anachronistic

10 The mayor was considered _____ by the council, who believed that she would have a(n) _____ term in office.

Ⓐ grating . . successful

Ⓑ reckless . . dangerous

Ⓒ kind . . notorious

Ⓓ asocial . . amicable

Ⓔ conventional . . established

11 The counselor was concerned by Jenna's _____ comportment; she hardly acknowledged her peers and seemed unconcerned about school.

Ⓐ saccharine

Ⓑ flippant

Ⓒ apathetic

Ⓓ baneful

Ⓔ erroneous

The passages below are followed by questions based on their content; questions following a pair of related passages may also be based on the relationship between the paired passages. Answer the questions on the basis of what is <u>stated</u> or <u>implied</u> in the passages and in any introductory material that may be provided.

The following passages consider the roles of two leaders of a group of plane crash survivors on an island.

Passage 1

Transformed by the plane crash and reborn on the island, John Locke is the true leader of the survivors of Oceanic 815. Once paralyzed and struggling with inner and outer demons, Locke
5   stood up from the crash on the beach and was able to walk. This physical epiphany restored his faith in people and changed his philosophy on life completely. This "man of faith" leads his fellow survivors on the path that saved him—
10 the path of the island. Now a strong believer in the power of the island, Locke knows that the place where they are stranded has a purpose for everyone. Following the will of the island, Locke guides others who are lost as he once
15 was, showing them hope for the future and a chance to start anew.

Passage 2

From the moment Oceanic Flight 815 crashes into the island, Dr. Jack Shepherd secures himself as the preeminent leader of the group of
20 survivors. A successful surgeon with a troubled history, Jack is a man based on principles and fact, giving his fellow survivors a sense of realistic optimism and security during a time of confusion and chaos. With a heavy emphasis
25 on logic and reason, Jack avoids hokey mysticism. Confronted by the mysterious and inexplicable challenges that the island presents him, he shows his leadership qualities in the democratic decisions that he makes in the best
30 interest of the group and for the ultimate goal of getting everyone rescued.

⑫ The passages share the common aim of

Ⓐ telling the story of the plane crash of Flight 815

Ⓑ analyzing the anatomy of a leader

Ⓒ describing the path of the island

Ⓓ identifying the leader on the island

Ⓔ describing inexplicable challenges faced on the island

⑬ The primary purpose of Passage 2 is to

Ⓐ tell the story of Oceanic Flight 815

Ⓑ demonstrate why Jack Shepherd is the true leader of the survivors

Ⓒ profile the personality of Jack Shepherd

Ⓓ examine the theme of challenge

Ⓔ argue for the merits of logic and reason

⑭ In Passage 1, line 13, "will" most nearly means

Ⓐ testament

Ⓑ stubbornness

Ⓒ being

Ⓓ ego

Ⓔ desire

⑮ Passage 2 indicates that the principle to which Shepherd is most loyal is

Ⓐ leadership

Ⓑ optimism

Ⓒ chaos

Ⓓ reason

Ⓔ democracy

⑯ The two passages suggest that a leader must do all of the following EXCEPT

Ⓐ inspire followers

Ⓑ govern democratically

Ⓒ provide hope

Ⓓ have faith in others

Ⓔ attempt to provide safety

⑰ In lines 13 to 16, the author of Passage 1 makes the assumption that

Ⓐ the survivors want to start anew as John Locke did

Ⓑ John Locke was once paralyzed

Ⓒ John Locke feels no hope

Ⓓ Jack Shepherd was a successful surgeon

Ⓔ Jack Shepherd makes democratic decisions

⑱ The author of Passage 1 would most likely regard Dr. Jack Shepherd with

Ⓐ absolute puzzlement

Ⓑ unabashed contempt

Ⓒ amusement

Ⓓ qualified disapproval

Ⓔ general admiration

⑲ The author of Passage 2 would most likely regard John Locke with

Ⓐ reverence

Ⓑ indifference

Ⓒ skepticism

Ⓓ caustic abhorrence

Ⓔ bitter jealousy

This passage is adapted from a film review written in 2006.

The most distinctly American of all genres, the Western has evolved and changed greatly over the past sixty years. After an initial "rebirth,"
marked by John Ford's *Stagecoach*, the genre's
5   moral conflicts and dominant ideologies have grown ever more complicated. We can see this progression in the contrast between the gloomy and existentially aimless *Dead Man* (1995) and the relatively idealistic and naïve *Stagecoach*
10 (1939). From one to the other, the myth of pure masculinity has become convoluted, the male hero less omnipotent, the not always moral White settler less a symbol of "Family Values," and America less of a pristine, idealized dream.
15 However, both films still adhere to some defining genre conventions, both aesthetically and thematically, so some aspects remain the same.

A close examination of the following points will
20 be adequate to illustrate this change. We shall see what form the roles and portrayals of Indians, women, white civilization, violence, and the hero's masculinity and mission take in each film. In the time between *Stagecoach* and
25 *Dead Man*, encompassing the bulk of WWII and the entirety of war in Vietnam, each category has grown progressively darker and less supportive of an idealized notion of "America the Beautiful." Jim Jarmusch's *Dead*
30 *Man*, featuring an effete, nearly-albino Johnny Depp as a banker named William Blake, is part of a larger trend that aims to besmirch a long-established Western legend that *Stagecoach* unambiguously supports. As the Western
35 serves largely to present a certain image of this country's foundations and of the men who laid them, these changes are significant not only within the film, but also as they serve to redefine film's role in society.

20 The passage is best described as
(A) an illustration of an ongoing relationship
(B) an introduction to a character
(C) a social commentary on the Western genre
(D) a nostalgic depiction of a Western hero
(E) a story of how one movie inspired another

21 In line 13, the quotation marks around the words "Family Values" serve to
(A) criticize the Western genre
(B) indicate an irony in the meaning of the words
(C) emphasize the uniqueness of the author's writing
(D) support the common use of the words
(E) emphasize that the words would be emphasized if read aloud

22 Which statement about Westerns, if true, detracts most from the author's assertions expressed in lines 15 to 18 ("both films . . . same")?
(A) Both films follow a similar style.
(B) Both films examine the theme of love and loss.
(C) *Dead Man* and *Stagecoach* each stick to predictable Western patterns.
(D) *Dead Man* and *Stagecoach* examine different subject matter.
(E) The films were filmed half a century apart.

23 In line 20, "this change" refers to
(A) the beginning and end of the Vietnam war
(B) the different representations depicted in the two films
(C) the loss of American values
(D) the changing role of film in society
(E) the mission of women

The following sentences test your ability to recognize grammar and usage errors. Each sentence contains either a single error or no error at all. No sentence contains more than one error. The error, if there is one, is underlined and lettered. If the sentence contains an error, select the one underlined part that must be changed to make the sentence correct. If the sentence is correct, select choice E. In choosing answers, follow the requirements of standard written English.

24 Even after she had healed physically, she <u>wants</u> somewhere <u>to heal</u>
        A   B

emotionally, and <u>chose</u> Winston College
              C

<u>for its</u> small community. <u>No error</u>
 D   E

25 At seven <u>in the morning</u> each and
    A   B

every day, Jimmy, with his closest

friends, <u>walk</u> the long way <u>to</u> school.
       C   D

<u>No error</u>
 E

26 <u>Though</u> George and Sam spent all
    A

day surfing together <u>in</u> Costa Rica, <u>he</u>
               B   C

did not <u>go to</u> the party at night. <u>No error</u>
       D   E

27 Although <u>it</u> is healthy, calming,
     A   B

and energizing, daily exercise,

<u>such as swimming</u>, walking, or biking,
           C

<u>is recommended</u> by doctors. <u>No error</u>
     D   E

28 This book <u>will help</u> you <u>confidently</u>
          A   B

answer sentence completion <u>questions</u>,
                   C

reading comprehension questions,

writing multiple-choice questions,

and <u>to write</u> the essay. <u>No error</u>
     D   E

29 The music <u>of</u> *The Matt Oestreicher Band*
        A

<u>sometimes called *The* MOB</u> <u>is</u> known for its
        B   C

uplifting effect and is often compared to

the <u>performer Krishna Das</u>. <u>No error</u>
       D   E

30 <u>By practicing</u> meditation every day, Rihana
      A

does not get obsessed <u>on</u> details
              B

and <u>therefore</u> experiences increased
     C

<u>peace and comfort</u>. <u>No error</u>
   D   E

31 Every day I walked <u>for</u> over an hour
        $\overline{}$A

down the Avenue Jean-Médecin <u>through</u>
       B   C

the <u>slow progressing</u> construction.
       D

<u>No error</u>
    E

The following sentences test correctness and effectiveness of expression. Part of each sentence or the entire sentence is underlined; beneath each sentence are five ways of phrasing the underlined material. Choice A repeats the original phrasing; the other four choices are different. If you think the original phrasing produces a better sentence than any of the alternatives, select choice A; if not, select one of the other choices.

In making your selections, follow the requirements of standard written English; that is, pay attention to grammar, choice of words, sentence construction, and punctuation. Your selection should result in the most effective sentence—clear and precise, without awkwardness or ambiguity.

---

32 Excited about our advancements, the school board <u>granted Khalif and I the funding to continue</u> our research for another two years.

Ⓐ granted Khalif and I the funding to continue

Ⓑ granted Khalif and me the funding to continue

Ⓒ granted Khalif and myself the funding to continue

Ⓓ granted myself and Khalif the funding to continue

Ⓔ granted us, Khalif and I the funding to continue

33 Nearly all of the critics agree that of the author's two published novels, <u>the first is the more readable</u>.

Ⓐ the first is the more readable

Ⓑ the first is the most readable

Ⓒ the first is of the two most readable

Ⓓ the first is the more readable than the second one is

Ⓔ the first one are more readable

34 Madonna released her first album <u>and the year was 1983</u>.

Ⓐ and the year was 1983

Ⓑ and it was 1983

Ⓒ when it was 1983

Ⓓ in 1983

Ⓔ it being 1983

35 After marching three hours in direct sun, <u>the locker room was where the band went</u> for a break from the heat.

Ⓐ the locker room was where the band went

Ⓑ the locker room was gone to be the band

Ⓒ the band went to the locker room

Ⓓ the band's locker room was where they went

Ⓔ the locker room was the place gone to by the band

36 If you want to bake good cookies, <u>the oven should be preheated</u> for several minutes.

Ⓐ the oven should be preheated

Ⓑ it's a good idea for the oven to be preheated

Ⓒ consider the preheating of the oven

Ⓓ the preheating of the oven is a good idea

Ⓔ you should preheat the oven

37 Which of the following is the best way to revise and combine the sentences reproduced below?

Professor Chen is a great instructor. He is known for his lucid explanations of even the most complex topics.

(A) Being a great instructor; lucid explanations for even the most complex topics are what Professor Chen is known for.

(B) A great instructor, Professor Chen is known for his lucid explanations of even the most complex topics.

(C) As being a great instructor, Professor Chen is known for his lucid explanations of even the most complex topics.

(D) Professor Chen is known for his lucid explanations of even the most complex topics, he is known to be a great instructor.

(E) As a great instructor; Professor Chen is known for his lucid explanations of even the most complex topics.

38 The protagonist of novelist Ahmadou Kourouma's first book was a <u>character which enabled</u> Kourouma to express his criticism of post-colonial governments in Africa.

(A) character which enabled

(B) character, she enabled

(C) character, she enables

(D) character who enabled

(E) character that was enabling

Skills 39 to 49: Essay
See Essay prompt on next page.

50 The night before the test you should

(A) stay up all night studying

(B) go to Jules' huge party

(C) get answers from someone who is 18 hours ahead in Australia and already took the test

(D) have a nice dinner, relax, go to bed at a reasonable hour

(E) spend time with your most freaked out grade-mongering friends

Essay

The essay gives you an opportunity to show how effectively you can develop and express ideas. You should, therefore, take care to develop your point of view, present your ideas logically and clearly, and use language precisely.

Your essay must be written on the lines provided on your answer sheet—you will receive no other paper on which to write. You will have enough space to write if you write on every line, avoid wide margins, and keep your handwriting to a reasonable size. Remember that people who are not familiar with your handwriting will read what you write. Try to write or print so that what you are writing is legible to those readers.

Important Reminders:

- **A pencil is required for the essay.** An essay written in ink will receive a score of zero.
- **Do not write your essay in your test book.** You will receive credit only for what you write on your answer sheet.
- **An off-topic essay will receive a score of zero.**

You have 25 minutes to write an essay on the topic assigned below.

Think carefully about the issue presented in the following excerpt and the assignment below.

> Economist Adam Smith espoused the idea that rational self-interest, pursued while adhering to moral obligations, leads to economic prosperity for all. In other words, he believed that if everyone is basically moral and rational and pursues what is best for them, then society will thrive.

Assignment: Does each individual pursuing self-interest best ensure the success of a society? Plan and write an essay in which you develop your point of view on this issue. Support your position with reasoning and examples taken from your reading, studies, experience, or observations.

Top 50 Skills: Sentence Completion

Each reading section of the SAT begins with a page of "sentence completion" questions. You are given a sentence with a missing word, and you have to choose the best word to fill the blank. These are a huge opportunity to gain points. The system described in the next 11 Skills will help you work more quickly, avoid careless errors, and get more questions right. Basically, any extra question that you get right will earn you 10 more points on your score.

Sentence completion questions are always organized from easiest to hardest. In each group of sentence completion questions, the first third of the questions are easy, the middle bunch are medium, and the last third are hard. The easy questions are worth just as much as the hard ones, so don't rush and risk a careless error just to reach the hard questions. Remember, you need to get to the hardest questions only if you are shooting for 700+.

Being aware of the order of difficulty is also important because easy questions are designed to be easy—easy to understand, easy to get right. Therefore, the correct answer choice for an easy question will not be a tough vocab word that you don't know. It will be an easy word that you've seen many times. The answer to a hard question, on the other hand, could be an obscure vocab word. If you have a hard question down to two choices and have nothing else to go on, choose the harder word or the simple word that has an unusual alternate meaning.

Don't Be Such a <u>Blank</u>

Here we go. Sentence completion step 1:

Read the sentence, saying "blank" when you get to a _____.

Then **before** you look at the answer choices, think of a word to fill the blank. Don't look at the answer choices until you have a word in mind. If you go straight to the choices, you can be tricked and seduced by a word that seems to fit the sentence but does not actually work for the blank.

The best way to choose a word is to borrow one right from the sentence. The sentences are designed to describe and define the missing word. In fact, many times the blank is followed by a phrase that defines the word that we need. This is an invitation to be lazy, to borrow a word right from the sentence.

Let's try this on the Pretest question.

1. Ryan's oral presentation on skiing was _____, full of liveliness and zeal.

   (A) verbose   (B) inaudible   (C) animated   (D) hesitant   (E) lackluster

Solution: What word would fit that blank? Rather than think of one ourselves, which takes time and could be off from the intention of the sentence, we pluck one right out of the sentence:
Ryan's oral presentation on skiing was <u>lively</u>, full of liveliness and zeal.

Choosing a word right from the sentence keeps us in line with the meaning of the sentence.

Now try the choices. Cross out any choices that definitely do not mean "lively." Then choose the best from the words that are left.

(A) ~~verbose~~—Nope, "verbose" means "long-winded" or "wordy."
(B) ~~inaudible~~—Nope, "inaudible" means "not hearable" or "impossible to hear."
(C) animated—Yes, "animated" means "lively."
(D) ~~hesitant~~—Nope, "hesitant" means "tentative" or "uncertain."
(E) ~~lackluster~~—Nope, "lackluster" means "bland."

Correct answer: C

SAT Reading/Writing Mantra #1
Read the question and think of a word you'd like to see to fill the blank.
Choose a word right from the sentence when possible.

Let's practice.

Don't Be Such a <u>Blank</u> Drills

Choose a word to fill each blank. Pluck out a word right from the sentence when possible. Remember, this is not a time for creativity. In this drill I am not giving you answer choices. The goal here is just to practice choosing a word to fill the blank. We'll select from answer choices later.

Easy

❶ Clients feel that Manny has a great combination of _____ and _____: he is both hard working and very reliable.

❷ Amit is so _____; he is always on time.

❸ Michael Jordan was the best ever; he had the perfect _____ of skills, ranging from speed and agility to strength.

❹ Kayla's description of skiing was _____, full of liveliness and zeal.

Medium

❺ Some animals seem _____ to onlookers who mistake fear for aggression.

❻ Brian's book is both _____ and _____: though hilarious, it is also the most effective book on the market.

❼ Ali is not a typical young person; in the 12 months that I have known her, I have witnessed how truly _____ she is.

❽ Many teens are _____ by peer pressure, afraid of what others think.

❾ Anna appreciated Georgetown for its close-knit community and the intimacy of its _____ classes.

❿ Senaii is very strong in acting, painting, singing, and other _____.

This Suit Is NOT Black

If I say "Lucia is quite _____, though she can be pretty wild, too," you know that we need a word that means the opposite of "wild," let's call it "not wild." So sometimes to fill the blank, we want a word that is the opposite of the one we pluck out. We can usually recognize these because there is a word such as "but," "although," "though," "however," or "yet" that tells us that the two parts of the sentence are opposites.

Let's look at the question from the Pretest.

2. Though occasionally he is on time, nine days out of ten, Jimmy arrives _____.

    (A) early   (B) tardy   (C) promptly   (D) rationally   (E) convincingly

Solution: Key words such as "but," "although," "though," "however," or "yet" indicate that we want the opposite of the word or phrase that we pluck out. In this sentence, "though" tells us that he is not usually "on time." Therefore, he is usually the opposite of "on time"; he is "not on time." He is "late." "Late" is easy to come up with, but if it isn't, just stick to "not on time," and don't even bother brainstorming for a concise word; just go to the choices, looking for "not on time." The closer you can stay to the words in the sentence, the better chance you have. Don't be a hero here; keep it simple. Then cross out choices that definitely do not mean "late."

(A) ~~early~~—Nope, we want the opposite of "early."
(B) tardy—Yes, "tardy" means "not on time" or "late."
(C) ~~promptly~~—Nope, "promptly" means "on time."
(D) ~~rationally~~—Nope, "rationally" means "reasonably" which is unrelated to "late."
(E) ~~convincingly~~—Nope, "convincingly" means "persuasively" which is unrelated to "late."

Correct answer: B

Key Words to Watch For		
But	Except	Instead of
Although	Even though	Unless
Though	Nevertheless	Far from
However	Ironically	Instead of
Yet	Despite	
While	In spite of	

SAT Reading/Writing Mantra #2
Watch for keywords ("but," "however," "though". . .) that tell you to look for an opposite.

This Suit Is NOT Black Drills

Choose a word to fill each blank. If possible, pluck a word right out of the sentence, and when you see a key word such as "but," "however," or "though," decide if you want the opposite. The goal here is to practice choosing the word to fill the blank. We'll start selecting from answer choices in the next section.

Easy

❶ Though Zoe was known to be _____, she was actually quite social.

❷ Many teens like hip-hop music; however, Diego _____ hip-hop, preferring classical music.

❸ Edward was the most adept chess player at Northampton High School, but he is _____ at Princeton University.

❹ Both in school and on the field, John is so _____ that his friends count on him never to lie.

❺ Marjorie has none of her sister's spitefulness; she is always _____.

❻ Ryan always showed up _____ to work, never lazy or complaining.

Medium

❼ While Sora feels that her ability to enjoy Brittney's music is hindered by the singer's rocky personal life, others feel that Brittney's exploits _____ their appreciation of her craft.

Hard

❽ Although critics decry the merger as _____, they consider it equally detrimental to local businesses and large out of town corporations.

Positive, Negative, or Neither

What if you can't think of a word to fill the blank? Freak out? No, when you can't come up with a word, just decide if it should be positive, negative, or neither. In other words, should it be nice, mean, or neither?

Also, and this is huge, many times students come into my office and say, "I skipped #5 because I don't know what 'gait' means." I have a great strategy for this! If you can't figure out the meaning of a word in the sentence, ax it. Just cross it out. This seems cheap, but it's actually what the SAT wants you to do. No one word matters that much for the sentence, and usually you can answer a question correctly based on the other words. The SAT purposely designs it this way. They are not really testing your vocab; they are trying to test how clever you are, how wily you are, and whether you get intimidated or not. So don't get intimidated. If you don't know a word in the sentence, cross the word out.

Let's look at the question from the Pretest:

3. Even at age two, Amrita moved with a _____ gait, gracefully handling hills, rocks, and uneven terrain.

(A) rational   (B) rocky   (C) mediocre   (D) difficult   (E) smooth

Solution: Many students get intimidated by "gait" and skip the question. If you do not know "gait," ax it. We do not need it to fill in the blank. Now, the question reads: "Even at age two, Amrita moved with a _____ ~~gait~~, gracefully handling hills, rocks, and uneven terrain." What word do we want for the blank? Pluck a word right from the sentence when possible; we want "graceful."

(A) ~~rational~~ —Nope, "rational" means "reasonable" and is not related to "graceful".
(B) ~~rocky~~ —Nope, "rocky" means "shaky" or "pertaining to rocks" and does not mean "graceful."
(C) ~~mediocre~~ —Nope, "mediocre" means "average" or "ordinary" and does not mean "graceful."
(D) ~~difficult~~ —Nope, "difficult" does not mean "graceful."
(E) smooth—Yes, "smooth" can mean "graceful."

Correct answer: E

> **SAT Reading/Writing Mantra #3**
> If you can't come up with a word to fill the blank, just decide
> if it should be +, −, or neither.
> And if there's a word that you don't know in the question, cross it out!

Positive, Negative, or Neither Drills

Here are some tough ones. If you can't think of a word for the blank, just write +, −, or neither. And if you can't figure out a word in the question, just cross it out. Then use the process of elimination; cross out any answer choices that are <u>definitely</u> not what you are looking for, and choose the best from what's left. This page of drills is tough. Unless you are aiming for 700+, I don't expect you to get them all.

Medium

❶ Stephen reported that the members of his family are _____ and very close with one another, and that they enjoy spending time together during holidays.

  Ⓐ devoted
  Ⓑ irate
  Ⓒ immense
  Ⓓ defunct
  Ⓔ doubtful

Hard

❷ After Gupta patently betrayed his teammates by giving away their plan to a girl from the opposition, they called him a (n) _____.

  Ⓐ sycophant
  Ⓑ deserter
  Ⓒ prophet
  Ⓓ imbecile
  Ⓔ expert

❸ Although Chloe receives incessant _____ from angry critics for her unconventional acting style, she never considers changing to please them.

  Ⓐ kudos
  Ⓑ appreciation
  Ⓒ tirades
  Ⓓ validation
  Ⓔ empathy

❹ Because of the professor's slow-paced didactic lecture style, many students felt bored and _____.

  Ⓐ patronized
  Ⓑ obsequious
  Ⓒ convivial
  Ⓓ inspired
  Ⓔ convinced

❺ Some psychologists argue that the internalization of disempowering messages from _____ cultural discourses is often at the source of an individual's psychological problems.

  Ⓐ affirming
  Ⓑ evasive
  Ⓒ diverting
  Ⓓ invigorating
  Ⓔ disenfranchising

❻ Bandura asserts that _____ reinforcement, the reinforcement that an individual observes rather than experiences, greatly influences behavior.

  Ⓐ brash
  Ⓑ experiential
  Ⓒ lucrative
  Ⓓ vicarious
  Ⓔ petulant

SAT Crashers Rule #4: Process of Elimination

SAT Crashers Rule #4: Never cross out an answer choice unless you're **absolutely** positive what it means and that it's wrong.

SAT Crashers Rule #45: No excuses. Test like a champion!

Once you have chosen a word that should fill the blank, go to the answer choices and cross out words that you are SURE do not fit. Cross out ONLY words that you are absolutely sure do not fit. This is very important; many people cross out words because they do not know them. Don't be crazy, cross out only words that definitely do not fit. Only after you have crossed out the choices that are definitely wrong, go through the remaining answer choices and choose the word that fits best.

The word you chose should make the whole sentence click into place—if there's a part of the sentence that doesn't fit with your word, then the word is wrong. It's like doing a jigsaw puzzle—you know when a piece fits in, and you know when you're forcing it.

Let's use the process of elimination on the question from the Pretest.

4. A scientist must stay alert; sometimes new technologies emerge from _____ instead of from planned experiments.

    (A) collaboration   (B) persistence   (C) accidents   (D) forecasts   (E) laziness

---

Solution: The key word "but" indicates that we want the opposite of "planned experiments," perhaps "unplanned." Use the process of elimination.

(A) ~~collaboration~~ Nope, "collaboration" means "working together" and is unrelated to "unplanned."
(B) ~~persistence~~ Nope, "persistence" means "resolve" and is unrelated to "unplanned."
(C) accidents—Maybe, "accidents" are "unplanned."
(D) ~~forecasts~~ Nope, "forecasts" means "predictions" and is unrelated to "unplanned."
(E) laziness—Maybe, "laziness" is sorta kinda the opposite of planning, but it's a stretch.

Cross out answer choices that are definitely wrong. Then choose the best answer from the remaining possibilities. Choice C is certainly the best answer.

SAT Reading/Writing Mantra #4
**Cross out answer choices that are definitely wrong. Then choose
the best from what's left.**
The correct answer should make sense with all the parts of the sentence.

SAT Crashers Rule #4: Process of Elimination Drills

Each sentence below has a blank indicating that something has been omitted. Beneath each sentence are five words labeled A through E. Choose the word that, when inserted in the sentence, <u>best</u> fits the meaning of the sentence as a whole.

Easy

❶ People who are always on time are by definition _____.

Ⓐ tardy
Ⓑ punctual
Ⓒ steadfast
Ⓓ dull
Ⓔ leaders

Medium

❷ To properly represent its _____ forms, Manpriya included, in her paper on the history of Renaissance art, over 20 sections, each describing a divergent style.

Ⓐ simplest
Ⓑ oldest
Ⓒ singular
Ⓓ diverse
Ⓔ solitary

❸ Friends often seek out Ben's _____: he is known for his ability to listen carefully and offer unbiased sagacious advice.

Ⓐ counsel
Ⓑ concern
Ⓒ trouble
Ⓓ empathy
Ⓔ ululation

❹ Zibby refused to believe her mom's admonition that the sweet and innocent-seeming demeanor of the salesman was a _____ for gaining her trust and taking advantage of her.

Ⓐ plea
Ⓑ ruse
Ⓒ denial
Ⓓ mood
Ⓔ challenge

Hard

❺ Behavioral theory is _____ in nature as it focuses on the observation and direct study of actions.

Ⓐ didactic
Ⓑ theoretical
Ⓒ obtuse
Ⓓ empirical
Ⓔ phlegmatic

❻ Al Gore's movie *An Inconvenient Truth* helped bring environmentalism into the spotlight, raising public awareness and inspiring environmental _____.

Ⓐ retraction
Ⓑ blame
Ⓒ recrimination
Ⓓ stockpiling
Ⓔ husbandry

Two Blanks

If there are two blanks in the sentence, get excited. Some people think that these must be harder, but they are actually much easier! Using the process of elimination, we are looking for wrong answers to cross out, so two blanks offer two opportunities to whittle the choices down. This means you can get questions correct even when you don't know a bunch of the vocabulary words!

When you see two blanks, answer one blank at a time. Start with whichever seems easier, usually the second. Think of a word you'd like to see for the blank. Eliminate choices that don't work. When you cross them out, cross out the whole answer choice, not just the one word. If one blank doesn't fit, it doesn't matter how good or bad the word for the other blank is.

Remember from Skill 4, cross off only answer choices that are **definitely** wrong. Leave any choices that could work or that you don't know. Then do the same for the other blank. Often, you are left with only one choice—the correct answer. If there are two or more choices left, try each pair of words in the sentence and choose the pair that fits best in the sentence.

Let's try this on the question from the Pretest.

5. The mindfulness program was designed to teach patients in remission from major depression to _____ awareness of their thoughts, feelings, and sensations in a non-judgmental and _____ way.

   (A) cultivate . . nonreactive   (B) lose . . unbiased   (C) reduce . . safe
   (D) build . . lavish   (E) grow . . deleterious

Solution: The second blank is easier; we need a word like "nonjudgmental."

(A) cultivate . . nonreactive—Yes, "nonreactive" is similar.
(B) lose . . unbiased—Yes, "unbiased" is a synonym for "nonjudgmental."
(C) reduce . . safe—Maybe, "safe" does not fit well, but I wouldn't eliminate it yet.
(D) build . . lavish—Nope, "lavish" means "generous" and is not related to "nonjudgmental."
(E) grow . . deleterious—Nope, "deleterious" sounds like "delete" and means "harmful."

We are left with A, B, and C. Now, think of a word for the first blank, perhaps "increase."

(A) cultivate . . nonreactive—Yes, "cultivate" means "develop" which is similar to "increase."
(B) lose . . unbiased—No, "lose" does not mean "increase," it's almost the opposite.
(C) reduce . . safe—Nope, "reduce" does not mean "increase," it's almost the opposite.

Correct answer: A

SAT Reading/Writing Mantra #5
When you see two blanks, answer one blank at a time, using the process of elimination.

Two Blanks Drills

Each sentence below has two blanks, each indicating that something has been omitted. Beneath each sentence are five sets of words labeled A through E. Choose the set of words that, when inserted in the sentence, best fits the meaning of the sentence as a whole.

Medium

❶ More influential and effective than any fraternity president before him, Reisner has _____ the tone for all subsequent _____ of the organization.

- Ⓐ provided . . defacers
- Ⓑ undermined . . antagonists
- Ⓒ set . . leaders
- Ⓓ reduced . . fellowships
- Ⓔ qualified . . critics

❷ The SAT author so impressed students with his jokes and lucid style that they wrote rave reviews of his book on Amazon that praised his _____ and _____.

- Ⓐ wittiness . . obtuseness
- Ⓑ humor . . clarity
- Ⓒ cleverness . . intemperance
- Ⓓ redolence . . eloquence
- Ⓔ practicality . . rhetoric

❸ Shortly after they began hiking into the scorchingly hot badlands of South Dakota, Zach and Rachel realized that the hike, instead of being _____, might be _____ and exhausting.

- Ⓐ strenuous . . insular
- Ⓑ grueling . . forbidding
- Ⓒ effortless . . amiable
- Ⓓ forbidding . . fascinating
- Ⓔ undemanding . . arduous

❹ The two biographies of abstract expressionist painter Jackson Pollock were published at the same time, so while _____ between the two is inevitable, all critics feel that Bak's is far superior and far _____ the other.

- Ⓐ comparison . . outclasses
- Ⓑ enmity . . rivals
- Ⓒ harmony . . outshines
- Ⓓ opacity . . surpasses
- Ⓔ rigidity . . allays

Hard

❺ Jimbo's teachers labeled him a(n) _____ because he constantly challenged authority and tradition; he deeply disliked _____.

- Ⓐ sycophant . . followers
- Ⓑ tyrant . . autocrats
- Ⓒ gadfly . . connoisseurs
- Ⓓ iconoclast . . conformity
- Ⓔ gourmand . . toadies

Vocab I: Compliment or Insult

Okay, right about now, you might be thinking, "Okay professional SAT teacher, you might know what 'sycophant' means, but I sure do not. How does looking for a + or − word help me? How do I know if sycophant is + or − ?" Well, the weird thing is that you can almost always tell if a word is + or −. I call this strategy "Compliment or insult." If someone called you a sycophant, would you feel happy or hurt? Think about it, it does not sound like a compliment, and it kinda sounds negative. You don't want to be called a sycophant. In fact, "sycophant" means "suck-up" and is definitely an insult, a negative word.

Here's another example. The word "lackluster" showed up as an answer choice on an SAT a few years back. We needed a positive word to fill the blank, but tons of kids got to lackluster and said, "I don't know that word." Maybe they never saw the word before, but there is no way "lackluster" is a positive word. It has "lack" in it. In fact, it basically says, "lacking luster" or "without shine." And, that's exactly what it means, "dull." So if you get a sense that a word is positive or negative, trust it. You can always test a word by asking, "Would I want to be called that? Would I feel complimented or insulted?"

Let's try to use this on the question from the Pretest.

6. Fans of the TV show *The OC* argue that critics who decry the show as _____ have not understood its deeper meaning and social significance.

    (A) insightful   (B) profound   (C) alleviating   (D) vapid   (E) lucid

Solution: Before you might have said, "I don't know some of these words; I'll just skip it." But now you say, "Well let's see, I don't know 'decry,' so I cross it out. I probably don't need it (Skill 3)." Then choose a word to fill the blank (Skill 1). If it's hard to do that here, decide if you want a + or – word (Skill 3). Since the blank is describing what the critics say, we want a negative word. Go to the choices and cross out any positive words (Skills 4 and 6), and then choose the best from what's left.

(A) ~~insightful~~—Nope, "insightful" sounds like a compliment. ("Insightful" means "perceptive.")
(B) ~~profound~~—Nope, "profound" sounds like a compliment. ("Profound" means "deep.")
(C) ~~alleviating~~—Nope, "alleviating" sounds positive. ("Alleviating" means "relieving.")
(D) vapid—Yep, "vapid" definitely sounds negative. You'd be irked if your girlfriend called you vapid.
(E) ~~lucid~~—Nope, "lucid" sounds like the Spanish or French word for light, it's either positive or neutral.

Correct answer: D

Reading/Writing SAT Mantra #6
If you don't know the meaning of a word, determine if it sounds positive, negative, or neither.

Vocab I: Compliment or Insult Drills

Before we use this strategy on SAT sentence completions, let's practice predicting if words are positive, negative, or neither. You'll be surprised how often you can tell, even when you think that you don't know the word. Look at these super-high-level vocab words and decide if they are a compliment or an insult. Look at each word and ask, "Would I be psyched or insulted if Jenny called me a(n) _____?" Write +, −, or neither. Then check the solutions to see if your feeling was correct.

a. peevish	j. flippant	s. dazzling
b. petulant	k. enthralling	t. resolute
c. sophisticated	l. vapid	u. pernicious
d. soporific	m. diminutive	v. disingenuous
e. saccharine	n. salutary	w. truculent
f. bombastic	o. magnanimous	x. diverting
g. magnificent	p. insipid	y. corrupt
h. abased	q. sagacious	z. charismatic
i. astute	r. baneful	

Now let's take this strategy out for a spin. For each question, think of a word you would like to fill each blank (and consider if it should be +, −, or neither). Then eliminate choices that do not mean what you are looking for. Use "compliment or insult" on words that you don't know—decide if they are positive, negative, or neither. Then choose the best of the remaining answers.

① To avoid being _____, the teacher often includes jokes and amusing anecdotes in her lectures.

- Ⓐ amusing
- Ⓑ insipid
- Ⓒ complex
- Ⓓ eccentric
- Ⓔ servile

② The miners of the gold rush dug so deeply into the mountain that any more excavation could have had _____ consequences, causing a cave-in or complete collapse.

- Ⓐ alienating
- Ⓑ rigid
- Ⓒ moderate
- Ⓓ worthy
- Ⓔ devastating

③ Despite the committee's efforts to _____ the discord between the two factions, no progress was made and the two groups remain sworn enemies.

- Ⓐ assuage
- Ⓑ intensify
- Ⓒ exploit
- Ⓓ excite
- Ⓔ scour

④ Just as a rhino's tough hide gives it both protection from predators and insulation from heat and cold, the exterior walls of old castles provided _____ from attackers and _____ from the wind.

- Ⓐ dispersion . . wadding
- Ⓑ admission . . convection
- Ⓒ safety . . conduction
- Ⓓ fortification . . transmission
- Ⓔ asylum . . sanctuary

Vocab II: Superbad Vocabulary

Some say that to build your vocabulary, you must munch your toast with *The New York Times* and take Shakespeare to the beach. These are great suggestions that will certainly benefit you in many ways, but even without *The New York Times* and Shakespeare you are already constantly surrounded by great vocabulary. So to build your vocab, you can also use what's already in front of you. Let's start with movies. Movies contain a ton of SAT vocab words.

Here' a great example from the movie *Juno* (Fox Searchlight Pictures, 2007):
Juno: No, this is not a food baby all right? I've taken like three pregnancy tests, and I'm forshizz up the spout.
Leah: How did you even generate enough pee for three pregnancy tests? That's amazing. . . .
Juno: I don't know, I drank like, ten tons of Sunny D. Anyway dude, I'm telling you I'm pregnant and you're acting shockingly **cavalier.**

What did Juno mean by "cavalier"? You can get it from the words around it. Juno is telling Leah that she's pregnant, which she is clearly upset about, and Leah doubts it and jokes around. Then Juno calls Leah "cavalier," so it must mean something like "too jokey" or "doubtful" or "not getting the seriousness here." And it does; "cavalier" means "too casual." Obviously, you might not memorize every new vocab word that comes at you while you munch popcorn, but if you keep your ears open, you'll pick up some of them.

Let's take a look at the Pretest question.

7. The primary purpose of the study was to find _____ proof; Salazar wanted to demonstrate that the findings of the original investigation were indisputable.

   (A) incontrovertible   (B) terminable   (C) supple   (D) imminent   (E) pertinent

Solution: What word do we want for the _____ ? Pluck a word right from the sentence if possible: "indisputable" works best. If you can't pluck, just say, "OK, the word should be 'good' proof." Then go to the choices and use the process of elimination.

(A) incontrovertible—Yup, "incontrovertible" means "indisputable." Skill 9 Preview: These are great words to break apart, "in" means "not," and "controvertible" looks like "controversy," so "incontrovertible" means "nocontroversy" or "definite."
(B) ~~terminable~~—Nope, "terminable" means "ending," like *The Terminator*.
(C) ~~supple~~—Nope, "supple" means "flexible."
(D) ~~imminent~~—Nope, "imminent" means "looming."
(E) pertinent—Maybe, "pertinent" means "relevant." It's the second-best answer, but choice A is better.

If you didn't know these words, don't fret, you soon will!

Correct answer: A

Vocab II: Superbad Vocabulary Drills

Let's take a look at some of the most important cinematic moments of all time and the SAT vocab we can learn from them. I'll give a quote from a movie, and you see if you can identify the movie and an approximate definition of the **bold** SAT vocabulary word.

1 Galadriel: . . . in the fires of Mount Doom, the Dark Lord Sauron forged in secret a master ring to control all others. And into this ring he poured all his cruelty, his **malice** and his will to dominate all life.

Movie _____

"Malice" means _____

2 El Guapo: Many pinatas?
Jefe: Oh yes, many!
El Guapo: Would you say I have a **plethora** of pinatas?
Jefe: A what?
El Guapo: A "plethora."
Jefe: Oh yes, you have a plethora.

Movie _____

"Plethora" means _____

3 The Emperor: [laughing] Perhaps you refer to the **imminent** attack of your rebel fleet? Yes, I assure you, we are quite safe from your friends here.

Movie _____

"Imminent" means _____

4 Bruce Wayne: Have you told anyone I'm coming back?
Alfred Pennyworth: I just couldn't figure the legal **ramifications** of bringing you back from the dead.
Bruce Wayne: Dead?
Alfred Pennyworth: You've been gone seven years.

Movie _____

"Ramifications" means _____

5 Evan: It's not just making them smaller. They completely reshaped them. They make them more **supple**, symmetrical.
Seth: I gotta catch a glimpse of these warlocks. Let's make a move.

Movie _____

"Supple" means _____

6 Elizabeth: Captain Barbossa, I am here to **negotiate** the **cessation** of **hostilities** against Port Royal.
Barbossa: There are a lot of long words in there, Miss; we're **naught** but **humble** pirates. What is it that you want?
Elizabeth: I want you to leave and never come back.
Barbossa: I'm **disinclined** to **acquiesce** to your request. Means "no."

Movie _____

"Negotiate" means _____

"Cessation" means _____

"Hostilities" means _____

"Naught" means _____

"Humble" means _____

"Disinclined" means _____

"Acquiesce" means_____

7 Red: Oh, Andy loved geology, I guess it appealed to his **meticulous** nature. An ice age here, million years of mountain building there. Geology is the study of pressure and time. That's all it takes really, pressure, and time.

Movie _____

"Meticulous" means _____

8 John Beckwith: [about Chaz] He lived with his mom til he was forty! She tried to poison his oatmeal!
Jeremy Grey: **Erroneous! Erroneous! Erroneous** on both accounts!

Movie _____

"Erroneous" means _____

⑨ The Architect: You have many questions, and although the process has **altered** your consciousness, you remain **irrevocably** human. **Ergo**, some of my answers you will understand, and some of them you will not. **Concordantly**, while your first question may be the most **pertinent**, you may or may not realize it is also the most **irrelevant**.

Movie _____

"Altered" means _____

"Irrevocably" means _____

"Ergo" means _____

"Concordantly" means _____

"Pertinent" means _____

"Irrelevant" means _____

⑩ Ballard: You're asking for one of us to disobey a direct order.
Morpheus: That's right, I am. But we all well know that the reason that most of us are here is because of our . . . **affinity** for disobedience.

Movie _____

"Affinity" means _____

⑪ Homer Simpson: Okay, **epiphany**, **epiphany** . . . oh I know! Bananas are an excellent source of potassium! [*gets slapped*]

Movie _____

"Epiphany" means _____

⑫ Soldier: Where'd you get the coconuts?
King Arthur: We found them.
Soldier: Found them? In Mercia? The coconut's tropical!
King Arthur: What do you mean?
Soldier: Well, this is a **temperate** zone
King Arthur: The swallow may fly south with the sun or the house martin or the plover may seek warmer climes in winter, yet these are not strangers to our land.

Movie _____

"Temperate" means _____

⑬ Murtogg: Someone's got to make sure that this dock stays off-limits to civilians.
Jack Sparrow: It's a fine goal, to be sure. But it seems to me . . . that a ship like that one, makes this one here seem a bit **superfluous**, really.
Murtogg: Oh, the *Dauntless* is the power in these waters, true enough. But there's no ship as can match the *Interceptor* for speed.
Jack Sparrow: I've heard of one, supposed to be very fast, **nigh** uncatchable: *The Black Pearl*.

Movie _____

"Superfluous" means _____

"Nigh" means _____

⑭ Brooks: [*to Andy*] Son, six wardens have been through here in my **tenure**, and I've learned one **immutable**, universal truth.

Movie _____

"Tenure" means _____

"Immutable" means _____

⑮ C-3PO: I am fluent in over six million forms of communication, and can readily . . .
EV-9D9: Splendid! We have been without an interpreter since our master got angry with our last **protocol** droid and disintegrated him.

Movie _____

"Protocol" means _____

⑯ The Architect: Your life is the sum of a remainder of an unbalanced equation **inherent** to the programming of the matrix. You are the **eventuality** of an **anomaly**, which despite my sincerest efforts I have been unable to eliminate from what is otherwise a harmony of mathematical precision. While it remains a burden **assiduously** avoided, it is not unexpected, and thus not beyond a measure of control. Which has led you, **inexorably**, here.

Movie _____

"Inherent" means _____

"Eventuality" means _____

"Anomaly" means _____

"Assiduously" means _____

"Inexorably" means _____

⑰ Dennis: Oh, king eh? Very nice. And how'd you get that, eh? By **exploiting** the workers. By hanging on to outdated **imperialist dogma** which **perpetuates** the economic and social differences in our society. . . . Come to see the violence **inherent** in the system! I'm being **repressed**!

Movie _____

"Exploiting" means _____

"Imperialist" means _____

"Dogma" means _____

"Perpetuates" means _____

"Inherent" means _____

"Repressed" means _____

⑱ V: Of course you can. I'm not questioning your powers of observation, I'm merely remarking upon the **paradox** of asking a masked man who he is.

Movie _____

"Paradox" means _____

⑲ Ferris: I do have a test today. That wasn't bullshit. It's on European **socialism**. I mean, really, what's the point? I'm not European. I don't plan on being European. So who cares if they're socialists? They could be **fascist anarchists**. It still doesn't change the fact that I don't own a car. Not that I **condone** fascism, or any **-ism** for that matter.

Movie _____

"Socialism" means _____

"Fascist" means _____

"Anarchist" means _____

"Condone" means _____

"-ism" means _____

⑳ The Architect: You are here because Zion is about to be destroyed. Its every living inhabitant **terminated**, its entire existence **eradicated**.

Movie _____

"Terminated" means _____

"Eradicated" means_____

㉑ V: But on this most **auspicious** of nights, permit me then, in lieu of the more commonplace **sobriquet**, to suggest the character of this dramatis persona.

Movie _____

"Auspicious" means _____

"Sobriquet" means _____

㉒ Albus Dumbledore: Cornelius, I **implore** you to see reason. The evidence that the Dark Lord has returned is **incontrovertible**.
Cornelius Fudge: He is not back!

Movie _____

"Implore" means _____

"Incontrovertible" means _____

㉓ Virginia "Pepper" Potts: What do you want me to do with this?
Tony Stark: That? Destroy it. **Incinerate** it.
Virginia "Pepper" Potts: You don't want to keep it?
Tony Stark: Pepper, I've been called many things. **Nostalgic** is not one of them.

Movie _____

"Incinerate" means _____

"Nostalgic" means _____

㉔ Kumar Patel: I fear that I will always be / A lonely number like root three / . . . I wish instead I were a nine / For nine could **thwart** this evil trick, / with just some quick arithmetic.

Movie _____

"Thwart" means _____

This is a great way to learn and review vocabulary. Watch for vocab in your favorite movies and add new ones to my list at www.BrianLeaf.com/superbadvocab. I'll include new quotes in future editions of this book.

Vocab III: Deodorant and Spanish Class

When I was 17, the word "panache" was on my SAT. I didn't know the word, but I remembered that there was a fancy restaurant near my town called Café Panache. I thought, "What is Panache?" Obviously this fancy restaurant is not called Café Smells Bad or Café I Hate You. Some cafes might be called those names, but they are not the places my parents go. So it must be Café Delicious or Café Exciting or Café Good Times. That insight was enough to vibe the word and get the question right. In fact, "panache" is similar to "exciting," it means "flair."

You can use anything around you to vibe out SAT vocab words. "Imperious" is an SAT word that stumps most kids. But you've definitely seen it around. You've heard of "Imperial Stormtroopers" or an "Imperial Cruiser" in *Star Wars* and the "Imperious Curse" in *Harry Potter*. From these references you can certainly conclude that "imperious" must mean something like "big" or "grand" or "important," and that's enough to get an SAT question right. "Imperious" actually means "domineering, bossy, or authoritative." Makes sense that, in *Star Wars*, the Empire would have an Imperial Cruiser or that J. K. Rowling would use the word to describe a curse that gives control over another person!

So when you don't know a word or aren't sure of its definition, see if you can remember seeing or hearing the word anywhere—a billboard, a TV commercial, history class, Spanish class, *Harry Potter*, a restaurant name, a comic book, or *Magic: The Gathering* cards. Use anything that you can to figure it out.

Let's try this out on the question from the Pretest.

8. Nita observed the deep connections that existed between the members of the band, and yearned for that kind of _____ in her life.

(A) treacle   (B) fellowship   (C) facile   (D) requiem   (E) alleviation

Solution: Plucking a word directly from the question, we want a word for "deep connection."

(A) ~~treacle~~—Who the heck knows the word "treacle"? Maybe you. Remember Ron stuffing his face with treacle tart in *Harry Potter*? Well, that's enough to get it. "Treacle" means "something too sweet or sentimental."

(B) fellowship—Don't know the word? What about Frodo, Sam, Aragorn, Gimli, Legolas, and the gang? "The Fellowship of the Ring." "Fellowship" means "a group or association."

(C) ~~facile~~—Most people think that they don't know this word, but if you take Spanish or French, it's easy. In Spanish "facil" means "easy," and in English "facile" means "too easy."

(D) ~~requiem~~—Tough word. But how about the Academy Award–winning movie *Requiem for a Dream*? "Requiem" means "remembrance."

(E) ~~alleviation~~—Seems like a maybe, cause we want a positive-sounding word. But you know this word. It sounds like the pain reliever Aleve, and in fact, it means "making something more bearable."

Correct answer: B

Vocab III: Deodorant and Spanish Class Drills

Here are some great SAT vocab words. Let's see if you can vibe them out. Even if you can't define them, try to come up with an association. That might be enough to know if it's the right or wrong answer on a sentence completion question. The goal here is not just for you to learn 13 new SAT words, but for you to become awake to all the great vocabulary that surrounds you.

Spanish

❶ "Diverting" might mean _____

❷ "Facile" might mean _____

French

❸ "Luminance" might mean _____

❹ "Clairvoyant" might mean _____

❺ "Comportment" might mean _____

❻ "Filial" might mean _____

The Grocery Store

❼ "Arid" might mean _____

Harry Potter

J. K. Rowling based the names of most charms and curses on English or Latin word parts. This is a font of SAT vocab; check out Wikipedia's entry for "Spells in Harry Potter."

❽ "Impervious" might mean _____

❾ "Stupefy" might mean _____

❿ "Conflagration" might mean _____

Dungeons & Dragons

All right, fess up and roll me a D20. D&D is a treasure chest of amazing SAT vocab words.

⓫ "Sagacious" might mean _____

⓬ "Sylvan" might mean _____

⓭ "Expeditious" might mean _____

Vocab IV: Splitting Words

Here's another great way to get a vibe for the meaning of a tough word. Many words in English break apart. For example, "anachronism" is a tough SAT word that most people don't know, but . . .

"A" or "an" means "not," like amoral, atypical, or asymptomatic.

"Chron" means "time," like chronological, chronology, or chronograph (a stopwatch).

And "ism" doesn't change the meaning of a word much; it's just an ending that means "a practice or system."

Thus, "anachronism" means something like "a system not time." What? Confusing? Maybe, but it's enough to know if the word applies or not. If you are looking for a word relating to time, it might be right; and if you are looking for a word meaning "pertaining to trees," cross it out. In fact, "anachronism" means "something placed in the wrong time period," like Amelia wearing her digital watch while acting the role of Ophelia in Shakespeare's *Hamlet*.

Let's look at the question from the pretest.

9. Certain types of cats are _____, and never leave the ground, while others climb trees to stalk prey.

   (A) philanthropic
   (B) phobic
   (C) sympathetic
   (D) terrestrial
   (E) anachronistic

Solution: This is a classic sentence completion setup. There is a _____ and then a clause that defines the _____. So we want a word related to "never leaving the ground" to fill the blank. Look at the answer choices for words related to the ground. (You'll learn all these word parts in the drills.)

(A) ~~philanthropic~~—Nope, "philanthropic" means "love of people."
(B) ~~phobic~~—Nope, "phobic" means "afraid."
(C) ~~sympathetic~~—Nope, "sympathetic" means "compassionate."
(D) terrestrial—Sure! "Terrestrial" means "pertaining to the earth."
(E) ~~anachronistic~~—Nope, you know that "anachronistic" means "in the wrong time."

Correct answer: D

Soon you'll know all these words. Let's take a look!

Vocab IV: Splitting Words Drills

Use a dictionary to define the words in each group below, and then conclude what the word parts must mean.

❶ sympathy _____
apathy _____
pathetic _____

"path" means _____
"anti" means _____

empathy _____
pathos _____
antipathy _____

"a" means _____

❷ philanthropy _____
technophile _____
technology _____

"phil" means _____
"soph" means _____
"phobe" means _____

philosophy _____
technophobe _____
phobia _____

"anthro" means _____
"tech" means _____
"ology" means _____

❸ terrestrial _____
extraterrestrial _____

"terr" means _____

terrain _____
extraordinary_____

"extra" means _____

❹ homogeneous _____
homologous _____
homosexual_____

"homo" means _____
"gen" means _____

heterogeneous _____
heterologous _____
heterosexual _____

"hetero" means _____

❺ circumscribe_____
circumvent _____
postscript _____
circumambulate _____
manuscript _____
transatlantic _____

"circum" means _____
"scribe" means _____
"re" means _____
"amb" means _____

circumnavigate _____
recirculate _____
transcribe _____
amble _____
manufacture _____

"post" means _____
"man" means _____
"trans" means _____

Here are a few more word parts. Can you define them?

"dis" means _____   "co" means _____   "sub" means _____

Couples Counseling

Approximately once per test, a sentence does not give you enough info to decide what the word in the blank should be. This is usually a "hard" rated question, near the end of the bunch of sentence completion questions. For these questions, the two blanks are related as synonyms, opposites, or cause and effect. To answer these, we read the question and determine if the words that fill the two blanks need to be synonyms, antonyms, or cause and effect.

Let's apply this on the question from the Pretest.

10. The mayor was considered _____ by the council, who believed that she would have a(n) _____ term in office.

   (A) grating . . successful   (B) reckless . . dangerous   (C) kind . . notorious
   (D) asocial . . amicable   (E) conventional . . established

Solution: We do not have enough info to determine either word, but the two blanks are connected and the definition of one will determine the other. We decide if they are similar words, like "nice" and "pleasant," or opposite words, like "good" and "bad." For this sentence, we need similar words. The mayor being a certain way will indicate that her term in office will be that way. (Skill 2 review: A key word like "but" might have told us that we are looking for opposites rather than similar words.) Then we go to the answer choices and cross off any pairs that are not similar words. From what's left, we choose the best fit for the sentence.

(A) ~~grating . . successful~~—Nope, "grating" means "annoying" and is unrelated to "successful."
(B) reckless. . dangerous—Yes, "reckless" and "dangerous" are similar.
(C) ~~kind . . notorious~~—Nope, "notorious" means "infamous," as in *The Notorious B.I.G.*
(D) ~~asocial . . amicable~~—Nope, "asocial" means "not social" and "amicable" means "friendly."
(E) conventional . . established—Maybe, "conventional" and "established" are synonyms. Remember, if you are not sure what a word means, leave it! Eliminate only words that you are sure of.

We have it down to choices B and D. Choice B is the better answer. "Reckless" and "dangerous" fit well. Even though "conventional" and "established" are synonyms, they do not fit into the sentence. Remember from Skill 4 that the correct answer should fit smoothly into the sentence and not feel forced. It should make sense with the whole sentence. If it sounds weird, it's probably wrong.

Correct answer: B

SAT Reading/Writing Mantra #10
When there is not enough info to determine the words for two blanks, decide if the two words should be synonyms, antonyms, or cause and effect.

Couples Counseling Drills

Hard

❶ In the field of psychology, "abnormal behavior" is defined to be behavior that creates _____ to the individual or that is _____ to others.

- Ⓐ distress . . harmful
- Ⓑ injury . . acceptable
- Ⓒ worry . . sympathetic
- Ⓓ calm . . agitating
- Ⓔ healing . . malicious

❷ Because the politician _____ his stance on policies so often, pundits labeled him _____.

- Ⓐ altered . . steadfast
- Ⓑ maintained . . mercurial
- Ⓒ condoned . . nostalgic
- Ⓓ changed . . irresolute
- Ⓔ vacillated . . reliable

❸ Onlookers noted that Helga held none of her sister's _____ nature, she was thoroughly _____.

- Ⓐ sympathetic . . selfless
- Ⓑ egotistical . . terrestrial
- Ⓒ whimsical . . staid
- Ⓓ nefarious . . malicious
- Ⓔ intense . . severe

❹ Ten years ago, the association was on the verge of financial _____, but now, a decade later, they are completely _____.

- Ⓐ renovation . . rebuilt
- Ⓑ renaissance . . innovative
- Ⓒ collapse . . solvent
- Ⓓ catastrophe . . bankrupt
- Ⓔ devastation . . complex

❺ After Richard Alpert went to India, he changed his name to Ram Dass and became one of the most _____ spiritual teachers in the United States, _____ by millions.

- Ⓐ revered . . adored
- Ⓑ amusing . . exploited
- Ⓒ moderate . . beloved
- Ⓓ sagacious . . dismissed
- Ⓔ dazzling . . despised

❻ Jason Franklin was famous for saying, "If in life you are _____, you will certainly _____."

- Ⓐ flippant . . stockpile
- Ⓑ phlegmatic . . thrive
- Ⓒ industrious . . fail
- Ⓓ assiduous . . succeed
- Ⓔ divisive . . be trusted

How to Be a Sentence Completion Master

Let's review. Here's what you've learned about sentence completion questions. Check the box next to each Skill when you've mastered it. Refer to the Skills if needed.

☐ **Skill 1.** Read the question and think of a word you'd like to see to fill the blank. Choose a word right from the sentence when possible.

☐ **Skill 2.** Watch for key words ("but," "however," "though" . . .) that tell you to look for an opposite.

☐ **Skill 3.** If you can't come up with a word to fill the blank, just decide if it should be positive, negative, or neither. If there is a word you don't know in the question, cross it out!

☐ **Skill 4.** Cross out answer choices that are **definitely** wrong, and choose the best from what's left. The correct answer should make sense with all the parts of the sentence.

☐ **Skill 5.** When you see two blanks, answer one blank at a time, using the process of elimination.

☐ **Skill 6.** If you don't know the meaning of a word, determine if it sounds positive, negative, or neither.

☐ **Skills 7 and 8.** If you don't know the meaning of a word, determine if you've ever seen or heard it in context—in a movie, on TV, in a song, in a Spanish word, as the name of a product or business, etc.

☐ **Skill 9.** If you don't know the meaning of a word, see if it has parts that you can dissect.

☐ **Skill 10.** When there is not enough info to determine the words for two blanks, decide if the two words should be synonyms, opposites, or cause and effect.

Let's put it all into action on the question from the Pretest.

11. The counselor was concerned by Jenna's _____ comportment; she hardly acknowledged her peers and seemed unconcerned about school.

    (A) saccharine   (B) flippant   (C) apathetic   (D) baneful   (E) erroneous

Solution: If you don't know the word "comportment," cross it off. To fill the blank, you want "not acknowledging" or "unconcerned." Then cross out answer choices that **definitely** do not means "unconcerned," and choose the best answer from what's left.

(A) ~~saccharine~~—Nope, "saccharine" means "too sweet."
(B) ~~sagacious~~—Nope, "sagacious" means "wise."
(C) apathetic—Yes, "apathetic" means "not feeling" or "not caring"
(D) baneful—Probably not, "baneful" means "bothering" instead of "unconcerned."
(E) ~~erroneous~~—Nope, "erroneous" means "wrong."

Choice C is the best answer. It fits the blank and helps the whole sentence make perfect sense.

Correct answer: C

How to Be a Sentence Completion Master Drills

Easy

❶ Matty is a _____ athlete; he excels at baseball and football and even gives his brother Wilson a good game of squash.

- (A) speedy
- (B) translucent
- (C) hearty
- (D) droll
- (E) versatile

❷ Clair has a _____ for collecting sea glass; from a distance she can spot beautiful pieces that other collectors _____.

- (A) hatred . . find
- (B) penchant . . ward
- (C) distaste . . miss
- (D) knack . . overlook
- (E) gift . . stockpile

Medium

❸ Although opponents decry the tax code as inequitable, the government has kept it in place for decades and argues that the code is _____.

- (A) antagonistic
- (B) evenhanded
- (C) sophisticated
- (D) petulant
- (E) shrewd

❹ Certain types of squirrels are _____, spending most of their time jumping from tree to tree.

- (A) arboreal
- (B) terrestrial
- (C) dramatic
- (D) homogeneous
- (E) circumscribed

Hard

❺ To reflect the _____ of people's interests, the community art association commissioned the mural to depict 31 professions and 62 hobbies.

- (A) uniqueness
- (B) astuteness
- (C) heterogeneity
- (D) transference
- (E) passion

❻ The candidate's supporters cite her _____ as her greatest asset, and claim that her opponent falls short with far less _____.

- (A) concordance . . pertinence
- (B) temperance . . peevishness
- (C) experience . . naïveté
- (D) resolve . . tenacity
- (E) acumen . . ignorance

Reading Comprehension

Many students believe that reading comprehension questions are tricky, with several answers that work. But in the next 12 Skills, I'll show you that they're not tricky and that, in fact, they're totally predictable. In English class you might discuss for 30 minutes what Walt Whitman meant when he wrote something, but on the SAT there can be only one right answer, no tricks, no debate. The reading passage will always provide clear proof for the correct answer. Your goal is to be a detective or a lawyer and find the proof. After learning these 12 Skills, most students enjoy the reading section; it becomes easy and predictable. Read, learn, and drill these Skills, and you'll raise your score, guaranteed!

Most reading passages are introduced by a line or two in italics. Many students say, "I just skip those lines to save time," but the lines can be very useful. Read them carefully. Sometimes they give away lots of info; sometimes we even get the main idea of the passage. I love this strategy; I love little changes like this that make a big difference. Reading the italics can help you better understand the passage, which will help you to stay focused while you read and to get more questions right! (This is also a great strategy when reading your high school history text or your future college philosophy books; the intro sentences or italics can tell you a lot.)

Here's an example:

This passage is from a memoir published in 2001. The author is a young boy in 1941 who has just emigrated with his family to the United States.

What do we learn? A lot. The book is a memoir, a story from the author's life. It took place in 1941, so we wonder if there are references to World War I. The author was new to the United States. Knowing all this will help us with main idea and tone questions, and it will help us stay focused as we read.

Let's try this out on the italics from the Pretest.

The following passages consider the roles of two leaders of a group of plane crash survivors on an island.

12. The passages share the common aim of

(A) telling the story of the plane crash of Flight 815
(B) analyzing the anatomy of a leader
(C) describing the path of the island
(D) identifying the leader on the island
(E) describing inexplicable challenges faced on the island

Solution: The italics in this case pretty much gives us the answer to the first question. It tells us that the passages "consider the roles of two leaders . . . ." The plane crash and survivors are important, but the "roles of the two leaders" are the primary purpose. Thus, the best answer is choice D. Choice B is about leadership, but the passage does not analyze what makes a leader in general; it analyzes who the leader is on the island. This also brings up an incredibly important point. You are no doubt a scholar on *Lost*, able to quote entire episodes and argue complex hypotheses, but you must answer a critical reading question only from evidence in the passage, and **not** from your outside knowledge. That's why I chose *Lost*, to demonstrate this point, and well, cause it's fun.

Correct answer: D

SAT Reading/Writing Mantra #12
Always begin a reading passage by reading the italics.

Italics Drills

Each of the following is an italicized intro to an SAT reading passage. What can you conclude from each?

❶ *Passage 1 was adopted from a 1976 article about environmentalism. Passage 2 was adopted from a 2005 analysis of the environmental movement of the 1970s.*

❷ *This passage was excerpted from a novel published in 1985. As the passage begins, three women are discussing their relationships.*

❸ *This passage is from a 1995 article by a doctor describing new medical technologies available in certain hospitals.*

❹ *In 1973, the U.S. Supreme Court case Roe v. Wade, a landmark case legalizing abortion, sparked tremendous debate. Each of the passages below was written in 1974.*

❺ *This passage is taken from an English novel written in 1820. Mr. Peabody works in Mrs. Primberly's shop. He desires to court Mrs. Primberly's only daughter, Josephine.*

❻ *In the following passage from a book written in 2005, a music historian discusses changes brought about by CDs and MP3 players.*

The SAT Reading Meditation

After you have digested the italicized intro, read the passage in a relaxed, yet very focused way. This is like meditating. When you notice your mind wandering, come back to the moment; bring your mind back to the reading. Anytime your mind wanders, bring it back. That will save time and energy and bring you closer to being a Zen master. For years, Zen monks in the mountains of Japan have been training with SAT reading passages.

Don't read to memorize details. Read to figure out the main idea and tone—what the passage is about and how the author feels about it. You don't need to memorize details because almost every detail question on the SAT tells you what line to look at. And when you look back, you'll know what question you're trying to answer, making it even easier to understand what you're reading and find the best answer.

Also, and this is huge, I give you permission not to reread hard lines or lines that you spaced out for. This is especially important for perfectionists. Either we won't need the lines and the time rereading would have been wasted, or we will need them and we'll reread later, knowing the question and knowing what to look for. You never need any one particular sentence to get the main idea and tone. Main idea and tone are expressed throughout the passage.

One more thing. Many students worry, "Can I read this whole passage? It'll take 10 minutes." I actually remember being 16 years old and preparing for the SAT and thinking the exact same thing. Then one day I was like, "Wait, this is ridiculous, how long can it take?" So I timed myself. It took like 2.5 minutes! Try it, and you'll see. Even for a slow reader, the passage takes only a few minutes, especially if you use my "Don't Reread Strategy."

Let's take a look at the next question from the Pretest.

13. The primary purpose of Passage 2 is to

(A) tell the story of Oceanic Flight 815
(B) demonstrate why Jack Shepherd is the true leader of the survivors
(C) profile the personality of Jack Shepherd
(D) examine the theme of challenge
(E) argue for the merits of logic and reason

Solution: As we discussed in Skill 12, the italics told us the main idea. Plus the passage continually expresses its purpose: to demonstrate that "Jack Shepherd is the true leader of the survivors." Use the process of elimination; the passage does express ideas mentioned in the other choices, but choice B is the **primary** purpose.

Correct answer: B

SAT Reading/Writing Mantra #13
Read the passage, looking for main idea and tone. That helps you stay focused; keep asking yourself, "What are the main idea and tone?" Don't try to memorize details and don't reread hard lines. If you need them, you'll reread later when you know the question and what to look for.

The SAT Reading Meditation Drills

What are the main idea and tone of each passage?

Drill 1

The following passage was adapted from a 1998 essay written by a psychology graduate student exploring his heritage.

While my mother's parents spent their lives in New York, my paternal grandparents were born and raised in neighboring villages of Austria. My grandfather's father owned a liquor store and was very religious. My grandfather was the academic of the family. He completed high school, college, and graduate degrees. He worked as a teacher and principal, much more respected positions then than now. I connected deeply with this grandfather, Herman. He and I are sensitive, loving, prone to worry, and innately talented teachers.

Though my grandparents and great grandparents were born in Austria, I am not Austrian. This, I believe, is the case for many Jews in the United States. Belonging to this religion is a cultural heritage as well as a faith. Though I rarely think of myself as Jewish and pay small heed to the holidays, Judaism is a large part of my identity.

What is the main idea?

How does the author feel about that?

Drill 2

The question of whether law is simply a series of rigid prescriptions and maneuvers or a system with an overarching theme of justice and mercy fuels political, social, and legal discourse. For the Western tradition, the relation between fairness and legal reasoning goes back to the ancient Greeks. In *The Statesman,* Plato recognized that legal universalities cannot be considered under every imaginable circumstance and situation.

Aristotle developed this line of thinking in the *Nicomachean Ethics,* arguing that when circumstantial particulars disrupt a universal mandate, then it is only right to modify the law to ensure equitability. Anything written in universal language will, by its nature, create some exception. Aristotle relayed that equity superceded purely legal justice in the sense that the value of equity went beyond even that of the written law. Aristotle did not create a framework for carrying out his claim when applied to intricate cases with many technicalities that required finesse in judgment. Despite the murkiness of the idea, fairness as a legal principle persisted through Roman law and into the early modern period.

What is the main idea?

How does the author feel about that?

"Plethora" Most Nearly Means

You've read the passage, continually asking yourself, "Self, what is the main idea and tone?" Now, go to the questions. Unlike the sentence completion questions, reading comprehension questions are not arranged in order of difficulty. Instead, they go in order of the passage, with main idea and tone questions either first or last.

If the questions begin with main idea, and you feel pretty sure what it is, answer it. If you feel unsure, do the "line number" questions first. These are the ones that tell you what line number to look back at. Since we read quickly and did not obsess, we have time now to go back and reread the lines. By the time we've done all the line number questions, we will have reprocessed the passage and be even more sure of the main idea and tone. This is an awesome strategy. This alone will raise your score.

When you answer a line number question, always go back and reread not only the lines that the question refers to, but also at least three lines before and after. The answer usually comes before or after. If I say, "Vince Vaughn, the big man, is one facetious dude," I am probably expounding on what I said in the previous line, or what I'm about to say in the next line. The next line would probably be: "Don't you agree, he's just the funniest guy," and now we know that "facetious" means "funny." That's how the SAT works. They always explain tough words nearby!

Let's take a look at the question from the Pretest.

14. In Passage 1 line 13, "will" most nearly means

    (A) testament   (B) stubbornness   (C) being   (D) ego   (E) desire

Solution: This is a type of line number question. It always says, "Blah blah most nearly means." The answer to this type of question is rarely the obvious word that you'd pick if you hadn't even read the passage. It's usually one of the less obvious choices. To answer this question, go back to the line and reread a few lines before and a few lines after. In this case, the lines before contain the answer. "Now a strong believer in the power of the island, Locke knows that the place where they are stranded has a purpose for everyone. Following the **will** of the island . . . ." The word "will" as it is used here is related to "purpose," and the best answer is choice E.

You can actually treat this question like a sentence completion. Pluck out a word you'd like to see, and then use the process of elimination as you look for it. Remember to eliminate only answer choices that you're sure are wrong.

Correct answer: E

SAT Reading/Writing Mantra #14
**To answer a "most nearly means" question, reread a few lines before
and a few lines after, and remember that the answer is usually
not the most common definition.**

"Plethora" Most Nearly Means Drills

The following is adapted from a 2006 essay about poet Edna St. Vincent Millay. The author of the essay is referring to one of Millay's poems.

This is the energy that defines the flair and appeal of Edna St. Vincent Millay. She was always playing with fire, and at the same time shedding her lovely light for the world to
5   admire. She was lucky to be born in a time when people were ready to accept change as Millay was always experimenting, and the world loved her for it. She was small in stature and had fiery red hair and a beautifully clear
10 voice. The public adored her charismatic, headstrong and passionate nature, and she fed their adoration with carefully crafted poems, articulating the thrill of her courageous and daring life.

15 She lived in Maine, by the sea, and her childhood was bleak. Her father left her mother when Edna was seven. They were incredibly poor, and her mother had to work hard to support the family. As a visiting nurse, young
20 Vincent's mother left her children alone a lot. They were given chores, and it was up to Millay, the oldest, to inspire play from the work to keep the others happy. From this pinched childhood sprouted Millay's ability to dramatize
25 and entertain.

1 In line 1, "flair" most nearly means

(A) signal
(B) panache
(C) flame
(D) conflagration
(E) yearning

2 In line 10, the term "public" refers to

(A) all citizens
(B) theater attendees
(C) Millay's readers
(D) a visiting nurse
(E) newspaper audiences

3 In line 11, "nature" most nearly means

(A) world
(B) chronicle
(C) environment
(D) life
(E) spirit

4 In line 12, "adoration" most nearly means

(A) respect
(B) desire
(C) charisma
(D) tenacity
(E) penitence

5 In line 16, "bleak" most nearly means

(A) austere
(B) bland
(C) weak
(D) lonely
(E) morose

6 "The others" in line 23 refers to

(A) Millay's public
(B) Millay's parents
(C) Millay's siblings
(D) Millay's readers
(E) the world

7 In line 23, "pinched" most nearly means

(A) twisted
(B) wan
(C) evil
(D) virtuous
(E) enigmatic

"He's playing **fetch** . . . with my kids . . . he's treating my kids like they're dogs."

Debbie, *Knocked Up* (Universal Pictures, 2007)

This type of question asks you to directly retrieve info from the passage. No interpretation, no inferring, no thinking even. The key here is to be a dog; just play fetch. And be a lawyer. Read a little before and a little after the line number, and find **evidence** for an answer. Prove your answer with info from the passage.

Let's take a look at the question from the Pretest.

15. Passage 2 indicates that the principle to which Shepherd is most loyal is

(A) leadership
(B) optimism
(C) chaos
(D) reason
(E) democracy

Solution: Always look for the evidence in the passage. Be a lawyer; find proof. This is true for all types of questions, and especially for these direct info questions. All the answer choices for this question show up in the passage, but the passage states that Jack is a man based on principles and fact and that he has a heavy emphasis on logic and reason. He does demonstrate leadership and optimism, and generally favor democracy, but according to the passage, **primarily** he is a man guided by reason.

Correct answer: D

SAT Reading/Writing Mantra #15
For a "direct info" question, always read before and after a line and find proof.

Direct Info Drills

The following passage is adapted from a scholarly paper that examines Yeats' poem "The Tower."

    The Tower's three parts correspond to three stages of life, or three modes of relating to the world, but not in a scheme as simple as youth, adulthood and old age. Rather, the first and
5 third parts—or the first and third poems in a three-poem sequence—chart the internal experiences of an accelerating mind within a decelerating body. The second part is a more external reminiscence, passing elegiacally over
10 the lore of the land. The dying poet is taking a nostalgic survey of his works. The first and third parts take place within a dreaming mind, while the second takes place within the dream.

    If we think of this poem as a ceremony, the first
15 part senses that the end is near, but is not ready to face it; the second part is a preparation ritual, and the third arrives at readiness and passes into nothing. If this passing is to have any meaning, the poet must propel himself
20 enthusiastically into the next world rather than fall, withered and bedraggled, out of this one. To do so, he must find the memories in which he was most alive, maybe the ones that still hurt the most. These moments were truly his,
25 and so are truly his to leave behind.

❶ In lines 1 and 2, "three stages of life" refers to

  Ⓐ youth, adulthood, and old age
  Ⓑ baby, teenager, adult
  Ⓒ the life cycle of a poem
  Ⓓ the birth of an idea
  Ⓔ three ways of being in the world

❷ "The first and third poems" (lines 4 and 5) differ from the second in that

  Ⓐ they are nostalgic
  Ⓑ they catalogue the poet's inner experience
  Ⓒ they are enthusiastic
  Ⓓ they are part of a cremation ceremony
  Ⓔ they are painful

❸ In lines 9 and 10, the phrase "passing elegiacally over the lore of the land" indicates that the poet was

  Ⓐ a slow runner
  Ⓑ taking stock of his life's work
  Ⓒ working for the Census Bureau
  Ⓓ speaking at a funeral
  Ⓔ orating ancient tales

❹ The author states that the poet must "find the memories . . . alive" (lines 22 and 23) in order to

  Ⓐ leave this world with significance
  Ⓑ not die
  Ⓒ regain memories
  Ⓓ become alive
  Ⓔ become a poet

❺ The author compares the poem as a whole to

  Ⓐ folklore
  Ⓑ a dying person
  Ⓒ a ceremony
  Ⓓ a memory
  Ⓔ a rocketship

What Are You Trying to "Suggest"?

This type of question asks you what the author "suggests" or "implies," or what we can "infer." Whereas Skill 15 concerns questions that ask for information directly from the passage, like "what color was Rosalie's convertible," this question asks for information that was not given in the passage, but hinted at.

When students see this, they think that they have to pull some crazy AP English logic. But, actually, the key is **not** to overthink the answer. For a "suggest" question, the correct answer will probably not be directly quoted from the passage, but it should be pretty darn close, and we must still have proof from the passage. The correct answer for any SAT question, even this type, should always be very close to what was directly stated in the passage.

Here's the question from the Pretest.

16. The two passages suggest that a leader must do all of the following EXCEPT

  (A) inspire followers
  (B) govern democratically
  (C) provide hope
  (D) have faith in others
  (E) attempt to provide safety

Solution: The word "suggest" tells us that the answer might not directly be stated. So we freak out? It's too hard for us? No sir, follow SAT Crashers Rule #16, "Don't look for problems, make answers!" Stay focused. Don't overthink it. The answer will be very close to something that's actually stated. Let's use the process of elimination.

(A) ~~inspire followers~~ —Nope, both suggest a leader must give "hope."
(B) govern democratically—Maybe, only Passage 2 mentions it.
(C) ~~provide hope~~ —No way, both directly suggest it.
(D) have faith in others—Maybe, do they both suggest it?
(E) ~~attempt to provide safety~~ —No, both basically suggest it with "hope" and "rescue."

Choice B is the best answer because only Passage 2 discusses governing "democratically." Choice D is not correct because "faith in others" is stated directly in Passage 1 and suggested in Passage 2 with democratic leadership.

Correct answer: B

SAT Reading/Writing Mantra #16
For "suggest" questions look for the answer that is hinted at in the passage; though it might have different language, it should be pretty close to what is actually said.

What Are You Trying to "Suggest"? Drills

Read the passage for main idea and tone, not to memorize details. We'll come back for those. Also, if you come to a crazy-hard sentence, don't reread, move on. It's very liberating!

The following passage was included in a 1999 master's thesis about stress management.

The concept of biological stress refers to the body's response to any real or perceived threat to equilibrium. This stress response produces changes in the body in preparation for engaging
5 or running from a physical threat. These changes can include increased heart rate and blood pressure, muscle tension, and suspended digestive activity. In a physically threatening situation, this response is essential and can be
10 life-saving. However, after the threat has passed, the changes should abate and the body should return to normal.

The stress response can also be triggered by threats that are not solved by physical
15 readiness: traffic, work deadlines, or thinking of difficult future events. These threats are not solved by the stress response, and can persist for long periods or occur repeatedly. Thus, the stress response that is intended to turn on and
20 then off can become chronically activated. In this case, when the physiological changes of the stress response persist, the changes can lead to disease. Chronic stress has been linked to suppression of the immune system, rises in
25 blood-cholesterol levels, calcium loss from bones, long-term increases in blood pressure, increased muscle tension, diarrhea or digestive organ spasms, and risk of arrhythmia.

As a result of these potential problems, people
30 have explored ways of managing stress so it does not become chronic. The goal of stress management is not to avoid all stress, as some stress is inevitable and even stimulating, but to experience the stress response only when it is
35 relevant and helpful. Scientists studying stress and its management have found that stressors and stress management modalities affect individuals differently. A stressor that brings distress to one person may be pleasant for
40 another. Similarly, a stress management technique might work for one person, but be ineffective or even distressing for another.

❶ The passage suggests that the "changes" described in lines 6 to 8 can be life-saving because they allow a person to

Ⓐ tense up at the possibility of danger

Ⓑ avoid heart attack

Ⓒ deal with work deadlines

Ⓓ deal with material danger

Ⓔ manage stress

❷ The reader can infer that the examples in lines 15 and 16 ("traffic . . . events.") are not solved by the stress response because

Ⓐ they require physical readiness, not thinking

Ⓑ they persist too long

Ⓒ traffic and work deadlines are worsened by stress

Ⓓ the ability to fight or flee does not solve these concerns

Ⓔ they lead to chronic activation of the stress response

❸ The last paragraph implies that stress management aims to

Ⓐ avert the stress response when it cannot solve a problem

Ⓑ affect individuals differently

Ⓒ avoid all stress

Ⓓ raise one's heart rate

Ⓔ reduce muscle tension

Skill Preview:

❹ (Skill 18) The author's attitude toward stress management is one of

Ⓐ qualified disapproval

Ⓑ resentment

Ⓒ ambivalence

Ⓓ unbiased appreciation

Ⓔ moral indignation

ASS of U and ME

Some questions will ask you to identify the assumptions that the author made in the passage. What's an SAT assumption? Here's an example. If I tell you that you must study to achieve your SAT goal, I have assumed that your goal is to do well on the SAT. We handle assumption questions as we do Skill 16's "suggest" questions; the correct answer will probably not be directly quoted from the passage, but it should be pretty darn close, and we must still have proof from the passage.

Let's take a look at the question from the Pretest.

17. In lines 13 to 16, the author of Passage 1 makes the assumption that

(A) the survivors want to start anew as John Locke did
(B) John Locke was once paralyzed
(C) John Locke feels no hope
(D) Jack Shepherd was a successful surgeon
(E) Jack Shepherd makes democratic decisions

Solution: Use the process of elimination, and remember to answer based on evidence in the passage.

(A) the survivors want to start anew as John Locke did—Maybe, seems like an assumption.
(B) ~~John Locke was once paralyzed~~—No, this is fact.
(C) ~~John Locke feels no hope~~—No, there is no mention of this.
(D) ~~Jack Shepherd was a successful surgeon~~—No, that is Passage 2, and not an assumption anyway.
(E) ~~Jack Shepherd makes democratic decisions~~—Nope, that is Passage 2, and not an assumption anyway.

It has to be choice A. Even when a question seems weird or difficult, if you stay focused and use the process of elimination, you can get it right, sometimes without even being sure of the right answer!

Correct answer: A

SAT Reading/Writing Mantra #17
For an "assumption" question, use the process of elimination.

ASS of U and ME Drills

The following was adapted from an exploration of polarity, written in 2007.

Polarity is more complicated than many seem to understand. Indeed, I myself was surprised by the depths to which we may pursue any case of opposites. One astonishing example of this
5 complexity is that one opposite may, at an extreme, become the other. As a child in Waldorf kindergarten I remember marveling with my friends at the water in which we washed the dishes from lunch, and how it was
10 so hot that it felt cold. We have all had the experience of laughing so hard that we cried, or feeling so happy that it hurt. In optics we see the color orange at the point where the top of a poorly lit window-frame meets the bright
15 sky. At the bottom of the window where dark and light meet, we see its complementary color, blue.

Albert Einstein once stated that "Imagination is more important than knowledge." Einstein's
20 fame as a scientist gives this quote tremendous meaning. In one of the greatest minds of the modern world, one might expect a preference for knowledge over creativity, or hard work over play. Einstein, however, tells us not to discredit
25 original thought, intuition, and the power of our own minds.

Einstein also said, "Science without religion is lame, religion without science is blind." It is interesting to think that the two might go hand
30 in hand, since we often think of science and religion as being at war. Einstein obviously believed in the idea of these two polar opposites being complementary, rather than clashing.

35 Furthermore, to Einstein there exists a whole new level of religious understanding. "There is a third stage of religious experience . . . even though it is rarely found in a pure form: I shall call it cosmic religious feeling." To Einstein, this
40 is the level of pure religious feeling, separate from any taught concept of religion. It is man's sense of right and wrong, his desire to do good and to help others.

❶ In the first sentence, the author assumes that

- Ⓐ no one can understand the true meaning of polarity
- Ⓑ people misunderstand polarity's implications
- Ⓒ others are not as intrigued as he about polarity's depths
- Ⓓ one opposite may become another
- Ⓔ people are not interested in polarity because it offends them

❷ Lines 21 to 24 ("In one of the . . . play.") indicate that the author believes people might assume Einstein

- Ⓐ respected human instinct
- Ⓑ was pensive
- Ⓒ hated intellectualism
- Ⓓ favored religion over science
- Ⓔ favored assiduous logical inquiry

❸ A major assumption of the third paragraph is that

- Ⓐ science and religion go hand in hand
- Ⓑ science and religion are important
- Ⓒ Einstein's experiments were invalid
- Ⓓ Einstein was devout
- Ⓔ science and religion are considered opposites

Review

❹ (Skill 14) In line 1, "polarity" most nearly means

- Ⓐ complications
- Ⓑ magnetism
- Ⓒ apex
- Ⓓ opposites
- Ⓔ southernmost point

Some Attitude

Remember from Skill 13 that as you read each passage, you are keeping in mind, "What is the main idea and what is the author's attitude?" In this Skill you will become an attitude master. An author's attitude is expressed through choice of words and punctuation. For example, what is the attitude expressed in each of the following?

❶ Politicians have once again overlooked the need for improvement in the infrastructure.
Attitude toward politicians: disapproval

❷ Overworked politicians cannot be expected to foresee every need of their community.
Attitude toward politicians: compassion, forgiveness

❶ Will Farrell is one funny guy.
Attitude toward Will Farrell: admiration, appreciation

❷ You're such a "funny" guy.
Attitude: criticism, sarcasm

Remember to answer attitude questions based on evidence in the passage, not your own attitude toward the subject or outside knowledge. If you need help, try rereading the first and last lines of each paragraph. Often, these lines convey the author's attitude.

The SAT favors mellow attitudes. An extreme answer with all-out hatred or complete unqualified worship is not usually correct. Usually the answer is more moderate. If fact, the correct answer often has moderate words such as "moderate," "tempered," "qualified," "veiled," "relative," "somewhat," or "generally."

Let's take a look at the question from the Pretest.

18. The author of Passage 1 would most likely regard Dr. Jack Shepherd with

    (A) absolute puzzlement   (B) unabashed contempt   (C) amusement
    (D) qualified disapproval   (E) general admiration

Solution: Use the process of elimination. The author of Passage 2 describes John Locke as the **true** leader of the group and appreciates Locke's faith-based approach to leadership. She would therefore, at least to some extent, disagree with Jack's logic-based approach. We have no evidence that she would hate Jack, only that she appreciates Locke's style more. So we are looking for something neutral or slightly negative.

(A) ~~absolute puzzlement~~ —Nope, the author does not seem puzzled, she seems sure.
(B) ~~unabashed contempt~~ —Nope, the author never mentions hating Jack.
(C) ~~amusement~~ —No, the author does not seem amused.
(D) qualified disapproval—Maybe, "qualified disapproval" means "limited disapproval."
(E) ~~general admiration~~ —Nope, the author admires Locke.

Correct answer: D

SAT Reading/Writing Mantra #18
Answer "attitude" questions based on evidence in the passage; an author's attitude is expressed through choice of words and punctuation.

Some Attitude Drills

The following is a monologue delivered in a 1998 movie. The speaker is about to scatter the ashes of his friend. (Courtesy of Universal Studios Licensing LLLP.)

Donny was a good bowler, and a good man. He was one of us. He was a man who loved the outdoors . . . and bowling, and as a surfer he explored the beaches of Southern California,
5   from La Jolla to Leo Carrillo and . . . up to . . . Pismo. He died, like so many young men of his generation, he died before his time. In your wisdom, Lord, you took him, as you took so many bright, flowering young men at Khe Sanh,
10 at Langdok, at Hill 364.[1] These young men gave their lives. And so would Donny. Donny, who loved bowling. And so, Theodore Donald Karabotsos, in accordance with what we think your dying wishes might well have been, we
15 commit your final mortal remains to the bosom of the Pacific Ocean, which you loved so well. Good night, sweet prince.

1 In this passage, the speaker's attitude toward Donny is primarily one of

- (A) mournful eulogy
- (B) unbiased detachment
- (C) clear hostility
- (D) elated nostalgia
- (E) friendly regret

2 The speaker's attitude toward bowling can best be described as

- (A) respect
- (B) disregard
- (C) contempt
- (D) indifference
- (E) earnest puzzlement

3 In context, the tone of lines 7 to 10 ("In your wisdom . . . Hill 364.") is best described as

- (A) anxious
- (B) impatient
- (C) baffled
- (D) ambivalent
- (E) resigned

4 The speaker's tone in the last two sentences is best described as

- (A) irritated
- (B) confused
- (C) solemn
- (D) encouraged
- (E) curious

Review

5 (Skill 14) In line 9, "bright" most nearly means

- (A) light
- (B) intelligent
- (C) vivid
- (D) dazzling
- (E) clear

6 (Skill 14) In context, "bosom" (line 15) most nearly means

- (A) chest
- (B) column
- (C) trunk
- (D) comfort
- (E) foam

7 (Skill 16) The reference in lines 9 and 10 to Khe Sanh and Langdok suggests

- (A) Donny will be buried at Hill 364
- (B) Donny died in combat
- (C) the speaker misses these places
- (D) the speaker also lost friends at these places
- (E) bowling is like war

[1]Battles of the Vietnam war.

Two Passages

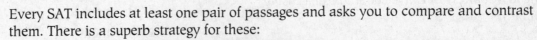

Every SAT includes at least one pair of passages and asks you to compare and contrast them. There is a superb strategy for these:

> **SAT Reading/Writing Mantra #19**
> **When there are two passages, read the first passage for main idea and tone and answer those questions. Then read the second passage for main idea and tone, and answer those questions. Finally, answer questions that compare and contrast the two passages.**

The questions usually contain trick answers from the other passage, and if you haven't even read it, then you can't be fooled by the tricks. They'll just seem irrelevant, and you'll immediately eliminate them.

After you read Passage 1, jot down or circle a phrase that identifies the main idea or the tone. Then after you answer Passage 1 questions, read Passage 2 for main idea and tone, and jot down or circle a phrase. This will help you keep the passages straight for the compare and contrast questions.

Also, generally, if the passages are about the same topic, they will have a slightly different take on it. And if they are about different topics, then they will share a common link uniting them. For example, if both passages are about MP3 players, they will have slightly different opinions or focus on different aspects of the topic, such as the benefits of portability versus the reduction in sound quality. And if they are on totally different topics, such as Shakespeare and Eminem, they will have something in common, such as praising the extraordinary poetry of each.

Let's look at the question from the Pretest.

19. The author of Passage 2 would most likely regard John Locke with

    (A) reverence
    (B) indifference
    (C) skepticism
    (D) caustic abhorrence
    (E) bitter jealousy

Solution: The author of Passage 2 respects Jack's logical nature and compliments Jack on avoiding "hokey mysticism." She would therefore disapprove of John Locke's faith-based approach to leadership on the island. Therefore, choices C and E are possible answers, but choice E is too strong. The author does not hate Locke; she just thinks that Jack is the better leader.

Remember, an extreme answer with all-out hatred or complete unqualified worship is not usually correct. Usually the answer is more moderate.

Correct answer: C

Two Passages Drills

Passage 1

Medicinal systems can be examined by using the three models, biochemical, bioenergetic, and biospiritual. The biochemical model is the dominant approach used in the United States.

5 Scientists using this approach analyze the chemical constituents of things. It views the human body as a chemical factory that can be adjusted according to the intake of the right chemicals. This model tends to employ

10 medicinal drugs, called pharmaceuticals. These drugs are made by identifying therapeutic substances and isolating their active ingredients. These drugs often have a stronger potency and a more immediate effect on the body than

15 nonisolated and natural remedies, but often, later, it is found that they have unanticipated side effects or that the pathogenic factors change, rendering the drug less effective.

Passage 2

Ayurveda is a 5000 year old natural healing

20 system from India. The word "Ayurveda" translates from Sanskrit as "the science of life or longevity." It can be described as a natural holistic medical system. Dr. Andrew Weil describes natural medical systems as having a

25 philosophy of healing based on the notion that the body has innate mechanisms of self-repair, for example, that a cut on the human body will naturally heal itself. The aim in Ayurveda is to observe and then encourage the self-repair

30 process: to empower the body's natural healing potential. Ayurveda is also a type of holistic medicine, as it considers the effect of a whole substance on the whole of a person, rather than only a body part or system.

❶ In Passage 1 the author cites which of the following as an example of a biochemical medicine?

Ⓐ nonisolated remedies

Ⓑ Ayurveda

Ⓒ holistic medicine

Ⓓ natural remedies

Ⓔ pharmaceuticals

❷ The author of Passage 1 would most likely regard the system of Auyrveda as described in lines 31 to 34 ("Aurveda . . . system.") in Passage 2 as

Ⓐ a biochemical system

Ⓑ inactive

Ⓒ superior to holistic models

Ⓓ inferior to the dominant approach

Ⓔ either bioenergetic or biospiritual

❸ Both passages serve to encourage

Ⓐ the body's self-repair

Ⓑ consideration of the whole effect of medicines on the body

Ⓒ need for medical reform

Ⓓ lack of continuity in medical systems

Ⓔ problems with alternative medicine

❹ A primary difference between the two passages is

Ⓐ the first begins to set up a basis to analyze any medical system whereas the second begins to detail one specific system

Ⓑ the first is specific and the second is general

Ⓒ the first encourages holistic health and the second discourages it

Ⓓ the first discusses one system and the second discusses several

Ⓔ the first cites authorities

❺ Unlike the author of Passage 1, the author of Passage 2 makes use of

Ⓐ generalizations

Ⓑ refuting a hypothesis

Ⓒ commonly held beliefs

Ⓓ citing an authority

Ⓔ technical terms

Main Idea

The main idea is the general topic of a passage, what it's trying to get across. It answers the question, So, what's your point? That's the question that you kept in mind as you read the passage. Reading with this question in mind helps you

- Stay focused
- Avoid getting caught up in memorizing details
- Gather an answer for the "main idea" question

After you have answered all the line number questions, go back to main idea and tone questions. Why wait? Because by the time you have completed the line number questions, you have reread and rethought the passage, and you have an even better understanding of main idea and tone.

Also, remember the italics. I showed you in Skill 12 that sometimes the italicized intro actually gives away the main idea! If you need more help, you can also reread the first and last lines of each paragraph for clues to the main idea.

Here's the question from the Pretest.

20. The passage is best described as

   (A) an illustration of an ongoing relationship
   (B) an introduction to a character
   (C) a social commentary on the Western genre
   (D) a nostalgic depiction of a Western hero
   (E) a story of how one movie inspired another

Solution: Think of a basic answer that you like to see and then use the process of elimination. Don't get thrown by a wrong answer that sounds fancy. Stay confident. Kids sometimes think, "Wow, that sounds fancy, I don't get it, but it must be right." No! The right answer should make sense to you. It should fit the evidence in the passage. Be a lawyer! Let's take a look:

(A) an illustration of an ongoing relationship—Maybe, but kinda weak, it is not really about an ongoing relationship.

(B) an introduction to a character—Maybe, but also weak, it seems more about Westerns in general than about any specific character.

(C) a social commentary on Western genre—Probably, it is certainly mostly about Westerns in general.

(D) a nostalgic depiction of a Western hero—No, it's not the story of a particular hero.

(E) a story of how one movie inspired another—No, it does compare the movies, but the main idea is not that one inspired another.

Choice C is the best answer. The passage is primarily about Westerns and the changes in the style over the years. You can see this very clearly be rereading the first and last lines of each paragraph!

Correct answer: C

SAT Reading/Writing Mantra #20
If you need help with a "main idea" question, reread the italics and the first and last lines of each paragraph.

Main Idea Drills

Olmsted foresaw the need for plans at a time when they were considered mysterious. He anticipated that city parks would ensure future prosperity for the cities by increasing the value of city real estate, as well as creating a more balanced and egalitarian life for city dwellers then and in the future. Olmsted possessed an ability to see into the future and address future needs of city-dwellers in his planning. In this way, his planning had a permanent effect on history that remains pertinent to our modern lifestyles. Even today, his concepts of city parks and landscaping are widely accepted and practiced.

❶ The author's main point in the passage is that

Ⓐ city parks are essential to city real estate

Ⓑ Olmsted was a man of vision

Ⓒ city park planning has not changed much since Olmsted's time

Ⓓ Olmsted sought egalitarian city park use

Ⓔ Olmsted has affected our modern lives

During the tower's construction many Parisian citizens complained about the tower's aesthetics, inconvenience and potential danger. Some people went so far as to testify in court. A number of well-known artists and musicians got together to sign a petition against the tower. They stated that it was, ugly, useless, costly and likely to fall in harsh weather. Gustave replied to the complaints by saying that he was as dedicated to the tower's aesthetics as they were, and that he designed the tower in such a way that the iron lattice work created almost no wind resistance, thus ensuring the tower's endurance.

❷ The primary purpose of the passage is to

Ⓐ depict an era

Ⓑ justify an expenditure

Ⓒ give an historical account

Ⓓ defend a decision

Ⓔ criticize an architectural work

Ma makes sassafras tea while Pa's boss compliments the tree. Then, they all sit down for grown-up talk while we gather round the tree to shake the copious presents. When carolers come by, we witness the enchanted looks on their faces as they too are inebriated by the magic of the gorgeous tree. Then Ma gives them some gingerbread and cider. If we had a tree like this, we'd never travel to Brooklyn to see Grandma; she'd come to us, despite the fact that she hates our dogs.

❸ The passage is best described as

Ⓐ an illustration of a lasting relationship

Ⓑ a nostalgic recollection

Ⓒ a pleasant fantasy

Ⓓ a story of imminent change

Ⓔ an introduction to a character through another's eyes

Skill 21
Gretchen Is "Such" a Good Friend

And you know she cheats on Aaron? Yes, every Thursday he thinks she's doing SAT prep, but really she's hooking up with Shane Oman in the projection room above the auditorium! I never told anybody that because I am "such" a good friend!

Gretchen, *Mean Girls* (Paramount Pictures, 2004)

Why are there quote marks around "such"? In this example, it's to show that the word is emphasized. The SAT loves to ask questions like this; questions about why the author choose a certain word or punctuation mark. These questions ask about the writer's choices and how a word functions, rather than about the main idea or what a word means.

Let's look at the question from the Pretest.

21. In line 13, the quotation marks around the words "Family Values" serve to

(A) criticize the Western genre
(B) indicate an irony in the meaning of the words
(C) emphasize the uniqueness of the author's writing
(D) support the common use of the words
(E) emphasize that the words would be emphasized if read aloud

Solution: Usually, on the SAT, when quotation marks are not used literally to quote something, they indicate that the word or phrase is used in an unusual way, such as ironically. In this case, the settler is described as "not always moral," so "Family Values" is being used ironically. You could convince yourself of several of the other answers, but choice B is the best answer and the one most clearly supported by evidence in the passage. Remember to base your answer on evidence in the passage, not your own outside knowledge or opinions.

Correct answer: B

SAT Reading/Writing Mantra #21
When quotes around a phrase are not used to literally quote something from another source, they indicate that the phrase is used in an unusual way, such as ironically. And words in parentheses usually function as a side note to the reader.

58

Gretchen Is "Such" a Good Friend Drills

This passage is from a 1998 movie. (Courtesy of Universal Studios Licensing LLLP.)

Way out west there was this fella I wanna tell ya about. Goes by the name of Jeff Lebowski. At least that was the handle his loving parents gave him, but he never had much use for it himself.
5 See, this Lebowski, he called himself "The Dude." Now, "Dude"—there's a name no man would self-apply where I come from. But then there was a lot about the Dude that didn't make a whole lot of sense. And a lot about where he lived, likewise.
10 But then again, maybe that's why I found the place so darned interestin'. See, they call Los Angeles the "City of Angels"; but I didn't find it to be that, exactly. But I'll allow it as there are some nice folks there. 'Course I ain't never been to
15 London, and I ain't never seen France. And I ain't never seen no queen in her damned undies, so the feller says. But I'll tell you what—after seeing Los Angeles, and this here story I'm about to unfold, well, I guess I seen somethin' every bit as
20 stupefyin' as you'd seen in any of them other places. And in English, too. So I can die with a smile on my face, without feelin' like the good Lord gypped me.

Now this here story I'm about to unfold took
25 place in the early '90s—just about the time of our conflict with Sad'm and the I-raqis. I only mention it because sometimes there's a man . . . I won't say a hero, 'cause, what's a hero? Sometimes, there's a man. And I'm talkin'
30 about the Dude here—the Dude from Los Angeles. Sometimes, there's a man, well, he's the man for his time and place. He fits right in there. And that's the Dude. The Dude, from Los Angeles. And even if he's a lazy man—and the
35 Dude was most certainly that. Quite possibly the laziest in all of Los Angeles County, which would place him high in the runnin' for laziest worldwide. Sometimes there's a man, sometimes, there's a man. Well, I lost my train
40 of thought here. But . . . aw, hell. I've done introduced it enough.

① The author misspells words in line 1 ("Way out . . . about.") in order to

(A) represent the narrator's accent
(B) indicate his disapproval of the accepted spellings
(C) emphasize the uniqueness of the author's writing
(D) criticize the character being described
(E) characterize the Dude

② In line 6, the quotation marks around the word "Dude" serve to

(A) emphasize the individuality of the author's style
(B) indicate the unusualness of the name
(C) indicate the narrator's disapproval of Lebowski
(D) criticize Lebowski's parents
(E) demonstrate the speaker's confusion about Lebowski's professional life

③ The repetition of the phrase "sometimes there's a man" in lines 27 to 29 emphasizes the

(A) virility of the Dude
(B) infrequent appearances of the Dude
(C) doubt as to the Dude's gender
(D) Dude's laziness
(E) narrator losing concentration

④ The author develops the passage by presenting

(A) a hypothesis and supporting details
(B) a common argument followed by counterexamples to disprove it
(C) description interspersed with tangential remarks
(D) several sides to a single issue
(E) explication of an unusual belief

Review

5 (Skill 14) In line 3, "handle" most nearly means

(A) grip

(B) inheritance

(C) ability to cope

(D) title

(E) personality

6 (Skill 15) The phrase "but I didn't . . . exactly" (lines 12 to 13) indicates that the narrator

(A) could not locate the city

(B) did not attend church in Los Angeles

(C) met few virtuous people in Los Angeles

(D) met several nice people in the city

(E) liked his trip to Los Angeles more than to London

This question type asks, Which of the following ideas or situations is most like (or unlike) the one from the passage? This type throws students because the choices are not details from the passage. They are new details that exemplify something from the passage, and we want the one that satisfies the question.

Kids get confused by these and say, "Oh, I don't recognize these choices, I must have missed this; I'll just skip this one." But, with our strategies you won't miss anything. Stay relaxed and focused and confident. And when you see this type of question, just recognize it as a "parallel" question and know that the choices may not be from the passage. Since you know to expect it, you'll recognize it and get it right.

Let's take a look at the Pretest.

22. Which statement about Westerns, if true, detracts most from the author's assertions expressed in lines 15 to 18 ("both films . . . same")?

(A) Both films follow a similar style.
(B) Both films examine the theme of love and loss.
(C) *Dead Man* and *Stagecoach* each stick to predictable Western patterns.
(D) *Dead Man* and *Stagecoach* examine different subject matter.
(E) The films were filmed half a century apart.

Solution: The author's assertions say that even though there are big differences, there are also **similarities** in style and theme. To detract most from this, you want an answer that says the opposite—that points out the style and/or theme **differences** of the two films. Choice D is the only choice that points out differences. On this type of question, make sure to stay confident, and as you look through the choices, remember whether you want differences or similarities.

Correct answer: D

> **SAT Reading/Writing Mantra #22**
> For a "parallel" question, don't get thrown if the choices are not from the passage.
> Stay relaxed and focused, and look for the choice that proves or disproves the statement.

Parallel Drills

The media makes you think that you have to be skinny or buff. The media makes you think that you have to get rich and own lots of things. But you don't. I see a whole generation; no, I see

5 generations working as slaves to consumption. Working, working too hard to buy disposable things they're told they need. Go sit by a tree in a calm place for two hours, maybe by a stream. You'll see what I mean. It's free and it's more

10 joy than that new designer watch can possibly give you.

Why is everyone depressed? Their latte is not making them happy. Two and a half hours of TV per day is not satisfying. People are confused by

15 TV; their expectations of life get skewed. No, there's a void. Relax, open, and let it fill up.

1 Which of the following individuals best exemplifies the narrator's assertion in lines 1 to 3 ("The media . . . things.")?

(A) A man who saves up to buy a new designer suit

(B) A man who hates his job and quits

(C) A man who finds a job he loves

(D) A slave in chains

(E) A middle child in a large family

2 Which of the following is the narrator likely to do next?

(A) Teach more about designer watches

(B) Give Latin names for specific trees

(C) Describe more about how individuals can take action to effect change

(D) Describe jobs that are available

(E) Enlist for military service

3 Which of the following, if true, would LEAST undermine the assertion in lines 13 to 15 ("Two and . . . skewed.")?

(A) Most people do not try to model what they see on television.

(B) Most people do not realize that what they see on television is unreal.

(C) Most people watch far less than 2.5 hours of television per day.

(D) A study showed that most people are very minimally affected by the values expressed on television.

(E) Most people realize that television is fantasy.

Review

4 (Skill 18) The general tone of the passage can best be described as

(A) humorous contempt

(B) worried vexation

(C) relieved acknowledgment

(D) begrudging empathy

(E) muted anger

Special Section: How to Read

Sometimes SAT passages are obscenely long and kids panic, "I can't do it! It'll take too long. It'll kill me." Relax, and remember your skills. Read the passage, looking for main idea and tone. Don't memorize details. Don't reread a confusing line. Don't reread if you spaced out and missed a sentence or two. There's no single sentence or even paragraph that you need to get the main idea and tone. As for details, you'll reread the lines later anyway.

All this will save you time and energy. And remember my story. When I was 16 years old and preparing for the SAT, I did well in school, but didn't read much. I was terrified. Then one day I was like "Wait, this is ridiculous, how long can it take?" So I took out a stopwatch and timed myself. It took 2.5 minutes! Try it, and you'll see. Even for a slow reader, the passage takes only a few minutes, especially if you use your skills.

So read the following huge passage. Read quickly, but stay relaxed. Pretend you love the topic. As you read, ask yourself, What are the main idea and tone? Use all the Skills. Time yourself. You'll see that reading even a ridiculously long passage takes only a few minutes. And remember that a passage this long would be the main passage of the section, so you'd have the rest of your time just to answer the questions.

How to Read
- **Read the passage, looking for main idea and tone.**
- **Don't memorize details.**
- **Don't reread a confusing line.**
- **Don't reread if you spaced out and missed a sentence or two.**

Directions: Read the absurdly long passage on the next page. Time yourself. If it takes you over 5 minutes, review the Skills above and reread the passage. Anyone can read quickly; remember, you are not reading to memorize details, just to get the gist. You'll see that even a disgustingly long SAT passage takes only a few minutes to read. When it takes you under 5 minutes, you're ready.

(If you absolutely cannot do it in under 5 minutes, no problem, here's your strategy: read for 4 minutes and stop. That'll be enough for you to get some main idea and tone info, without spending too much time. But you have to practice watching the clock and knowing when it's been 4 minutes.)

This passage describing a certain type of spider was written in 2006.

The Brown Recluse spider is a potentially dangerous species that inhabits the southeastern part of the United States. A bite from the Brown Recluse can cause a severe wound. As a result, the spiders cause much fear; however, in reality, Brown Recluse spiders cause few grave injuries to humans, and you are more likely to get struck by lightning than critically hurt by a Brown Recluse spider.

Including its legs, the Recluse spider is roughly the size of a quarter. Females have a slightly larger body than the males, however the males make up for this with longer legs—better for hunting. The only way for an everyday person (not a trained scientist) to identify this spider is the darker brown fiddle-shaped marking on the back of the abdomen. This is how they acquired their nickname Fiddler Spider.

The Recluse spider lives about two years, taking about a year to fully mature, molting clear bridal exoskeletons several times on their way to adulthood. The females lay their eggs in white silky sacks, each containing roughly forty spider-larva. A female can lay several sacks a season, sometimes even producing up to 300 individual eggs. The mother remains in her web to guard the eggs until the spiderlings emerge. During this period of twenty to thirty days, the mother doesn't eat or drink, not letting her attention waver at all from her offspring.

The spiderlings abandon the web immediately after they hatch; they leave to find their secluded hideaways and to give their mother back her preferred solitary life. The young spiders enter the world as immature lentil-sized versions of their parents. Their only major defense is their freakish ability to fast for up to six months without food or water—their poison hasn't even peaked in its potency. Most of them will die on their eleven-month journey to adulthood. Come next year the small handful of time-tested troopers will be mature in time to take part in breeding season. This is most likely their first of two breedings.

The Brown Recluse spider uses its web as a private day lodging. They do not use it as a hunting palate like most spiders do. Their web is also unusual in that it doesn't have a pleasing symmetrical spiral pattern of tightly woven clean threads. On the contrary it is rough, lacking order, comprised of loose strands of off-yellow silk sagging in all directions. The web seems to be of little use to these spiders and the project of building can even be abandoned if a soft nesting place, such as stored linens or clothes, is available.

The spiders tend to leave their lone retreats at sundown to hunt for insects. They kill their prey by initially using their legs to trap the insect and then injecting their venom to finish the job. Although they can hunt and have evolved venom to do so, their weak physical constitution renders hunting second to scavenging. Their legs fall off easily, and if a spider is not quick enough to inject the venom, it is possible for the prey to shred it to pieces. This often happens with crickets. Changing habitats have also fostered their growing love of dead insects. With more and more Recluses living in human environments, dried out bugs are all around them and easily picked up during the night when the inhabitants are sleeping.

The spiders tend to spin their webs in dark reclusive sheltered areas, and consequently man-made buildings meet their needs perfectly. They can be invasive pests, monopolizing attics, barns, cellars, and crawl spaces with their ugly webs. Their need for private spaces quickly disperses a colony throughout a building.

In North America the Brown Recluse spider ranks with the rattlesnake, black widow, cougar, and grizzly in its threat to people. Yet, problematic injuries actually rarely happen. In fact, you are more likely to croak in your bathtub than from a bite from a Brown Recluse spider. However I don't buy it, I'm the first to avoid grizzly bear territory, and next time I go South, I plan on sleeping in a body bag with microscopic breathing holes.

How to Be a Reading Ninja

You've now learned the 11 reading Skills that you need for the SAT. The Mantras remind you what to do for each type of question. Let's make sure you've memorized them. Drill them until you are ready to teach them. Then do that. Find a willing friend and give a little SAT course.

Learning the Mantras is like learning martial arts. Practice until they become part of you—until you follow them naturally: When you see a passage, you read for main idea and tone, and when you answer questions, you recognize most questions types and know what to do. This will definitely raise your score. It might even fundamentally change you as a student. After SAT prep many students have better study habits. They read the intros in their history book, they read faster and with better comprehension, they are able to anticipate quiz questions. Homework becomes less intimidating, easier, and more fun. So go to work—your SAT score and probably even your school grades will go up!

Here are the 11 SAT reading Mantras. Check the box next to each Skill when you have mastered it. Reread the Skill sections if you need to.

☐ **Skill 12.** Always begin a reading passage by reading the italics.

☐ **Skill 13.** Read the passage, looking for main idea and tone. That helps you stay focused; keep asking yourself, What are the main idea and tone? Don't try to memorize details and don't reread hard lines. If you need them, you'll reread later when you know the question and what to look for.

☐ **Skill 14.** To answer a "most nearly means" question, reread a few lines before and a few lines after, and remember that the answer is usually not the most common definition.

☐ **Skill 15.** For a "direct info" question, always read before and after a line and find proof.

☐ **Skill 16.** For "suggest" questions, look for the answer that is hinted at in the passage; though it might have different language, it should be pretty close to what is actually said.

☐ **Skill 17.** For an "assumption" question, use the process of elimination.

☐ **Skill 18.** Answer "attitude" questions based on evidence in the passage; an author's attitude is expressed through choice of words and punctuation.

☐ **Skill 19.** When there are two passages, read the first passage for main idea and tone and answer those questions. Then read the second passage for main idea and tone, and answer those questions. Finally, answer questions that compare and contrast the two passages.

☐ **Skill 20.** If you need help with a "main idea" question, reread the italics and the first and last lines of each paragraph.

☐ **Skill 21.** When quotes around a phrase are not used to literally quote something from another source, they indicate that the phrase is used in an unusual way, such as ironically. And words in parentheses usually function as a side note to the reader.

☐ **Skill 22.** For a "parallel" question, don't get thrown if the choices are not from the passage. Stay relaxed and focused, and look for the choice that proves or disproves the statement.

Here's the question from the Pretest.

23. In line 20, "this change" refers to

   (A) the beginning and end of the Vietnam war
   (B) the different representations depicted in the two films
   (C) the loss of American values
   (D) the changing role of film in society
   (E) the mission of women

Solution: This is a direct info question. Just read a few lines before and a few lines after "this change." The answer is evident both sentences before and in one sentence after. Each demonstrates that "this change" specifically refers to the change in the depiction of American values as seen in the two films. Choice B is the best answer. Several other answers are close or have words recognizable from the passage, but they do not express the author's intention for "this change." Remember, the whole answer must work, not just the first few words.

Correct answer: B

How to Avoid the Six Most Common Careless Errors on SAT Reading Questions

1. Don't select an answer based on just the first few words; the whole answer should make sense.
2. Be mindful on EXCEPT questions; you are looking for the choice that does **not** work.
3. Be mindful on LEAST/MOST questions.
4. Find evidence for your answer; be a lawyer.
5. Use evidence from the passage, not your own outside knowledge or opinions.
6. Don't get intimidated. If it seems hard, look for the evidence, decide what type of question it is, use your Mantras, and remember:
   SAT Crashers Rule #45: No excuses. Test like a champion!

Identify each question type, and then choose the best answer.

The following passage examines certain themes of the Disney movie The Little Mermaid.

Among the most important themes in *The Little Mermaid* are those of questioning conventional thinking, and pursuing a dream. Not only is Ariel, the little mermaid, demonstrating original
5 thought (something that many seem to think she is lacking), but she is rebelling against her speciesist father. When Ariel expresses her love for the human prince, King Trident is furious. When Ariel points out angrily that he does not
10 understand her, or even know the man whom she loves, Trident retorts, "Know him? I don't need to know him! He's a human!" In a very real way Disney is encouraging children to question preconceived ideas that we may have
15 against a certain group.

Disney also teaches children to pursue what they love. We see that Ariel's love for Prince Eric is more important than all else. In turning to the Sea Witch, Ursula, for help, Ariel makes
20 a mistake, but no true hero or heroine is flawless. Ariel puts herself, her family, and all merfolk in danger, but we see that with the help of her prince, she is able to put everything to right.

25 At the end of the film, when Ursula has forced King Trident to sacrifice his kingdom for his daughter's soul, the Sea Witch rises out of the water, gigantic and terrifying, wearing the king's crown and holding his magic trident. She
30 laughs evilly and declares that she is the ruler of all mermen and women. "So much for true love!" she screams victoriously. Eric, however, succeeds in piloting the prow of his ship straight through her belly, vanquishing her. The
35 moral here is that while we all make mistakes, what is truly important is how we right the wrongs we may do to others.

❶ The author's main point in the passage is that

Ⓐ Ariel should not have been allowed to marry Prince Eric

Ⓑ only Prince Eric truly understood Ariel

Ⓒ Ariel demonstrated original thought

Ⓓ *The Little Mermaid* teaches children to follow their hearts

Ⓔ Disney movies teach that love is stronger than hate

❷ Why does the author use parentheses around the comment in lines 5 to 6 ?

Ⓐ to indicate a side comment to the reader

Ⓑ to indicate that it is unimportant

Ⓒ to indicate a humorous tone

Ⓓ to indicate a shift in meaning

Ⓔ to indicate a change in tone

❸ In line 7, Ariel's father is called "speciesist" because he

Ⓐ does not know Eric

Ⓑ is king of his people and pursuing what he loves

Ⓒ is rebelling against preconceived notions

Ⓓ is furious

Ⓔ opposes Ariel's love based only on Eric being human

④ Which fictional plot line would best to illustrate the assertion made in lines 13 to 15 ("Disney is . . . group.")?

Ⓐ A movie about a boy who hates donkeys

Ⓑ A movie about the development of the iPod

Ⓒ A movie about a girl who overcomes her fear of snakes

Ⓓ A movie that details the horrors of war

Ⓔ A movie that documents the travels of a rock band

⑤ Ursula's quote in lines 31 and 32 primarily suggests that

Ⓐ the marriage was unacceptable to her

Ⓑ she is mocking true love

Ⓒ she is speciesist

Ⓓ she was hurt in a prior relationship

Ⓔ Eric is her true love

⑥ In line 34, "vanquishing" most nearly means

Ⓐ loving

Ⓑ succeeding

Ⓒ besting

Ⓓ squashing

Ⓔ vanishing

⑦ The author's attitude toward *The Little Mermaid* is primarily one of

Ⓐ frustration

Ⓑ stoicism

Ⓒ ambivalence

Ⓓ respect

Ⓔ wonder

Alternate Nostril Breathing and Meditation

Alternate Nostril Breathing

This is a sweet technique. It will calm your mind and help you think clearly. And in yoga circles it's considered a fast track to enlightenment. See, mom was right—SAT prep can fulfill all your dreams!

To try it, sit in a chair or on a cushion. Sit up straight, but relaxed. Bring your right hand to your nose. With your thumb close the right nostril and inhale through the left. Then with your pinky and ring finger, close your left nostril and exhale slowly through the right. A slow relaxed exhalation. Then, still covering the left nostril, inhale through the right.

Then cover the right, and exhale slowly through the left. Inhale left, and switch. Continue alternating between right and left nostrils for several minutes. Slow, relaxed, deep, comfortable breaths.

According to yoga philosophy, you should end this practice with an exhale through the left nostril, and then allow your breathing to return to normal.

Meditation

Running builds your endurance. Bench-pressing builds your pecs. Sit-ups tone your abs. Similarly, meditation builds your concentration "muscles" and strengthens your ability to stay focused.

How do you strengthen your concentration? It's easy, although, like weight lifting, it takes work and repetition. If you do the following exercise 5 minutes every morning and every night, I guarantee that you will build your ability to focus. This will make homework easier, improve your grades, and bring up your SAT score. It will probably even improve your social life.

Here's how to meditate. Sit in a comfortable position on a chair or cushion. You need not imitate a swami with your legs twisted together. Then close your eyes. Relax your face. Relax your body. Sit up straight, but relaxed. Become aware of your breathing. Find a spot where you notice your breathing, either the rise and fall of your belly or the in and out of air through your nostrils. Bring your attention to this place. Now, count 10 normal breaths. Unless you are already a Zen monk or a superhero, your mind will probably wander. That's okay. You'll start counting, "One, two, three, . . ." and then wander off and think about breakfast, the SATs, or yesterday's game. Whenever you notice that your mind has wandered, gently come back to counting the breath. Start over at 1. If ever you make it to 10, start over at 1. Do this for 5 minutes.

Five minutes of this every morning and every night will change your life. Your concentration will improve. Your grades will go up. Your SAT score will go up. Your stress level will go down. It's a win-win.

Writing Multiple-Choice

Writing multiple-choice questions are arranged from easiest to hardest. On the "easy" and "medium" questions, trust your ear. You know the error when you hear it. If something sounds wrong, it probably is. If something is difficult to read, it's probably wrong. The purpose of good grammar is to make writing easy to read and understand, so if it's not, if it trips up your tongue or you can't get its meaning, don't say, "Boy, I can't do this." Say, "I can't understand this, so it must be bad grammar." Notice where your tongue gets tied up, where you have to pause and say, "what the . . . ?" That's where the error is, and there's your answer.

**When something trips up your tongue or you
can't get its meaning, it's probably wrong.**

For questions where your ear can't pick up the answer, we have Skills. Many kids who wind up scoring 700+ on the Writing section started out saying, "I suck at these." I don't know where this attitude comes from. Maybe grammar seems very hard the way it's taught in school, or maybe it's not taught, but either way, on the SAT it's easy and totally predicable! The SAT has chosen only a few concepts to test. Memorize these concepts in the next 15 Skills, and your score will go way up, guaranteed!

The SAT Writing Multiple-Choice sections contain three types of questions:

"Identify the error" questions where you just identify the error
"Correct the error" questions where you correct the error
"Edit the passage" questions where you answer questions about editing a passage

The first two types of questions (Skills 24 to 36) are arranged in order of difficulty, easiest to hardest, like sentence completion questions. The "edit the passage" questions (Skill 37) are arranged, like reading comprehension questions, in order of the passage, not order of difficulty.

Subject/Verb Agreement

This is one of the most common types of SAT writing questions, and it's very easy. Basically, in a sentence, subject and verb must match. There is no fancy rule that I need to teach you; you already know this stuff, just from speaking and reading. What I need to teach you is to train and then trust your ear for "easy" and "medium" questions, and to identify the subject of the verb for "hard" questions or when in doubt. In this Skill, we'll look at some straightforward questions. Then in Skill 25 we'll look at the two tricks that the SAT always tries.

Let's take a look at this on the Pretest.

24. Even after she had healed physically, she <u>wants</u> somewhere to <u>heal</u> emotionally,
                                            A   B

and <u>chose</u> Winston College <u>for its</u> small community. <u>No error</u>
    C   D   E

Solution: Listen to your ear; "Even after she had healed physically, she <u>wants</u>" does not sound correct. The "she had healed" implies that the "she wants" should be past tense, "she wanted." You can hear that if you know to listen for it. That's our goal, to train you to listen for it.

Correct answer: A

SAT Reading/Writing Mantra #24
When a verb is underlined, trust your ear. When in doubt, identify its subject and make sure singular/plural and tense match the subject.

Subject/Verb Agreement Drills

Easy

1 Thousands <u>of years</u> <u>after</u> the
              A   B
development of yoga in India, over
<u>twenty-one styles</u> of yoga are
      C
currently <u>practices</u> by millions of
         D
Americans. <u>No error</u>
           E

2 The school council <u>is negotiating</u> a
                A
resolution <u>with the labor union</u> <u>that</u>
          B   C
<u>will meet</u> the requirements set
  D
forth by both the teachers and the
administrators. <u>No error</u>
             E

3 The school association <u>are</u> leading a
                A
day <u>of remembrance</u> <u>for soldiers</u>
      B   C
<u>who perished</u> in World War II in
  D
Europe. <u>No error</u>
       E

4 Twenty-four days after <u>they were</u>
                   A
marooned on an island, the survivors
had split into two <u>groups</u>, one
            B
<u>lives</u> <u>on</u> the beach and the other living in
 C D
caves. <u>No error</u>
      E

Medium

5 Because he <u>is out of town</u> when the
          A
committee voted <u>for</u> the park proposal,
           B
Manuel <u>is concerned</u> about missing any
       C
<u>future</u> Park Planning Committee
  D
meetings. <u>No error</u>
        E

6 The vote of the council, "yes" by all
fourteen members, <u>indicate</u> <u>that</u> the
            A   B
group <u>strongly</u> <u>favors</u> reducing its
     C   D
carbon footprint. <u>No error</u>
         E

7 <u>Running</u> quickly is highly <u>advisable</u> to
  A   B
the tourist who <u>taunt</u> mating lions <u>in the</u>
          C   D
Sahara Desert. <u>No error</u>
        E

8 After Neal <u>had swam</u> across
         A
the lake, he <u>was disappointed</u>
          B
<u>to realize</u> that the giant red dragon still
 C
<u>followed</u> him. <u>No error</u>
   D   E

Subject/Verb Agreement Tricks

The SAT is tricky, but we know and expect their shenanigans. It's like a bad magician whose tricks you can totally predict. The SAT loves two kinds of subject/verb agreement tricks. Every test has at least one of them. They're always rated as "hard" questions, but since we expect them, they're easy for us.

We saw the first trick on the Pretest.

25. At seven in the morning each and every day, Jimmy, with his closest friends, walk the
     A   B   C
    long way to school. No error
         C   E

Solution: Great question. The SAT loves these. Every test has at least one! The trick is that "Jimmy" is the subject, not "friends." "Friends **walk**" sounds correct, but the subject of the verb is "Jimmy," so it should be "Jimmy **walks**."

Correct answer: C

"How can I ever tell that?" you say. Ahh, my friend, easy. A prepositional phrase, such as "with his closest friends," NEVER counts as the subject. Prepositional phrases always begin with a preposition ("on," "above," "below," "with," "by," "during," "until," . . . just Google "prepositions" for a full list) and end with a noun, such as "friends." Here are a few more prepositional phrases: "of awards," "with six kids," and "on the table."

So when you are identifying the subject of an underlined verb, if there is a prepositional phrase, cross it out! Then subject/verb agreement is obvious, and a "hard" question becomes an "easy!"

Jimmy ~~with his friends~~ walks
The number ~~of awards~~ proves
Billy ~~along with six kids~~ goes

The SAT's other trick is to put the subject after the verb. How do you catch these? When you see a verb underlined, look for its subject—notice what is doing the action of the verb. It's easy to tell, as long as you know to look. I love these, they are tricky, but we know they are coming!

SAT Reading/Writing Mantra #26
When a verb is underlined, identify the subject and cross out any prepositional phrases; a prepositional phrase NEVER counts as the subject of the verb. Also, ask what is doing the action of the verb and watch for the second trick, where the subject comes after the verb.

Subject/Verb Agreement Tricks Drills

Cross out any prepositional phrases between the subject and verb, and underline the subject of the bold verb in each of the following sentences.

1 Stephen for two more weeks **is** single.

2 Margarita with her sisters currently **runs** a marketing firm.

3 Running from the bulls **is** Jimmy with his friends.

4 The way of samurais **is** a strict path.

5 Around the corner **are** a dog and a cat.

6 The PTA through generous donations **is** building a new school building.

7 The boys with their dog Alfred **walk** to school.

Now, let's see these tricks on a few SAT questions.

Medium

1 Only recently has the careful craftsmanship of Mabel Seeley's mystery novels been appreciated by readers and critics.

  Ⓐ Only recently has the careful craftsmanship

  Ⓑ Only recently have the careful craftsmanship

  Ⓒ Recently only has the careful craftsmanship

  Ⓓ While recently only have the careful craftsmanship

  Ⓔ Only recently becoming fully appreciated, the careful craftsmanship

2 Though the music of the Boudreaus
    A
has been enjoyed for years, only
  B   C
this past year has it received proper
  D
credit. No error
      E

Hard

3 Hanging on the wall in his office is
  A   B   C
Frank's trophies from years
of dominating amateur spitting
      D
competitions all over Massachusetts.
No error
E

4 The number of milligrams
of various minerals demonstrate
    A   B
the healthfulness of these delicious
      C   D
granola bars. No error
          E

Skill 26

Pronoun Clarity and Agreement

When a pronoun (such as "he," "she," "it," "they," "them," "him," or "her") is underlined, we must be totally sure what noun it is referring to. If it is unclear, in any way, it is incorrect. You're smart, so you might be able to figure out which noun a pronoun refers to, but ask yourself, If Borat were translating this sentence, what would he think? If it's at all unclear, it's wrong. Also, once you know what the pronoun refers to, make sure that it matches—singular or plural.

Let's see this on the question from the Pretest.

26. <u>Though</u> George and Sam spent all day surfing together <u>in</u> Costa Rica, he did not <u>go</u> to the
    A   B   C   D

party at night. <u>No error</u>
                E

Solution: We cannot be sure who "he" (choice C) refers to, so it's wrong. As you learn all of our writing multiple-choice Skills, use them to analyze each underlined word. If the underlined word is a verb, ask, What is its subject? If it's a pronoun ask, Want does it refer to and does it match?

Correct answer: C

SAT Reading/Writing Mantra #26
When a pronoun is underlined, we must be totally sure what noun it is referring to. If it is unclear in any way, it is incorrect. The underlined pronoun must also match (singular or plural) the noun that it refers to.

Here Are Most of the Pronouns That the SAT Uses		
All	I	Some
Both	It	Them
Each	Many	These
Few	Neither	They
He	Nobody	We
Her	None	Who
Him	One	You
His	She	Me

Pronoun Clarity and Agreement Drills

Easy

1 Bill and Edward <u>were convinced</u> to
          A

become <u>a doctor</u> <u>after watching</u> open
       B   **C**

heart surgery <u>on their uncle.</u> <u>No error</u>
              D   **E**

2 If you want to improve <u>your score,</u>
                            A

you <u>should use</u> Brian's SAT prep books;
    B

it is absolutely the best <u>on the</u>
C   **D**

market. <u>No error</u>
        E

Medium

3 Anne Frank is remembered more for
accomplishments in her early years than <u>for</u>
<u>those in her later years.</u>

   Ⓐ for those in her later years

   Ⓑ for they in her later years

   Ⓒ for them occurring in her later years

   Ⓓ for occurrences in their later years

   Ⓔ for those in their later years

4 <u>When</u> the nonprofit organization
     A

started publishing a newsletter
electronically instead of on paper, <u>they</u>
                                    B

brought <u>awareness</u> to this simple and
        C

<u>powerful</u> environmental action. <u>No error</u>
D   **E**

Hard

5 The reason first songs are often their singers'
best work <u>is that it happens</u> more sponta-
neously than later, more processed efforts.

   Ⓐ is that it happens

   Ⓑ is their first songs happening

   Ⓒ is since they happen

   Ⓓ is because these first songs happen

   Ⓔ is because that these happen

6 Until <u>it</u> can be swapped for a
          A

<u>more sustainable</u> and economical form
B

of fuel, petroleum products <u>remain</u> the
                            C

primary source of power used

<u>in transportation.</u> <u>No error</u>
D   **E**

Correct Transition Word

When a transition word (such as "although," "since," "but," "therefore," or "however") is underlined, see if it works in the flow of the sentence. Words like "therefore" express a direct cause and effect. Opposition words like "but" express a cause and effect where the second part opposes the first. For example:

Brian is funny; <u>therefore</u>, he makes you laugh.
        The second part results from the first part.
Brian is funny, <u>but</u> sometimes he is tired and dull.
        The second part opposes the first part.

When a transition word is underlined, check if it's the right transition word for the sentence. These are great. If you didn't know to look for them, you might miss 'em. You might think, "That was weird, but I guess it's okay." But it's not okay.

Let's take a look at the one from the Pretest.

27. <u>Although</u> <u>it</u> is healthy, calming, and energizing, daily exercise, <u>such as swimming,</u>
    A   B   C
    walking, or biking, <u>is recommended</u> by doctors. <u>No error</u>
                        D   E

Solution: Doctors recommend that people exercise **since** it's healthy, not **although** it's healthy. "Although" implies opposition, so we want a different word, such as "since." If you weren't looking for this, you might miss it, but we expect it and we catch it. This is where my job is easy, I just tell you what to look out for. Then you get them right and it makes me look good!

Correct answer: A

SAT Reading/Writing Mantra #27
When a transition word (such as "although," "since," "but," "therefore," or "however") is underlined, see if it works in the sentence.

Direct Cause-and-Effect Words			Opposition Words		
Therefore	Thus	So	However	Although	But
Ergo	And	Since	Still	Though	
Because			Nevertheless	Even though	

Correct Transition Word Drills

Easy

① Since Iron Man is quite a hearty fellow, he certainly would not stand a chance against Superman.

- Ⓐ Since Iron Man is quite a hearty fellow, he certainly
- Ⓑ Being such a hearty fellow, Iron Man would certainly
- Ⓒ Though Iron Man is quite a hearty fellow, he certainly
- Ⓓ Being as that he is such a hearty fellow, Iron Man would certainly
- Ⓔ Though being quite a hearty fellow, Iron Man would certainly

② The doubles team of Immerman and
  $\overline{}$
  A

Sun has won eight straight matches, but
    $\overline{}$ $\overline{}$
    B   C

they will of course be picked

to represent the school at the tennis
$\overline{}$
D

tournament. No error
          $\overline{}$
          E

Medium

③ Many businesses and government agencies are offering flu vaccines as part of their health offerings, even though the vaccines help reduce employee sick days.

- Ⓐ of their health offerings, even though the vaccines
- Ⓑ of the offerings for your health, even though the vaccines
- Ⓒ of its health offerings, though the vaccines
- Ⓓ of their health offerings; since the vaccines
- Ⓔ of their health offerings, as the vaccines

④ In four years she has never missed a
                  $\overline{}$
                  A

vote, so some say the young senator
    $\overline{}$
    B

from Rhode Island makes up in gusto
                 $\overline{}$
                 C   D

what she lacks in experience. No error
                           $\overline{}$
                           E

⑤ Having invented the piano style
    $\overline{}$
    A

known as emotive catharsis, Matt
$\overline{}$
B

Oestreicher will nevertheless be
          $\overline{}$
          C

remembered for this ground-breaking
$\overline{}$
D

advancement. No error
           $\overline{}$
           E

Brave, Honest, and Relaxed

Words in a list must match. The fancy name for this is "parallel structure," but we don't need that term for the SAT. Your ear can tell if the words match, as long as you watch for it. That's the key on so many of these Skills. You already know the material; you just need to practice watching for it.

Look at these examples:

These match:
- When I traveled cross-country, I followed the motto, "**brave, honest, and relaxed**."
- Sanaa is **beautiful, funny, and kind**.
- Omar will **run, jump, and swim**.
- To test the endurance of their warriors, the ancient Spartans held contests involving **running, fighting, and enduring** pain.

These do not match:
- When I traveled cross-country, I followed the motto, "**brave, honest, and be relaxed**."
- Sanaa is **beautiful, funny, and acts kindly**.
- Omar **runs, jumps, and will swim**.
- To test the endurance of their warriors, the ancient Spartans held contests involving **running, fighting, and to endure** pain.

In this last example, the first two members of the list do not have the "to" in front of them. All members of the list must match. Either they all have a "to" or none do; it's like bringing cupcakes to school in third grade—either you have enough for everyone or don't you bring 'em!

Let's apply this on the Pretest.

This book will help you confidently answer sentence completion questions, reading
    A   B   C

comprehension questions, writing multiple-choice questions, and to write
                           D

the essay. No error
    E

Solution: Easy, when you have a list, all the words must match. The list is "sentence completion questions, reading comprehension questions, writing multiple-choice questions, and to write . . ." The first three parts match (they are nouns), and the fourth part "to write" does not match. So the fourth part must also be a noun, such as "the essay."

Correct answer: D

SAT Reading/Writing Mantra #28
When words in a list are underlined, make sure they match.

Brave, Honest, and Relaxed Drills

Easy

1 The storm tore through the new forest, uprooting saplings, leveling huts, and <u>animals' homes were disturbed.</u>

(A) animals' homes were disturbed

(B) animals' homes disturbing

(C) animals' homes disturbed

(D) disturbed animals' homes

(E) disturbing animals' homes

2 <u>Now,</u> Kathy <u>feels</u> healthy, grounded and
   A   B

   <u>is ready</u> <u>to broaden</u> her environment. <u>No error</u>
     C   D   E

Medium

3 Ian's four weeks at language school <u>had been interesting, informative, and had opened his eyes;</u> he gained new insights and a new appreciation of relationships.

(A) had been interesting, informative, and had opened his eyes

(B) were interesting and informative, and had opened his eyes

(C) had been interesting, informative, and eye-opening

(D) had been interesting, informative, and opened his eyes

(E) had been interesting, informative, and was opening his eyes

4 <u>Each time</u> Billy <u>enters</u> the vault, the
    A   B

   guard checks Billy's key, then his ID card,

   and then <u>examines his tattoo</u> before
               C

   <u>Billy can</u> enter. <u>No error</u>
    D   E

5 <u>A skilled and versatile musician,</u>
             A

   Satyajit <u>has been</u> a guitarist, <u>vocalist,</u>
         B   C

   drummer, and <u>worked as a soundman.</u>
                    D

   <u>No error</u>
     E

6 A skilled and versatile musician, Satyajit has been a guitarist, vocalist, drummer, <u>and worked as a soundman.</u>

(A) and worked as a soundman

(B) and been working as a soundman

(C) and working as a soundman

(D) and has worked as a soundman

(E) and soundman

Comparison

In Skill 28 I taught you that words in a list must match; similarly, words being compared must match. There are three ways that this shows up on the SAT.

- **Doing** yoga is as cool as **acing** the SAT.
- **John's singing** is better than **Ed's**.
- Aunt Frances is not only **smart**, but also **athletic**.

Let's take a look at the question from the Pretest.

29. The music of The *Matt Oestreicher Band*, sometimes called *The MOB*, is known for its
    <u>A</u>   <u>B</u>   <u>C</u>
    uplifting effect and is often compared to the <u>performer Krishna Das.</u> <u>No error</u>
                                                  D   E

Solution: Great question. Nearly every SAT has one like this. Most kids get it wrong; know to look for it, and you'll get it right! The problem with the sentence is that it compares the "music" with "the performer." If should compare music to music or performer to performer, for example, "The **music of** "The Matt . . ." compared to the "**music of** the performer Krishna Das."

Correct answer: D

SAT Reading/Writing Mantra #29
When words being compared are underlined, make sure they match.

Comparison Drills

Easy

1 Anyone <u>who has extra time or great interest</u> can learn the tricks and illusions that a successful magician needs.

   Ⓐ who has extra time or great interest

   Ⓑ who has extra time or is in fact very interested

   Ⓒ who has extra time or very interest

   Ⓓ who has extra time or who has interested

   Ⓔ who has extra time or who is of great interest

2 <u>Because they</u> paint for fun, rather than
       A

<u>for profiting</u>, <u>many</u> young painters
   B   C

particularly <u>enjoy</u> their craft. <u>No error</u>
       D   E

Medium

3 One day, David will be known not only as an honored graduate of Harvard University, but also <u>he writes many important</u> works of American fiction.

   Ⓐ he writes many important

   Ⓑ he then will write many important

   Ⓒ will he write many important

   Ⓓ as an author who writes many important

   Ⓔ because he will write many important

4 Taking the bus is one <u>way of</u>
              A

saving energy; <u>to bike</u> to work <u>is</u>
         B   C

<u>another</u>. <u>No error</u>
  D   E

Hard

5 Businesses rely more on consumer <u>spending than do they rely on government subsidies</u> to meet their yearly expenditures.

   Ⓐ spending than do they rely on government subsidies

   Ⓑ spending than them relying on government subsidies

   Ⓒ spending than they rely on government subsidies

   Ⓓ spending than businesses rely on government subsidies

   Ⓔ spending than on government subsidies

6 The novel *A Walk in the Woods* <u>by</u>
                      A

Bill Bryson is <u>funnier</u> and <u>more widely</u>
        B   C

read <u>than Karl Marx</u>. <u>No Error</u>
     D   E

The College Board calls this one "correct idiom." I love their term; you just don't hear people using the word "idiom" nearly enough. It makes me think of *Monty Python and the Holy Grail* when Sir Lancelot receives a call of distress from the singing Prince of Swamp Castle. Lancelot's squire wants to come along for the daring rescue, but Lancelot says that he must rush the castle "in his own particular . . . idiom."

Instead of "correct idiom," which I can't say without laughing, I call it "correct preposition." I do this for three reasons:

❶ I don't feel like looking up what "idiom" means.
❷ I'm not sure if I'd have to pay College Board to use their term.
❸ The words that we are looking for are always prepositions, so it's much easier than looking for the "correct idiom."

Remember from Skill 25 that prepositions are words like: "up," "above," "of," "into," "on," "below," "with," "by," "during," "until." You can Google "prepositions" for a full list. When a preposition is underlined, ask if it's the correct preposition. How do you know? The correct one will make sense and sound smooth. The wrong one will sound weird or jarring. This is another great place to practice trusting your ear. If it sounds jarring, it's probably wrong. We'll train on the drills.

Here are some examples:

Correct	Incorrect
Zann went **to** the movies.	Zann went **onto** the movies.
Giancarlo sat **on** the couch.	Giancarlo sat **in** the couch.
Malaria is a threat **to** travelers.	Malaria is a threat **of** travelers.
Focusing **on** your studies will bring you success.	Focusing **with** your studies will bring you success.

Let's practice on the question from the Pretest.

30. By practicing meditation every day, Rihana does not get obsessed on details and therefore
    A   B   C
    experiences increased peace and comfort. No error
                          D   E

Solution: "Rihana does not get obsessed **on** details" sounds weird. "Rihana does not get obsessed **with** details" sounds better. This is a great topic; knowing to watch for the correct preposition turns a hard question into easy points.

Correct answer: B

SAT Reading/Writing Mantra #30
When a preposition is underlined, ask if it is the right preposition to use.

Correct Preposition Drills

Medium

1 In the opinion of certain chocolate
     A   B

lovers, nuts and berries get in the way
                             C

for the true enjoyment of the chocolate.
           D

No error
  E

2 The new virus protection software,

which uses complex algorithms
      A

in the catching of computer viruses and
         B

worms, may help prevent some of the
          C

more harmful computer bugs. No error
      D   E

3 Polio, a disease that has been virtually
eliminated, was once a major threat of both
travelers and Americans at home.

  Ⓐ of both travelers and Americans
  Ⓑ of two travelers and Americans
  Ⓒ being travelers and Americans
  Ⓓ and travelers and Americans
  Ⓔ to both travelers and Americans

4 Ian Curtis takes justifiable pride in his
education, which has included rigorous
academic work as well as intensive artistic
endeavors.

  Ⓐ pride in his education,
  Ⓑ pride in his schooling;
  Ⓒ pride of his education,
  Ⓓ pride in the educating of him,
  Ⓔ pride on his education,

Hard

5 Some instructors say that genuine love
                  A

for the music is as important as
 B   C

conscientious dedication on technique.
                        D

No error
  E

6 Howard Zinn's *A People's History*

of the United States argues that we ought
               A   B

to look more closely at how history was
       C

defined and told by the elite. No error
          D   E

Adverbs End in "ly"

Read the following message:

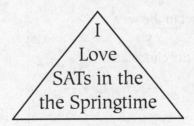

I
Love
SATs in the
the Springtime

What did it say?

"I Love SATs in the Springtime?" Yes, we do love SATs, and they're so great in the springtime. But that's not what it said. Read it again.

Did you catch it? It says, "I love SATs in **the the** springtime."

Cheap, right? But this is perfect practice for what the SAT does with "ly." Sometimes, they leave off the "ly" on an adverb and you need to catch it. Almost impossible if you're not watching for it, easy if you are! "Nasty, tricksy" SAT makers, but we know and expect their tricks, so we get the questions right!

Did you catch it on the Pretest?

31. Every day I walked for over an hour down the Avenue Jean-Médecin through
     _____   _____   _____
      A   B   C
    the slow progressing construction. No error
        _____   _____
               D   E

Solution: The construction is progressing "slowly," not "slow." This is easy if you know to watch for it. I'm not sure why the SAT chose to test this, but we know to watch for it, so they're easy points!

Correct answer: D

| SAT Reading/Writing Mantra #31 |
| Make sure to read the sentence as it really is. |
| Don't correct it in your head; i.e., watch for a missing "ly." |

Adverbs End in "ly" Drills

Medium

❶ If I am understanding this article
   $\overline{\text{A}}$

   correct, it is saying that we should all be
   $\overline{\text{B}}$ $\overline{\text{C}}$

   kind to one another. No error
        $\overline{\text{D}}$ $\overline{\text{E}}$

❷ The large green trucks that pass constant
                                 $\overline{\text{A}}$

   through Paris immaculately clean everything
     $\overline{\text{B}}$ $\overline{\text{C}}$

   in sight. No error
   $\overline{\text{D}}$ $\overline{\text{E}}$

❸ In this town I had avoided taking buses, which,
   due to the overall disorganization of the place,
   brought me places more slow than my feet.

   Ⓐ brought me places more slow than my feet

   Ⓑ brought me places that were more slow than
      my feet

   Ⓒ brought me places more slow than my feet
      would bring me

   Ⓓ brought me places slower than my feet

   Ⓔ brought me places more slowly than my feet

❹ The place was crowded, and I quickly
              $\overline{\text{A}}$ $\overline{\text{B}}$

   became separated from my friends in the
        $\overline{\text{C}}$

   attempt to advance toward a table. No error
          $\overline{\text{D}}$ $\overline{\text{E}}$

❺ Sometimes hand gestures, miming, and
   charades are involved when a tourist tries
   desperate to communicate in order to find a
   bank, restaurant, or bathroom.

   Ⓐ when a tourist tries desperate to
      communicate

   Ⓑ when a tourist tries to communicate
      desperately

   Ⓒ for a tourist to try desperately to
      communicate

   Ⓓ when a tourist tries desperately to
      communicate

   Ⓔ when of communication and desperate

Hard

❻ A relationship between therapist and
   $\overline{\text{A}}$

   patient promotes healing more quick
                          $\overline{\text{B}}$

   than when a patient is told
   $\overline{\text{C}}$

   how to feel and what to do. No error
   $\overline{\text{D}}$ $\overline{\text{E}}$

I vs. Me

I've noticed, over the years, that pretty much anytime "I" is underlined on an SAT writing question, it's wrong. No need just to go by that, though; we have an incredibly easy and effective way to test if it's correct. If <u>I</u> is underlined, test it by putting it first or dropping the other person and then trusting your ear.

Let's try this on the question from the Pretest.

32. Excited about our advancements, the school board <u>granted Khalif and I the funding to continue</u> our research for another two years.

   (A) granted Khalif and I the funding to continue
   (B) granted Khalif and me the funding to continue
   (C) granted Khalif and myself the funding to continue
   (D) granted myself and Khalif the funding to continue
   (E) granted us, Khalif and I the funding to continue

Solution: To test if "I" is correct, just swap the "I" and "Khalif" or drop "Khalif," and then trust your ear. Sometimes swapping makes the answer more obvious, and sometimes dropping does. You'll hear it. It works so well. For this question, either way works. When you swap, the answer is obvious: "the school board granted I and Khalif the funding" sounds weird, and "the school board granted me and Khalif the funding" sounds great.

Correct answer: B

SAT Reading/Writing Mantra #32
To test "I vs. Me," try putting the I/Me first or drop the other person and trust your ear.

This strategy applies to
I vs. Me
He vs. Him
She vs. Her
We vs. Us
They vs. Them
Who vs. Whom

I vs. Me Drills

Medium

1 The other runners and <u>him</u> <u>quickly</u> ran
     A   B   C

from the starting line through the course and

<u>to the finish</u> in a record four minutes. <u>No error</u>
     D   E

2 Quincy passed the ball to <u>Josh and I</u>,
                           A

and <u>together</u> we <u>skillfully</u> brought <u>it</u>
     B   C   D

down court for two points. <u>No error</u>
                     E

Hard

3 For <u>us</u> kids, concern <u>about</u> the environment
     A   B

is <u>even more acute</u> than fears about
          C

the economy. <u>No error</u>
     D   E

4 The postal clerk asked, "This is being mailed <u>to</u> <u>who, your father or your brother</u>?"

Ⓐ to who, your father or your brother

Ⓑ to whom, your father or your brother

Ⓒ to who; your father or your brother

Ⓓ to whom; your father or your brother

Ⓔ to where; your father or your brother

5 No one is <u>more happier than me</u> that Asha won the spelling bee.

Ⓐ more happier than me

Ⓑ more happy like me

Ⓒ happier than I

Ⓓ as happy like I am

Ⓔ happier than me

A Few More Rules

Skill 33

Each of the nine writing Skills that you've learned so far appears on every single SAT. The three in this Skill appear less often, but often enough that you should memorize them.

❶ **"-er" vs. "-est"**

Use "more" or "-er" when comparing two things.
Use "most" or "-est" when comparing three or more things.
Examples: Of cats and dogs, dogs are the **lazier** animal.
              Of all animals, cows are the **laziest**.
              (P.C. notice: Neither the author nor the publisher believe cows or dogs are lazy.)

❷ **"Which" is for things; "who" is for people.**

Examples: Sierra is a girl **who** runs everyday.
              Computers are things **which** people love or hate.

❸ **Certain words go together, such as**

Neither . . . nor
Either . . . or
Not only . . . but also
As . . . as

Examples: I like **neither** ham **nor** venison.
              I will eat **either** organic turkey **or** wild-caught fish.
              Organic meat is **not only** free-range, **but also** antibiotic-free.
              Trevor is **as** tall **as** a giant.

Now, let's look at the one from the Pretest.

33. Nearly all of the critics agree that of the author's two published novels, <u>the first is the more readable</u>.

    (A) the first is the more readable
    (B) the first is the most readable
    (C) the first is of the two most readable
    (D) the first is the more readable than the second one is
    (E) the first one are more readable

Solution: Simple. Since we are comparing **two** books, "more" is correct.

Correct answer: A

> ### SAT Reading/Writing Mantra #33
> "-Er" or "more" is used to compare two things, and "-est" or "most"
> is used to compare more than two things. "Who" is for people, and
> "which" is for things.
> Watch for pairs of words such as "not only . . . but also" and "either . . . or."

A Few More Rules Drills

Easy

❶ Many environmentalists <u>are</u> motivated
                A

by either concern <u>for their health</u> <u>and</u>
           B   C

concern for the future, <u>though some</u>
                      D

seem to simply love the planet. <u>No error</u>
                              E

❷ Theodor Geisel <u>transformed</u> children's books,
                  A

<u>who have</u> been used to teach children
 B

<u>to read</u> <u>for over</u> fifty years. <u>No error</u>
 C   D   E

Medium

❸ Between the two candidates, many students felt
<u>that Angino was the most qualified to win</u> the
election and serve as president.

  Ⓐ that Angino was the most qualified to win

  Ⓑ for Angino being the most qualified to win

  Ⓒ that Angino was the one more qualified for
     winning

  Ⓓ of Angino was the more qualified for winning

  Ⓔ that Angino was more qualified to win

❹ Sam, a man <u>whose</u> Costa Rican background
            A

has <u>influenced</u> his world view, <u>likes</u> to live life
     B   C

<u>fully</u>. <u>No error</u>
 D   E

Hard

❺ Stephenie Meyer was honored not only for the
success of her <u>books, but inspiring</u> young
people to read.

  Ⓐ books, but inspiring

  Ⓑ books, but also she was honored for her
     inspiring

  Ⓒ books, but also for inspiring

  Ⓓ books, and for inspiring

  Ⓔ books, though also for her inspiring

❻ The politician <u>was offended</u> by the
               A

comedian's mocking tone, <u>but could</u>
                    B

deny neither the <u>truth of</u> the jabs <u>or</u> the
             C   D

accuracy of the imitation. <u>No error</u>
                      E

Direct, to the Point, Not Redundant

The SAT is not testing to see if you are the next J. K. Rowling, Judd Apatow, or William Shakespeare. It is merely testing to see if you can write a clear and concise memo from your cubicle at Dandar Mifflin Corporation. Not that there's anything wrong with writing a clear and concise memo. In fact, whether you're the CEO of Sony or a published novelist, it's great to be able to write in a variety of styles—personal, creative, and professional. Then you can adjust your style to the task.

It's also helpful, on the SAT and in life, to know the rules and the expectations of the task. Imagine that Michael Jordan had never seen a hoop before. If you placed him on a court, he'd still have the potential to be the best ever, and yet he wouldn't even know how to score. Acknowledging rules and expectations gives you freedom and choice; you can chose whether you follow them, but at least the choice is yours.

So the secret rule for the writing multiple-choice "sentence correction" questions is to choose the answer that is most clear, concise, direct, and nonredundant. Now, you can identify the best answer choice and be the Michael Jordan of the SAT.

Let's see this on the Pretest.

34. Madonna released her first album and the year was 1983.

(A) and the year was 1983
(B) and it was 1983
(C) when it was 1983
(D) in 1983
(E) it being 1983

Solution: We always want the answer that is most clear, concise, direct, nonredundant, and of course grammatically correct. In fact, for a "sentence correction" question, if you've used all of the Skills and the process of elimination and still can't decide between a few choices, pick the shortest one! In this question, "and the year was 1983" can be replaced by "in 1983," since "the year was" is redundant.

Correct answer: D

SAT Reading/Writing Mantra #34
The correct answer on a "sentence correction" question will always be the most clear, concise, direct, and nonredundant choice.

Direct, to the Point, Not Redundant Drills

Easy

1 One of Akshaya's most favorite novels is the book *Pride and Prejudice* by Jane Austen.

(A) One of Akshaya's most favorite novels is the book

(B) One of Akshaya's most favoritist novels is the novel

(C) One of Akshaya's most favorite novels of all time is the book

(D) One of the books Akshaya feels is her most favorite is

(E) One of Akshaya's favorite novels is

2 Newspapers should show both sides of an issue fairly and yet stimulate thought and discussion.

(A) and yet stimulate

(B) and yet be stimulating to

(C) and yet to stimulate both

(D) and yet stimulating

(E) and yet to stimulate

Medium

3 The retirement of musician Jay-Z, arguably the most successful hip-hop artist of all time, only lasting a total of three years.

(A) artist of all time, only lasting a total of three years

(B) artist of all time, only lasted three years

(C) artist of all time, and who only retired for a total of three years

(D) artist of all time, only did so for three years

(E) artist of all time, and only lasting a total of three years

4 There are currently many inspiring movies, such as *The Matrix* and *What the Bleep Do We Know!?*, in the cinema and for rent these days.

(A) in the cinema and for rent these days

(B) in the cinema and for renting these present days

(C) at the cinema and for rental currently

(D) in the cinema and for rent

(E) cinematically and rentwise these days

5 The group protested in front of the corporate headquarters, and passing pedestrians were asked by them to boycott the company's products.

(A) and passing pedestrians were asked by them to

(B) and passing pedestrians by them were asked to

(C) and asked passing pedestrians to

(D) and asking passing pedestrians by them to

(E) and asked pedestrians passing by them to

6 Being as he is a talented musician, Kyle is asked to play many venues.

(A) Being as he is a talented musician

(B) As being a talented musician

(C) A talented musician

(D) Playing music talentedly

(E) Although he is a talented musician

35 Misplaced Phrases

Look at this sentence:

A beloved children's story, Ethel read *The Three Little Pigs* to her son.

The sentence makes it sound like Ethel is a beloved children's story. That's how Borat would read it. "A beloved children's story" is misplaced. It should be closer to the thing it's describing, "*The Three Little Pigs*." This is a great strategy that will definitely earn you points—the SAT uses this type of question several times per test.

It's particularly important for "sentence correction" questions.

Let's see this on the Pretest.

35. After marching three hours in direct sun, <u>the locker room was where the band went</u> for a break from the heat.

   (A) the locker room was where the band went
   (B) the locker room was gone to be the band
   (C) the band went to the locker room
   (D) the band's locker room was where they went
   (E) the locker room was the place gone to by the band

Solution: The way the sentence is set up, it seems that "After marching three hours in direct sun" is describing the locker room. Of course it is not, you're smart and know that, but someone translating the sentence would be misled. That's the point of good grammar, to make writing completely clear. So "After marching . . . sun" should be as close to the thing that it describes ("the band") as possible, and choice C is the best answer. Choice C also makes the sentence more clear and direct.

Correct answer: C

> **SAT Reading/Writing Mantra #35**
> **A descriptive phrase on the SAT must be clearly associated with (and usually placed right next to) the noun described.**

Misplaced Phrases Drills

Easy

❶ Pressed for time, <u>running was the only choice Devon had</u> if she wanted to catch her flight.

   Ⓐ running was the only choice Devon had

   Ⓑ Devon had to run

   Ⓒ Devon's running was the only choice she had

   Ⓓ running to the plane was the only choice Devon had

   Ⓔ the choice Devon had was running

❷ Carrying three pieces of tiramisu, <u>Seth's search for a new Home Ec partner was frantic.</u>

   Ⓐ Seth's search for a new Home Ec partner was frantic

   Ⓑ Seth's frantic search for a new Home Ec partner

   Ⓒ a new partner was what Seth frantically searched for

   Ⓓ a Home Ec partner for which Seth frantically searched

   Ⓔ Seth searched frantically for a new Home Ec partner

Medium

❸ Having played third base for four years, <u>that she was being dropped to second string upset Abigail tremendously.</u>

   Ⓐ that she was being dropped to second string upset Abigail tremendously

   Ⓑ Abigail's tremendous upset resulted from her being dropped to second string

   Ⓒ Abigail's upset at being dropped to second string was tremendous

   Ⓓ Abigail was tremendously upset that she was being dropped to second string

   Ⓔ the dropping to second string was tremendously upsetting to Abigail

Hard

❹ <u>Returning to Northampton after three years, the small liberal town seemed much friendlier to Graham</u> than it had when he had lived there as a monk.

   Ⓐ Returning to Northampton after three years, the small liberal town seemed much friendlier to Graham

   Ⓑ Having returned to Northampton after three years, it seemed a much friendlier town to Graham

   Ⓒ After Graham returned to Northampton in three years, the small liberal town seemed much friendlier

   Ⓓ Graham returned to Northampton after three years, the small liberal town was seemingly much friendlier

   Ⓔ When Graham returned to Northampton after three years, the small liberal town seemed much friendlier

Jedi Master Yoda

"Named must your fear be before banish it you can."
Jedi Master Yoda

Great advice. True for Jedi training. True for the SAT. But unless you're an 800-year-old Jedi master, don't try speaking or writing in the passive voice; the SAT always favors the active voice. "Active voice" is just fancy grammar language for "be direct and to the point." This is actually part of Skills 34 and 35, but it comes up so much on the SAT that I wanted to give it its own section of drills. Look at these examples.

Active Voice	Passive Voice
I run.	Running is what I do.
Kumar ate a hamburger.	Eating a hamburger is what Kumar did.
The Hulk is incredible.	Incredible is what the Hulk is.

Let's see it on the Pretest.

36. If you want to bake good cookies, <u>the oven should be preheated</u> for several minutes.

   (A) the oven should be preheated
   (B) it's a good idea for the oven to be preheated
   (C) consider the preheating of the oven
   (D) the preheating of the oven is a good idea
   (E) you should preheat the oven

Solution: ". . . The oven should be preheated" uses "passive voice." You can hear it; it sounds weak, passive, indirect, and wordy. Choice E is in active voice; it sounds much more powerful and direct. This is a great tool for your own writing. Writing in the active voice sounds more powerful and clear.

Correct answer: E

SAT Reading/Writing Mantra #36
On an SAT writing question, always choose active over passive voice.

Jedi Master Yoda Drills

Medium

1 Passing the CPA exam is what Juana did last June, so now she practices accounting and can sign tax returns.

Ⓐ Passing the CPA exam is what Juana did

Ⓑ Of passing the CPA exam is something that Juana did

Ⓒ What Juana did was pass the CPA exam

Ⓓ In passing the CPA exam, Juana in

Ⓔ Juana passed the CPA exam

Hard

2 Indicating the time and effort the artist had put into making it, was the intention behind the high price of the painting.

Ⓐ Indicating the time and effort the artist had put into making it, was the intention behind the high price of the painting

Ⓑ To indicate the time and effort the artist had put into making it, was the intention behind the high price of the painting

Ⓒ The painting's high price was intended to indicate the time and effort the artist had put into making it.

Ⓓ Intending to indicate the time and effort the artist had put into making the painting, was the reason for the high price of the painting

Ⓔ The intention behind the high price of the painting was to indicate the time and effort the artist had put into making it.

3 Learning to cope with stress more effectively is the reason that many teenagers have started practicing yoga.

Ⓐ Learning to cope with stress more effectively is the reason that many teenagers have started practicing yoga.

Ⓑ Many teenagers have started practicing yoga to learn to cope with stress more effectively.

Ⓒ Starting to practice Yoga is what many teenagers have started doing; their reason being to learn to cope more effectively with stress.

Ⓓ Learning to cope with stress is the more effective reason why many teenagers have started practicing yoga.

Ⓔ To learn to cope with stress more effectively is the reason that many teenagers have started practicing yoga.

4 In *Monty Python and the Holy Grail*, before King Arthur lobbed the Holy Hand Grenade of Antioch, five is the number he counted to.

Ⓐ before King Arthur lobbed the Holy Hand Grenade of Antioch, five is the number he counted to

Ⓑ after counting to five, King Arthur then did the lobbing of the Holy Hand Grenade of Antioch

Ⓒ five being the number he counted to he then lobbed the Holy Hand Grenade of Antioch

Ⓓ King Arthur counted to five before he lobbed the Holy Hand Grenade of Antioch

Ⓔ counting to five is what King Arthur did before he lobbed the Holy Hand Grenade of Antioch

The last of the three types of writing multiple-choice questions on the SAT asks you to edit a paragraph. Once students get used to the format, these questions are very easy. You are given a paragraph that includes lots of errors, and then you answer six questions about improving the errors. You don't need any new strategies to answer these questions; they are all based on the same Skills that you use for the other two types of writing questions.

Some kids don't read the passage; they skip it and go right to questions. But my students always gain points when they read the passage first. Even though you are not being tested on reading comprehension, sometimes you need the context.

Let's review the question from the Pretest.

37. Which of the following is the best way to revise and combine the sentences reproduced below?

Professor Chen is a great instructor. He is known for his lucid explanations of even the most complex topics.

(A) Being a great instructor; lucid explanations for even the most complex topics are what Professor Chen is known for.
(B) A great instructor, Professor Chen is known for his lucid explanations of even the most complex topics.
(C) As being a great instructor, Professor Chen is known for his lucid explanations of even the most complex topics.
(D) Professor Chen is known for his lucid explanations of even the most complex topics, he is known to be a great instructor.
(E) As a great instructor; Professor Chen is known for his lucid explanations of even the most complex topics.

Solution: You can see that this is simply a combination of several Skills. The reproduced sentences are not too bad, but the question asks us to combine them. That makes sense, since the SAT loves conciseness. To find the correct answer, use the process of elimination. You know from Skill 35 that choice A makes it seem that the "lucid explanations" are the instructor, a misplaced descriptive phrase. Choice C sounds wordy and awkward. Choice D needs a semicolon instead of a comma, since both parts could stand alone. And choice E needs a comma instead of a semicolon, since the parts of the sentence could not stand alone. Choice B is best. It is clear and direct.

Correct answer: B

> **SAT Reading/Writing Mantra #37**
> For "edit the passage" questions, read the passage first.

Editing Paragraphs Drills

(1) Among all the books I've read, one of my favorites is the Harry Potter series. (2) There are seven books in that series. (3) I have three favorites. (4) This report is on Book One.

(5) For starters let's take a look at the Dursleys. (6) The Dursleys are normal, extremely normal, in fact their own brave but failing crusade to be utterly, fully, completely normal alienated them from those around them, consequently getting them more looks, stares, and whisperings-behind-backs then they would have gotten if they hadn't tried so hard.

(7) A truly remarkable boy with messy black hair, green eyes and a lightening shaped scar on his forehead and, as far as the Dursleys are concerned, a slug. (8) Harry is known as "the boy who lived" because he survived a dark curse cast by the evil Lord Voldemort. (9) His parents were killed and their house was destroyed, but Harry, a baby, survived.

(10) No one knows how Harry did it, how could a baby survive the same curse that killed so many powerful wizards far more powerful than Harry? (11) Very little is known, and that that is known is not known at all; it is only guesswork.

❶ In context, which of the following is the best way to revise and combine sentences 2 and 3 (reproduced below)?

There are seven books in that series. I have three favorites.

Ⓐ I have three favorites of the seven book series.

Ⓑ Seven books in the series, I have three that are favorites.

Ⓒ Three favorites I have and there are seven total in the series.

Ⓓ Of the seven books in the series, I have three favorites.

Ⓔ I favor three books and there are seven in the series.

❷ Which of the following, if inserted before sentence 5, would make a good transition from the first paragraph?

Ⓐ The book has many interesting characters.

Ⓑ Where to start?

Ⓒ Book Seven was good too.

Ⓓ Harry Potter is a fascinating character.

Ⓔ The "boy who lived."

❸ Which of the following sentences, if inserted before sentence 7, would best improve the third paragraph?

Ⓐ So, that's the Dursleys.

Ⓑ Why not be normal?

Ⓒ Next, there's Harry Potter.

Ⓓ How did Harry survive?

Ⓔ Relying on guesswork, we know Harry Potter.

❹ Which of the following would be most effective as a concluding sentence for the essay?

Ⓐ Such intriguing story lines make *Harry Potter* such a fun series!

Ⓑ The Dursleys and Harry Potter.

Ⓒ So, we keep guessing.

Ⓓ And that's Book One!

Ⓔ Slug, or no, he's a heck of a kid!

How to Think Like a Grammar Genius

You've now learned all the Skills that you need for SAT writing multiple-choice questions. The Mantras remind you what to do and when to do it. Let's make sure you've memorized and integrated the Mantras. Drill them until you are ready to teach them. Then do that.

Learning Mantras is like learning martial arts. Practice until they become part of you, until you follow them naturally: when you see an underlined verb, you look for its subject; when you see an underlined transition word or preposition, you ask if it fits; when you see an underlined pronoun, you check for clarity and agreement; you watch for "ly" on adverbs; you train and trust your ear; and you use the process of elimination. This will raise your SAT Writing score dramatically, and it will improve your actual writing too.

Check the box next to each Skill when you have mastered it. Reread the Skill sections if you need to.

☐ **Intro.** When something trips up your tongue or you can't get its meaning, it's probably wrong.

☐ **Skill 24.** When a verb is underlined, trust your ear. When in doubt, identify its subject and make sure singular/plural and tense match the subject.

☐ **Skill 25.** When a verb is underlined, identify the subject and cross out any prepositional phrases; a prepositional phrase NEVER counts as the subject of the verb. Also, ask what is doing the action of the verb, and watch for the second trick where the subject comes after the verb.

☐ **Skill 26.** When a pronoun is underlined, we must be totally sure what noun it is referring to. If it is unclear in any way, it is incorrect. The underlined pronoun must also match (singular or plural) the noun that it refers to.

☐ **Skill 27.** If a transition word (such as "although," "since," "but," "therefore," or "however") is underlined, see if it works in the sentence.

☐ **Skill 28.** When words in a list are underlined, make sure they match.

☐ **Skill 29.** When words being compared are underlined, make sure they match.

☐ **Skill 30.** When a preposition is underlined, ask if it is the right preposition to use.

☐ **Skill 31.** Make sure to read the sentence as it is. Don't correct it in your head; that is, watch for a missing "ly."

☐ **Skill 32.** To test "I versus Me," try putting the I/Me first or drop the other person and trust your ear.

☐ **Skill 33.** "-Er" or "more" is used to compare two things, and "-est" or "most' is used to compare more than two things. "Who" is for people, "which" is for things. Watch for pairs of words such as "not only . . . but also" and "either . . . or."

☐ **Skill 34.** The correct answer on a "sentence correction" question will always be the most clear, concise, direct, and nonredundant choice.

☐ **Skill 35.** A descriptive phrase on the SAT must be clearly associated with (and usually placed right next to) the noun described.

☐ **Skill 36.** On an SAT writing question, always choose active over passive voice.

☐ **Skill 37.** For "edit the passage" questions, read the passage first.

Let's apply this on the question from the Pretest.

38. The protagonist of novelist Ahmadou Kourouma's first book was a <u>character which enabled</u> Kourouma to express his criticism of post-colonial governments in Africa.

    (A) character which enabled
    (B) character, she enabled
    (C) character, she enables
    (D) character who enabled
    (E) character that was enabling

Solution: The "character" should be followed by "who" instead of "which." Recall from Skill 33 that "who" is used for people and "which" is used for things.

Correct answer: D

How to Think Like a Grammar Genius Drills

The following sentences test correctness and effectiveness of expression. Part of each sentence or the entire sentence is underlined; beneath each sentence are five ways of phrasing the underlined material. Choice A repeats the original phrasing; the other four choices are different. If you think the original phrasing produces a better sentence than any of the alternatives, select choice A; if not, select one of the other choices.

In making your selections, follow the requirements of standard written English; that is, pay attention to grammar, choice of words, sentence construction, and punctuation. Your selection should result in the most effective sentence—clear and precise, without awkwardness or ambiguity.

Easy

❶ Judd Apatow is a director and actor that is able to be making money by doing the directing and acting that he loves.

Ⓐ Judd Apatow is a director and actor that is able to be making money by doing the directing and acting that he loves.

Ⓑ By directing and acting is how Judd Apatow is able to make money doing what he loves.

Ⓒ Able to make money from doing it, Judd Apatow directs and acts and loves it.

Ⓓ Judd Apatow is able to make money by doing what he loves, directing and acting.

Ⓔ By directing and acting, Judd Apatow found the things that he loves to do which make him money.

Medium

❷ However repeatedly asking the security guard for permission to park in the teachers' lot, Moshe decided to go straight to the principal.

Ⓐ However repeatedly asking the security guard for permission to park in the teachers' lot

Ⓑ After repeatedly asking the security guard for permission to park in the teachers' lot

Ⓒ He having repeatedly asked the security guard for permission to park in the teachers' lot

Ⓓ Repeatedly asking the security guard for permission to park in the teachers' lot

Ⓔ While repeatedly asking the security guard for permission to park in the teachers' lot

❸ Every mathematician must master the basic skills of addition, multiplication, and subtracting before moving on to more involved operations.

Ⓐ addition, multiplication, and subtracting

Ⓑ adding, multiplication, and subtracting

Ⓒ addition, multiplication, and to subtract

Ⓓ to add, multiply, and subtract

Ⓔ addition, multiplication, and subtraction

Hard

❹ Soon to be a famous artist, critics will hail Colette for her beautiful, functional, and complex work.

Ⓐ critics will hail Colette for her

Ⓑ critics will soon be hailing Colette for her

Ⓒ Colette will be hailing to critics for her

Ⓓ Colette will be hailed by critics for her

Ⓔ Colette's work will be hailed for its

The following sentences test your ability to recognize grammar and usage errors. Each sentence contains either a single error or no error at all. No sentence contains more than one error. The error, if there is one, is underlined and lettered. If the sentence contains an error, select the one underlined part that must be changed to make the sentence correct. If the sentence is correct, select choice E. In choosing answers, follow the requirements of standard written English.

Easy

5. Mark felt that Mr. Okin's assignment

   of Chad <u>as the first speaker</u> <u>being unfair</u>,
       A   B

   so <u>he prepared</u> his argument and made
       C

   an appointment <u>to discuss</u> it. <u>No error</u>
              D   E

Medium

6. Perhaps no one can anticipate

   what <u>types</u> of movies <u>will succeed</u> in the
       A   B

   decades to come because fads change

   and themes either get outdated <u>and</u>
                        C

   <u>become overused</u>. <u>No error</u>
       D   E

7. Because <u>of its</u> useful advice,
          A

   <u>clear presentation</u>, and humor, Pausch's
       B

   book <u>sold</u> more copies and changed
        C

   more lives than <u>did most other books</u>.
                  D

   <u>No error</u>
     E

8. As teachers gain experience, often

   their teaching skills <u>improve</u>, their
               A

   knowledge <u>for their</u> subjects expands
           B

   and their connection <u>to children</u> <u>deepens</u>.
                C   D

   <u>No error</u>
     E

9. Famous for <u>its</u> beautiful feathers,
          A

   the <u>peacock</u> <u>actually</u> uses these feathers
       B   C

   <u>to scare</u> off potential attackers and
     D

   attract a mate. <u>No error</u>
             E

Hard

10. Ayurveda, the Indian science

    <u>that examines</u> ways <u>of enriching</u> and
       A   B

    prolonging peoples' lives, <u>were</u>
                   C

    developed over a period <u>of many</u> years.
                     D

    <u>No error</u>
      E

11. <u>Even though</u> it is not as well
      A

    respected nationally as it once <u>was</u>, each
                     B

    year Miller High School still celebrates

    <u>their</u> ranking <u>as the best</u> high school in
      C   D

    the district. <u>No error</u>
            E

Essay

Like Writing Multiple-Choice, the essay is not testing to see if you are the next William Faulkner. It tests whether you can write an organized four- or five-paragraph essay with intro, body, and conclusion paragraphs. The essay is graded by two readers, who each give a score from 1 to 6, yielding a total essay score from 2 to 12. The SAT essay seems a mystery to many kids. But it turns out that graders are trained to look for very specific elements. If you give graders those elements, you ace the essay. In the next 10 Skills, I'll show you exactly what graders look for.

Okay, you're at the test center. It's 8:16 a.m. The room smells like high school French fries and feet. The proctor has finished reading the initial instructions and tells you to open your test booklet to section 1, the essay. What do you do? (1). Open your booklet. (2). Read the essay topic. Then what? Decide if you agree or disagree? Okay, not bad. Even better, start by thinking of **specific** examples that demonstrate or disprove the question. The question has no right answer, so brainstorm examples, and then take the side supported by your strongest examples.

Brainstorming **specific** examples also avoids the biggest problem that kids face on the essay—using generalizations and too few details to support their point. Going straight to brainstorming **specific** details prevents you from an essay of generalizations. So brainstorm for details—names, places, dates, people, etc.

Using details is good advice for proving any point or winning any argument. Let's say you want to convince your parents to let you go to Ed's party. What works better? "Commme onnnnn mommmm!" or "Ed's parents will be home. His dad is head of the county chapter of Parents Against Drunk Driving and his mom is an emergency room doctor. They plan to supervise the whole time." Details are always more powerful.

Let's look at the question from the Pretest.

39. Does each individual pursuing self-interest best ensure the success of a society?

Solution: Okay, let's brainstorm. There is of course no right answer here. There's no right position to take and no right or wrong examples to use. You just need to choose specific details and support your position, whatever it is. The key is to brainstorm for specifics, not generalizations. Make that small change right here, in this step of the process, and your score will go up. Brainstorm from personal experience, books you've read, papers you've written for history class, whatever. Just look for specific examples.

Alex, a student of mine who faced this essay question, realized that he had recently written a paper on Columbus coming to America, and that he could contrast the nonindividualist Native Americans with the greedy explorers. We'll look at his essay in the Skills to come.

> **SAT Reading/Writing Mantra #39**
> **Brainstorm for specific details, not generalizations.**

Brainstorm Drills

Read each of the following essay topics and then brainstorm for specific examples that prove or disprove the assignment. Based on the examples that you come up with, choose a position.

---

1. Think carefully about the issue presented in the following excerpt and the assignment below.

> Some say that society defends the current way of doing things, known as the status quo, even after the current ways are outdated, wrong, or even unjust. Yet others argue that the stability of society relies on its members following the current norms and not questioning convention.

Assignment: Is it better to be compliant or to challenge the status quo? Plan and write an essay in which you develop your point of view on this issue. Support your position with reasoning and examples taken from your reading, studies, experience, or observations.

---

2. Think carefully about the issue presented in the following excerpt and the assignment below.

> Materialism is the tendency to consider physical objects as more important than spiritual ideals. Some say that modern society's focus on materialism is responsible for not only economic success, but also unprecedented religious freedom and social equality.

Assignment: Has materialism helped society? Plan and write an essay in which you develop your point of view on this issue. Support your position with reasoning and examples taken from your reading, studies, experience, or observations.

Brain Freeze Help

Many kids fear brainstorming. "I might freeze!" they lament. We can absolutely prevent this. Guaranteed. The essay questions are broad, and so much of what you study in school can be applied to any SAT essay topic!

For example, the reason we still read Shakespeare in schools is that each play covers so many themes: love, death, jealousy, striving, etc. The same is true of any major event in history or any important piece of literature. I have seen students who knew an awful lot about some slightly unusual piece of history use that topic on every essay they wrote. One student, whom you will meet later in this book, had written a paper on the history of the Fourth Republic of Nigeria for history class. Sounds fancy, right? It sounded fancy to the essay graders too. He used this topic every time that he wrote an SAT essay, and every time he got a perfect 12!

In the drills on the next page, I'll ask you to recall history and English papers that you've recently written. You'll be able to use these for any essay question.

Do the drills on the next page, and then come back to the question from the Pretest.

40. Does each individual pursuing self-interest best ensure the success of a society?

Solution: After you have completed the drills on the following page, you come armed with potential essay details, and you can breathe a huge sigh of relief. If something else brilliant occurs to you, of course use that; but if not, use whichever of the examples that you planned applies best. We will practice applying them more in the next few Skills. Ironically, because you come with planned details, you are more likely to be relaxed and more likely to come up with brilliant new examples that are perfect for the essay topic.

SAT Reading/Writing Mantra #40
When you brainstorm for details, if something new that perfectly fits the assignment occurs to you, of course use it. If not, use whichever of your planned examples applies best.

Brain Freeze Help Drills

❶ Recall a recent paper you wrote for history class. The more specific the topic was, the better. The more unusual the topic was, the better. Why? 'Cause the readers are bored; give them something interesting, something different, and they are happy. Plus obscure or specific topics are impressive. They make you sound smart! For example, a general paper about the life of Mahatma Gandhi is great, and you'll be able to use that for almost any SAT essay topic; but a detailed paper about Gandhi's particular policy of nonviolent protest will guarantee you even more points. Find a paper, and go reread it if you need to. Then write down some key details below: names, dates, places, numbers, statistics, etc.

What happened:

Full names of people involved:

Dates:

Places:

Statistics:

Other specific details:

❷ Recall a recent paper you wrote for English class, for example, about a book or poem that you read. Again, the more specific and/or obscure the better. Reread the paper if you need to, and write down some key details:

Author's full name:
Book or poem's full title:
Date written:

Characters' full names:
Setting:
Themes:

Plot:

Other specific details:

Outline

Okay, you've read the assignment, you've brainstormed for details, and you've started to ignore the French fry and feet smell in the cafeteria as well as the guy next to you chomping his gum. (This is why, when you do practice tests, you should hire a few people to tap pencils, chomp gum, and talk to themselves. Then you'd be truly prepared.)

So, now what? Do you make a long, extensive outline? That would be nice, but really there's not time. All you need to do is to write out a word or two for each example that you'll use, something that will remind you of the specifics. There's no time or need to jot all the details. You know them, they are safely in your head, and you'll remember them when you need to. And if you can't recall one detail, use another. The graders don't know what's in your head. They have no expectations; so don't be attached to using any specific piece of information.

Let's outline from our brainstorm for the Pretest.

Does each individual pursuing self-interest best ensure the success of a society?

Solution: Jot down or circle the best details from your brainstorm. The best details are the ones that most powerfully demonstrate your position. For example, Alex used the non-self-interest of Native Americans at the time of Columbus versus the self-interest of our current society. These examples form the outline for the body paragraphs of his essay. Each is the main idea of a paragraph.

SAT Reading/Writing Mantra #41
Jot down or circle the best details from your brainstorm. These details form the outline for the body paragraphs of the essay.

Outline Drills

See if you can apply your planned examples from Skill 40 to our two essay topics. Then circle or jot down the best details as your outline.

1. Think carefully about the issue presented in the following excerpt and the assignment below.

   Some say that society defends the current way of doing things, known as the status quo, even after the current ways are outdated, wrong, or even unjust. Yet others argue that the stability of society relies on its members following the current norms and not questioning convention.

   Assignment: Is it better to be compliant or to challenge the status quo? Plan and write an essay in which you develop your point of view on this issue. Support your position with reasoning and examples taken from your reading, studies, experience, or observations.

2. Think carefully about the issue presented in the following excerpt and the assignment below.

   Materialism is the tendency to consider physical objects as more important than spiritual ideals. Some say that modern society's focus on materialism is responsible for not only economic success, but also unprecedented religious freedom and social equality.

   Assignment: Has materialism helped society? Plan and write an essay in which you develop your point of view on this issue. Support your position with reasoning and examples taken from your reading, studies, experience, or observations.

Write Your Intro

Your introductory paragraph should be short, maybe three or four sentences. Make the first sentence interesting if you can—a question, a quote, a surprising statement, something clever. If you can't, that's okay; just ask or answer the question from the assignment. Then use a sentence or two to link that exciting statement or provocative question to your thesis; basically lead us to your opinion. Then end the intro with your thesis. The thesis clearly states your opinion and cites the specific examples that will be the focus of the body paragraphs. Use opener, link, and thesis as the format, and within that format be you, let your style come through. Don't try to mimic someone else's style; let your own shine through.

Let's apply this to the Pretest question.

42. Does each individual pursuing self-interest best ensure the success of a society?

Solution. Did the intro that you wrote accomplish opening, link, and thesis? Here's what Alex wrote for his perfect 12:

> If you define the success of a society by the amount of things achieved and conquered by that community, then limitation of self-interest is not necessary. However, if you measure the success of a group by the way it functions, its organization, and compassion for ideals, then limiting self-interest becomes more important. The success of a community should be measured through the overall happiness of its members, not by the amount of things the group achieves. In this way, each individual pursuing self-interest threatens, rather than ensures, a society's success.

Alex began by flushing out the assignment and examining what success means for a society. He implied that before we can determine if self-interest ensures success, we must define success. He made the link and then gave his opinion that self-interest threatens, rather than ensures, the success of a society. His exploration of success gave the essay depth that graders loved.

Remember that "opener, link, thesis" is a structure that, depending on your confidence as a writer, you can play with. You can see that Alex used the structure, but improvised. That's good. Use opener, link, and thesis as the format, and within that be you. Don't try to mimic someone else's style; let your own shine through.

SAT Reading/Writing Mantra #42
Your intro paragraph should be 3 to 4 sentences: an opener, a link, and a thesis.

Write Your Intro Drills

Now that you have your details and your outline planned, write your intro paragraph for each of the essay topics. Use opener, link, and thesis as the format; and within that be you, let your style come through. *Note:* To provide space for your writing, I have not copied the full prompts; refer to Skill 41 Drills if you need to reread them.

1. Assignment: Is it better to be compliant or to challenge the status quo?

_____

_____

_____

_____

_____

_____

_____

_____

_____

_____

2. Assignment: Has materialism helped society?

_____

_____

_____

_____

_____

_____

_____

_____

_____

_____

_____

Transition Sentences

Each paragraph should end with a closing sentence of some kind. I'm not telling you to be totally boring and predictable. Just make sure each paragraph is tied up in some way. And begin each new paragraph with a link to the previous one—a sentence that transitions/links the reader smoothly from one paragraph to the next. You can do this in a number of brilliant and creative ways.

This brings up an important point: essay design. I have noticed over the years that the middle (body) paragraphs for the highest-scoring essays follow one of the following formats (more on this in Skill 44):

- One topic, first paragraph setting the scene and the second proving the thesis
- Two connected examples from the same historical period or literary work
- Two chronological events, usually "cause and effect" or "before and after"
- Chronological personal observation

Any of these setups allows for easy transition statements because the paragraphs flow organically from one to the next. In fact, if a transition statement is very tough to come up with, perhaps the paragraphs and the thesis are too scattered. Don't worry, we will practice this so that your paragraphs flow smoothly and are not scattered.

So, like I said, within this framework, make your transition statements your own and make them brilliant. If you are not feeling brilliant and creative, you can just mention the previous paragraph and then introduce the main idea of the next, such as: "Now that you know that transition sentences are important, let's take a look at one that Alex used to get a perfect score."

Once again here's the question from the Pretest.

43. Does each individual pursuing self-interest best ensure the success of a society?

Solution: Look at the transition sentences that you wrote. Do they introduce the main idea of the paragraph, link to the previous paragraph, and remind us of your thesis? Each one need not necessarily fulfill all three of these goals, but should nail at least one or two of them.

Here are a few nice transition sentences from Alex's essay. You've seen his intro. Then he began his first paragraph with. "In Native American culture, the individual is essentially nonexistent." This transitioned nicely from the intro to the first paragraph, which is about Native American culture. Later in the essay, Alex began his last body paragraph with. "Society today is less physically brutal, but just as mentally brutal, more so, some might argue." This was a great link to the previous paragraph, a great clue to the direction of this paragraph, and a reminder of his thesis. Finally, he began his conclusion with "But what have these successes cost us?" This was a great opener for the conclusion and great link ("these successes") to the previous paragraph. To see these transition sentences in context, refer to his complete essay on page 134.

SAT Reading/Writing Mantra #43
Use transition sentences to begin each paragraph, link it to the previous paragraph, and/or remind the reader of your thesis.

Transition Sentences Drills

Okay, look back at the intro that you wrote in the drills of Skill 42. The next paragraph is the first "body" paragraph, which uses the specific examples that you brainstormed to demonstrate your thesis. Your transition sentence should introduce the main idea of the paragraph, link to the previous paragraph, and/or remind the reader of your thesis. Now let's see a transition sentence to introduce the second paragraph:

1. Assignment: Is it better to be compliant or to challenge the status quo?

_____

_____

_____

_____

_____

_____

_____

_____

2. Assignment: Has materialism helped society?

_____

_____

_____

_____

_____

_____

_____

_____

_____

Body Paragraph I

Each "body" paragraph can begin with a link to the previous paragraph. Then as you write it, keep it focused on a single main idea. It's easiest to write it around a single important specific example, with lots of details about the example. That avoids the two biggest problems that I see in students' essays: lack of details and lack of focus. Organizing around one example automatically corrects both of these!

As I said earlier, the highest-scoring essays that I have seen use one of the following designs for the body paragraphs. These are nice because they have organic organization and connection, rather than two examples that demonstrate your point but are totally unrelated. (Of course, if you try, you can relate any two examples with a clever transition sentence.)

• One topic, first paragraph setting the scene and the second proving the thesis
• Two topics from the same historical period or literary work
• Two chronological events, usually "cause and effect" or "before and after"
• Chronological personal observation

Let's look at what you did with your body paragraphs.

44. Does each individual pursuing self-interest best ensure the success of a society?

Solution: Make sure your body paragraphs are very detailed; the more details, the better. Usually, open with a transition sentence. You can remind the reader how this example demonstrates your thesis.

Here's what Alex did for his first two body paragraphs:

In Native American culture, the individual is essentially nonexistent. Any and every action taken by an individual should be to benefit the whole. Native life, primitive looking to early pioneers, stressed peace and harmony with nature, something that kept them alive for thousands of years. In this they were successful.

When Christopher Columbus and other explorers came looking for riches in the new world, they facilitated their groups with force. Spice trading was a dangerous business, and sailors were threatened by having their tongues cut off if they talked to the wrong person. The punishment for mutiny was often worse, death perhaps. Why then, did so many people come with Columbus and others on such a dangerous journey? They came for the money. Money they knew could only come with the assistance of others. A ship cannot sail across the Atlantic with only one man.

Alex began by writing that Native Americans did not emphasize the individual. Then he took us to Columbus and the explorers who were brutal and forced to act as a team, also deemphasizing the individual, but for greed, not for the benefit of the whole. Graders appreciated the logical connection between the two examples and the depth of analysis. Details get points, and so does depth.

SAT Reading/Writing Mantra #44
Begin each "body" paragraph with a link to the previous paragraph, and write each around a single main idea.

Body Paragraph I Drills

You've already written the transition sentence. Now, let's see that first body paragraph for each topic.

1. Assignment: Is it better to be compliant or to challenge the status quo?

_____

_____

_____

_____

_____

_____

_____

_____

_____

_____

_____

_____

2. Assignment: Has materialism helped society?

_____

_____

_____

_____

_____

_____

_____

_____

_____

_____

_____

_____

Skill 45 Body Paragraph II

The next body paragraph should finish demonstrating your thesis. Like other body paragraphs, it should be organized around a specific example. Ideally, it smoothly links to your previous body paragraph(s).

> Let's see what you did.
>
> 45. Does each individual pursuing self-interest best ensure the success of a society?

Solution: The paragraph that you wrote should revolve on one main idea, contain specific details, and demonstrate your thesis. Let's look at Alex's 12:

> Society today is less physically brutal, but just as mentally brutal, more so, some might argue. Our Capitalist society is run by greed and competition. Businesses achieve so much because their competitors are always right on their tails. It's a continuous scramble to the top, and the first one there's the winner. Our government is a system of checks and balances because nobody trusts anybody else. Our society is founded on the presumption that mankind is inherently evil. And that presumption has brought our society power and riches.

Alex began with a great transition linking this to the previous paragraph. He made several generalizations, but followed up with specific references such as "checks and balances" and "founded on the presumption . . . " This paragraph demonstrates his point that self-interest motivates people and that "our society" is run by greed.

Notice that Alex's essay is awesome, but not perfect. You cannot make a perfect essay in 25 minutes. They know that and allow for it. They call this allowance "holistic grading." They don't have a checklist, grade each item, and add up your points. Instead, they look at the essay as a whole and say, "Okay, he had good solid organization, a few spelling errors, but wow, he blew me away with details and depth. I'll give it a 12." If you give them what they want (structure, transitions, details, depth), you get a high score. This makes the essay easy to ace.

SAT Reading/Writing Mantra #45
The second or third body paragraph should finish demonstrating your thesis. It should be organized around a specific example of your thesis. Ideally, it smoothly links to your previous body paragraph(s).

Body Paragraph II Drills

Let's see the next body paragraph(s) for each topic:

1. Assignment: Is it better to be compliant or to challenge the status quo?

_____

_____

_____

_____

_____

_____

_____

_____

_____

_____

_____

2. Assignment: Has materialism helped society?

_____

_____

_____

_____

_____

_____

_____

_____

_____

_____

_____

Skill 46

Conclusion

Your conclusion should wrap it up. Generally it should follow the format: restate thesis, link, and end with a bang. The bang is like the opener. It can be a question, a quote, a surprising statement, or something else clever. The conclusion is your last chance to prove your thesis. If you have noticed that your essay is a hair off the topic or that you have not clearly proved your thesis, you can correct this with a sentence or two connecting your examples to the assignment.

Also—and this is so important—watch your pacing and leave time for the conclusion. You'd think that they would say, well she or he only had 25 minutes so I can see why she or he didn't get to it. But, no, you lose points for leaving it out. Remember, the basic thing they are testing is organization. Without a conclusion, they assume you didn't know that you needed it. So when there is, maybe, 5 minutes left, close up the body paragraph and write the conclusion. Brilliant is good, but even a modest sentence or two of a conclusion will get you points.

Let's see what you did with your conclusion.

46. Does each individual pursuing self-interest best ensure the success of a society?

Solution: The conclusion that you wrote should wrap up the essay. You can use restate thesis, link, and bang. Make sure you have proved your point.

Let's look at Alex's:

But, what have these successes cost us? We have psychologists, and medication, and jazzercise, and drug use, all to fill that big empty hole where happiness should be. Our greater civilization is thriving because of each member's indulgence in their own interests. Yet strangely, each member is suffering for it. The Native population was successful, for thousands of years, at the goals they put forth. We are the new Rome, and it's only a matter of time before we fall.

Nice conclusion. He definitely answered the question, and he ended with a really big bang. Notice, again, that his essay is not perfect. No doubt with a few more hours he could clean it up. But it's very good, and most importantly it accomplishes what the SAT wants—the things that we know they give points for. It's organized, detailed, deep, and interesting, and that made it a perfect 12!

SAT Reading/Writing Mantra #46
Structure your conclusion by restating your thesis, linking, and ending with a bang.

Conclusion Drills

Write a conclusion for each topic. Try using "restate, link, and bang."

1. Assignment: Is it better to be compliant or to challenge the status quo?

_____
_____
_____
_____
_____
_____
_____
_____
_____
_____

2. Assignment: Has materialism helped society?

_____
_____
_____
_____
_____
_____
_____
_____
_____
_____

Other Stuff That Matters

You've got the format—the intro, body, body, conclusion essay that uses tons of specific details, avoids too many generalizations, and has nice transition sentences. What else do you need? Here are five more things that the SAT loves. Add them, and I guarantee you'll gain points!

❶ **Depth of analysis**. Don't be afraid to be deep—within the safe framework of intro, body, body, conclusion and with each paragraph focused on a specific example, analyze things, make insights, state your observations, make conclusions, go out on a limb.

❷ **Length**. Longer is better; it makes you look eager and smart. All else equal, longer essays score higher than shorter ones.

❸ **Big words**. The SAT loves big vocab words, so use a bunch. (But make sure to use them correctly.) If this does not come easily to you, plan a few words that you will always use. We'll practice this in the drills. This is a great way to review and learn vocab words, and it's guaranteed points!

❹ **Varied sentences**. Don't use all short choppy sentences and don't use all long complex sentences. Use a variety. It makes an essay easier and more interesting to read. Variety keeps a reader awake and interested.

❺ **Readable handwriting**. Technically they don't grade for handwriting, but of course they do need to be able to read it. Try not to annoy them with handwriting that looks like the footprints left by a dying chicken. Do the best you can. Put a little extra effort into neatness. But don't stress, I have seen some pretty bad handwriting get perfect scores! Bottom line: make it readable.

❺ **Few or no grammar and spelling errors**. Make sure to proofread. Leave two or three minutes for proofing. More about this in Skill 48.

Back to the Pretest.

47. Does each individual pursuing self-interest best ensure the success of a society?

Solution: In your essay, did you get deep, write at least 1.5 pages, use some impressive vocab, vary your sentences, write readably, and avoid basic grammar and spelling errors? You'll have a chance to practice these in the drills and in the next few Skills. Adding any one of these will earn you points.

SAT Reading/Writing Mantra #47
In your essay, get deep, write at least 1.5 pages, use some impressive vocab, vary your sentences, write readably, and avoid basic grammar and spelling errors.

Other Stuff That Matters Drills

How do you use more impressive vocab in your essay? I learned this strategy from a student who would plan several big words that he knew he would use. He got a perfect 12 every time. Obviously some words will be easier to use than others. Ululation (a howl) might be hard to work in, but inherently (naturally occurring) or incontrovertible (unquestionable) could be used in **any** essay. For example, "These examples demonstrate incontrovertibly that self-interest is inherent in the success of any society." Try this. Below are a bunch of great essay words. Use these or choose a few of your own from the sentence completion skills, and try to incorporate them in the drill below. Then use them again in the practice essay in Skill 49. This is also, of course, a terrific way to review vocab words.

❶ Define each of the following great essay words:

Immutable_____   Concordant_____

Eradicated_____   Pertinent_____

Auspicious_____   Thwart_____

Superfluous_____   Ramification_____

Affinity_____

❷ Let's practice incorporating these tips. In the space below, take one of the body paragraphs that you wrote for Skill 44 or 45 and rewrite it, incorporating more of the following: depth of insight, length, impressive vocab, sentence variety, neatness, and proofreading.

_____

_____

_____

_____

_____

_____

_____

_____

_____

_____

_____

_____

_____

_____

Skill 48

Proofread

"Write the first draft as a free write," Mrs. Schwartzonagel always said. "Don't worry about spelling and grammar, just get your ideas on paper." This was great advice, and I still use it. But for the SAT essay, it creates a mess. On the SAT, attend to spelling and grammar as you write. Write quickly enough to capture your creative ideas as they come to you and quickly enough to finish in 25 minutes, but slowly enough to catch careless errors.

This is another one of those cool life skills. It's great to have the freedom and flexibility to meet different demands with appropriate measures. Like when Big Sally gets up to bat and you say, "Back it up in the outfield!" For a long-term project, do a creative free-write. But when you are writing a 25-minute timed essay, attend to spelling and grammar as you go.

Then when you have 5 minutes left, make sure you've done your conclusion, and use a few minutes to proofread. This is not a complex reanalysis, just a basic read over to find and correct big errors. This will definitely get you points.

Here's what you are looking for:

1. **Omitted words.** Because you are writing quickly, your hand may leave out a word that you meant to write. Example: Critics contend that the government overspends—superfluous items.
2. **Obvious misspellings.** Some words you may not be sure of; do the best you can. But look for words that of course you know how to spell, and yet writing furiously, you made a careless error.
3. **Obvious punctuation errors.** Some commas you may not be sure of; do the best you can. Fix any obvious errors.
4. **Indenting.** Make sure you indented clearly.
5. **Paragraphs.** Make sure you started new paragraphs when you meant to.
6. **Details.** Make sure you wrote what you meant to and not accidentally something else.

Back to the Pretest.

48. Does each individual pursuing self-interest best ensure the success of a society?

Solution: Check over your Pretest essay or Drills essays. Practice looking for and correcting the most common careless errors listed above.

SAT Reading/Writing Mantra #48

Leave a few minutes to proofread your essay for omitted words, misspellings, and punctuation errors, and to make sure that you represented details accurately and started new paragraphs where you meant to by indenting.

Proofread Drills

In the space below, quickly write a few paragraphs describing one of the topics that you wrote about and planned in the Brain Freeze Help drills of Skill 41. Include details and write mindfully but quickly, just like you would for the SAT essay.

_____

_____

_____

_____

_____

_____

_____

_____

_____

_____

_____

_____

_____

_____

_____

_____

_____

_____

_____

_____

_____

_____

Now, take a few minutes to proofread your essay for omitted words, misspellings, and punctuation errors, and to make sure that you indented, started new paragraphs when you meant to, and wrote details accurately. This is great practice and it will definitely improve your score.

How to Be a Writing Monster

Review the Mantras below for our 10 essay Skills. Go back and reread the Skills for any that you feel unsure of. Then check the box next to each Skill when you have mastered it.

☐ **Skill 39.** Brainstorm for specific details, not generalizations.

☐ **Skill 40.** When you brainstorm for details, if something new that perfectly fits the assignment occurs to you, of course use it. If not, use whichever of your planned examples applies best.

☐ **Skill 41.** Jot down or circle the best details from your brainstorm. These details form the outline for the body paragraphs of the essay.

☐ **Skill 42.** Your intro paragraph should be 3 to 4 sentences: an opener, a link, and a thesis.

☐ **Skill 43.** Use transition sentences to begin each paragraph, link it to the previous paragraph, and/or remind the reader of your thesis.

☐ **Skill 44.** Begin each "body" paragraph with a link to the previous paragraph, and write each around a single main idea.

☐ **Skill 45.** The second or third body paragraph should finish demonstrating your thesis. It should be organized around a specific example of your thesis. Ideally, it smoothly links to your previous body paragraph(s).

☐ **Skill 46.** Structure your conclusion by restating your thesis, linking, and ending with a bang.

☐ **Skill 47.** In your essay, get deep, write at least 1.5 pages, use some impressive vocab, vary your sentences, write readably, and avoid basic grammar and spelling errors.

☐ **Skill 48.** Leave a few minutes to proofread your essay for omitted words, misspellings, and punctuation errors, and to make sure that you represented details accurately and started new paragraphs when you meant to by indenting.

That's it. You are ready to write a freakishly good essay. Let's go to the drills.

How to Be a Writing Monster Drills

Take 25 minutes to write an essay on the topic assigned below.

Think carefully about the issue presented in the following excerpt and the assignment below.

> General Robert E. Lee said that truth is "a quality that will carry you through this world much better than policy, or tact, or expediency, or any other word that was ever devised to conceal or mystify a deviation from the straight line." Yet, often, speaking the truth causes ourselves or others humiliation, uneasiness, or even injury. Should we speak the truth in these situations?

Assignment: Should one always tell the truth? Plan and write an essay in which you develop your point of view on this issue. Support your position with reasoning and examples taken from your reading, studies, experience, or observations.

Use This Space to Brainstorm for Your Essay

Studies show that sleeping and eating healthfully two days before the test (or any important event) is as important as sleeping and eating healthfully the night before. So Thursday night eat a healthy dinner and go to bed early—not so early that you're lying in bed at 7:00 p.m. tense, hungry, and staring at the cracks in the ceiling, but normal early, maybe 10:00 p.m.

Friday, have a normal day, no need to cram or stress. If you have completed this book and one or more timed practice tests, you are ready. Go to school, play sports or do whatever you do after school, have a healthy dinner, and do something fun and relaxing. Don't hang out with anyone who stresses you out or obsesses over the test. Read, play a game, or watch a funny movie—I recommend *Fletch, Wedding Crashers,* or *40-Year-Old Virgin*—and go to bed at a sensible time. If you live in a household where, in the morning, everyone roams the house screaming for a clean shirt and the car keys, then gather your snack, drink, admission ticket, ID, sharpened pencils, watch, and calculator in the evening.

You should eat breakfast and pack a snack because it's a long day, and you have to feed the brain. For snack I recommend a cheese sandwich or two Luna bars; they are high in protein and not too high in sugar, good brain food. If you need an extra special boost, in India some people take a few drops of almond oil on the morning of a test.

Let's take a look at the question from the Pretest.

50. The night before the test you should

   (A) stay up all night studying
   (B) go to Jules' huge party
   (C) get answers from someone who is 18 hours ahead in Australia and already took the test
   (D) have a nice dinner, relax, go to bed at a reasonable hour
   (E) spend time with your most freaked out grade-mongering friends

Solution: Relax and sleep well, you are prepared. Now, go get'em!

Correct answer: D

Test Day Checklist	
2 Protein bars	Sharpened #2 pencils
Beverage	Calculator
Your admission ticket	A watch (to keep track of time)
Photo ID (driver's license, school ID, or passport)	

Brian's Friday Night Spiel: Recommendations for the Days Preceding the Test Drills

Here is your last drill section. Your last assignment is to be able to stay relaxed, even under pressure. So here is a little tool that you can use anytime, even during the test.

In the 1970s Herbert Benson, a researcher at Harvard Medical School, published work on what he called the *relaxation response*, a physiological response where the body and mind relax. Benson reported that the relaxation response was triggered by practicing 20 minutes of a concentration exercise, basically meditation. Apparently, Yale, always in competition with Harvard, decided to one-up them. "We need a way to trigger the relaxation response, but in less than Benson's 20 minutes!" they might have bemoaned. They researched, and they tried as hard as they could to relax; it was quite stressful. Finally, someone came up with the following goofy exercise. And it is goofy, but the thing is, it works! It totally works. Do it and you'll see.

Follow these steps:

1. Breathing through your nose, become aware of your breath.
2. Relax your shoulders and face.
3. Allow your exhale to be longer than your inhale.
4. Now, drop your shoulders and head and smile, and then bring your head back up.
5. Repeat: Drop your shoulders and head and smile, and then bring your head back up.
6. Notice how you feel.

That's it! Anytime you feel stressed, even during the test, try this very simple exercise to trigger your "relaxation response."

Score is tied: Yale, 1. Harvard, 1.

Bonus Skill: Writing the Perfect 12 Essay

Life goes by pretty fast. If you don't stop and look around once in a while, you could miss it.
Ferris Bueller, *Ferris Bueller's Day Off* (Paramount Pictures, 1986)

Want that perfect 12 essay? Here are the four steps to do it.

But first you have to promise me that you are doing this because you want to, and not out of some obsessive, sleep doesn't matter, gotta please my parents, if I don't go to Tufts I'm nothing misunderstanding. Strive to do well, yes. Also stay balanced. Sleep. Eat well. Exercise. Be true to yourself. Be brave. Be honest. Be relaxed. Breathe. And from that place, give it all that you got.

1. Make sure you understand all 10 essay writing Skills and all 14 writing multiple-choice skills; this is the same grammar that they are looking for on the essay. Don't just look at them and say, "Yeah, I can do that." Practice. Do the drills. For the grammar Skills, make sure you can answer every question correctly on every Skill. If you can't, reread the section, reread the solutions, and keep redoing the drills until they make perfect sense. Then teach them to a friend.

2. Master posttests I, II, and III (posttests II and III are on the CD-ROM). Take each test, read the solutions, and redo any questions that you missed. When you master these questions, your grammar is up to the task!

3. Then get a copy of *The Official SAT Study Guide* published by the College Board. It contains eight practice tests. Take all eight timed practice essays. Use our essay Mantras to check each essay, and ask a friend, parent, or teacher to use the checklist on page 113. Practice brainstorming. Practice pacing. Practice applying the Skills.

4. I've noticed over the years that writing an organized intro, body, conclusion essay will earn you a score of at least 8. Proofreading, using lots of specific details, depth of analysis, great vocab, and connected examples get you a 9 to 12. Connecting your examples seems to be very important; it gives your essay cohesiveness and organically adds depth of analysis. Connecting examples can mean the methods listed in Skills 43 and 44 and/or having a thread or theme running through the whole essay.

Let's see this all put into action on another essay that received a perfect score. Notice again that this essay is not error-free, but contains what graders are looking for. Also don't be intimidated by this essay (or Alex's or Kyle's). I think that if an essay could get a score higher than 12, these would!

Ian's Perfect 12

Think carefully about the issue presented in the following excerpt and the assignment below.

> The first problem for all of us is not to learn but to unlearn. We hold on to ideas that were accepted in the past, and we are afraid to give them up. Preconceptions about what is right or wrong, true or false, good or bad are embedded so deeply in our thinking that we honestly may not know that they are there. Whether it's women's role in society or the role of our country in the world, the old assumptions just don't work anymore.
>
> Adapted from Gloria Steinem, "A New Egalitarian Lifestyle."

Assignment: Do people need to "unlearn," or reject, many of their assumptions and ideas? Plan and write an essay in which you develop your point of view on this issue. Support your position with reasoning and examples taken from your reading, studies, experience, or observations.

On the first day of my Historical Symptomatology class, my teacher asked us all to think about a belief that we held without question. As I thought, I realized that we all hang on to many dogmas in our everyday lives. These dogmas take the form of religious beliefs, our conceptions of our roles in society, or simply our understanding that as students we must go to school. Although we cannot help taking a certain portion of what we "know" for granted, it is pivotal that we question convention and challenge past ways of thinking in order to progress and develop as people.

In Johan Koëstler's piece "The Sleepwalkers", he describes the Pythagorian universe. In Pythagorian thought, the planets produced a heavenly music as they revolved around the sun, each plant's pitch resonating in accordance to the others like harmonic intervals on the strings of a 'cello. For a long time it was believed that this was how the universe functioned; through heavenly music with God as its composer. C. S. Lewis tells us even Aristotle, one of the western world's greatest mind was in agreement with this line of thought.

Later, during the age of enlightenment, Isaac Newton told the world that the planets did not make music. With his laws of gravity Newton explained that the universe was guided by a set of rules. We still use Newton's laws of gravity today in modern science. A questioner of past convention, Newton helped to bring people to a greater understanding.

Renée Descartes is a man who has questioned dogmas more than perhaps anyone else. Confined to a small room during a serious snow storm that he experienced while serving in the military in Germany, Descartes began the arduous process of "unlearning" everything that he did not know for himself to be true. He began at one simple truth, which was that, in merely questioning his own existence, he had proved it, or more famously stated, "I think, therefore I am." Although Descartes was never fully able to relearn his entire conception of the world through deductive reasoning, he developed ideas about questioning dogma that philosophers still consider to be brilliant.

Through the ingenuity of these famous minds, we can see that the attempt to unlearn a certain outdated practice has lead the human race to a high, more enlightened place.

I remember when I saw Ian after he wrote this essay. When he told me that the assignment fit what he was studying in Historical Symptomatology class, I knew he would get a 12. (I had never heard of Historical Symptomatology!) He blew them away with organization, details, vocab, connected examples, and depth.

Alex's Perfect 12

Assignment: Does each individual pursuing self-interest best ensure the success of a society? Plan and write an essay in which you develop your point of view on this issue. Support your position with reasoning and examples taken from your reading, studies, experience, or observations.

If you define the success of a society by the amount of things achieved and conquered by that community, then limitation of self-interest is not necessary. However, if you measure the success of a group by the way it functions, its organization, and compassion for ideals, then limiting self-interest becomes more important. The success of a community should be measured through the overall happiness of its members, not by the amount of things the group achieves. In this way, each individual pursuing self-interest threatens, rather than ensures, a society's success.

In Native American culture, the individual is essentially nonexistent. Any and every action taken by an individual should be to benefit the whole. Native life, primitive looking to early pioneers, stressed peace and harmony with nature, something that kept them alive for thousands of years. In this they were successful.

When Christopher Columbus and other explorers came looking for riches in the new world, they facilitated their groups with force. Spice trading was a dangerous business, and sailors were threatened by having their tongues cut off if they talked to the wrong person. The punishment for mutiny was often worse, death perhaps. Why then, did so many people come with Columbus and others on such a dangerous journey? They came for the money. Money they knew could only come with the assistance of others. A ship cannot sail across the Atlantic with only one man.

Society today is less physically brutal, but just as mentally brutal, more so, some might argue. Our Capitalist society is run by greed and competition. Businesses achieve so much because their competitors are always right on their tails. It's a continuous scramble to the top, and the first one there's the winner. Our government is a system of checks and balances because nobody trusts anybody else. Our society is founded on the presumption that mankind is inherently evil. And that presumption has brought our society power and riches.

But, what have these successes cost us? We have psychologists, and medication, and jazzercise, and drug use, all to fill that big empty hole where happiness should be. Our greater civilization is thriving because of each member's indulgence in their own interests. Yet strangely, each member is suffering for it. The Native population was successful, for thousands of years, at the goals they put forth. We are the new Rome, and it's only a matter of time before we fall.

This is the essay that we looked at in the essay Skills. Alex gave graders organization, vocabulary, details, connected examples, and amazing depth for a perfect 12.

Kyle's Perfect 12

Assignment: Has materialism helped society? Plan and write an essay in which you develop your point of view on this issue. Support your position with reasoning and examples taken from your reading, studies, experience, or observations.

Our American culture pivots on our materialistic values. The "modern" society that we see daily is saturated with unecessay and wastful objects. The Amerian idealism that we hold so dear, as our identity, is slowly decaying admist a storm of consumption and over production. Perhaps Aristotle was right when he said that the best life is the most simple life. Modern society is much too concerned with amassing material wealth, that materialism has blinded our vision and blocked our paths to becoming a truly productive American society.

The average american life is fraught with consumption. Part of our identity that makes us so different is our extravigant and excessive lifestyles. However over the years of our frivolous wasting, we have aquired a feeling of hubris, and eminency when we should be ashamed and remorseful. America's modern mass-producing society will inevitably collapse if our materialistic values are not tamed. Our great country will inevitably fail if our American instinct emerges victorious over our inteligence and understanding. Our current battle against the monster of materialism resembles the 1920's conflicts. A time of flappers, bootleggers, flagpole sitters, and speakeasies was a short lived period of progressivisim and materialism. The collide between rural, traditional values and America's new defiant generation resulted in violence and ultimately The Great Depression. Our history shows what can potentialy happen when we remain naïve and let our encumbering burden of production weigh us down. We will be crippled!!

However, perhaps there are some positive aspects of the quest to material affluence. The fourth republic of nigeria, established by president Obasanjo in 1999 has created a economy based on mass production and consumption rather than its one scarce commodity, oil. Nigerias culturaly fragmented interior, that is infamous for extreme tribal violence, has been calmed. A history of military coups, ethnic riots, and civil warfare as been forgotten with the newly established, progressive attitude of materialism. In 1989, after the death of conservative dictator Sani Abach, Nigeria presented a united front between all ethnic groups (Iboo, Yoruba, Hausa-fulani), on the basis of increased economic production. Perhaps materialism isn't always a curse, but a cure.

However, there are obvious differences between Nigeria's fragil economic situation and the U.S.A.'s. But it is undeniable that without some measures to increase stringency on modern society, we will inevitable cripple, Perhaps Aristotle was on to something.

This is the essay that we looked at in the Drills solutions. There are spelling errors, but graders know that you have 25 minutes and don't expect perfect. Kyle's depth of reasoning, awesome details, varied sentences, and incredible vocabulary blew the graders away for a perfect 12!

Easy, Medium, Hard, and Guessing Revisited

Let's revisit what I told you way back at the beginning of the book. It will probably make even more sense now.

The SAT is not graded like an English test at school. To get a 500, the average score for kids across the country, you need to get about half the questions correct. To get a 600, the average score for admission to schools like Goucher and University of Vermont, you need about 75% correct. And for a beautiful 700 on the SAT, the average for kids who got into Georgetown, U.C. Berkeley, Emory, and Wesleyan, you must answer 89% of the questions correctly.

Use this info to determine how many questions you need to answer on the SAT. Remember that on sentence completion and writing multiple-choice questions, the first third of the questions are "easy," the middle bunch are "medium," and a little less than the last third are "hard." In other words, of 8 questions, perhaps 3 are easy, 3 are medium, and 2 are hard.

Knowing this order of difficulty is important because if you need only half correct or 70% correct, don't rush through the easies and mediums just to get to the hard ones. All questions are worth the same amount. Not rushing is the best way to avoid careless errors. In school you might need to finish tests in order to do well. Here you do not. **You need to get to the very hardest questions only if you are shooting for 700+**.

Guessing? Don't randomly guess, but if you are unsure of a question, sometimes you can get it correct by the process of elimination. When you can confidently eliminate at least one answer choice, take an educated guess. If you get it right, you gain four times as much as you lose if it's wrong. So educated guesses pay off. Of course, now that you've completed this book, you'll barely need to guess! When you feel stumped, take another look and ask yourself, Which reading/writing Skill can I use?

Now What?

Take the Posttest. It contains questions that review our 50 Skills. Check your answers and review the Skills for any questions that were difficult. Then take the additional Posttests found on the CD-ROM that came with this book. Again, check your answers and review the Skills for any questions that were difficult.

After you have completed the Posttests, go to your guidance office and pick up the free packet entitled "SAT Preparation Booklet: Get Ready for the SAT," which contains a full practice test with answers and scoring instructions. Or you can download a free test at www.collegeboard.com.

Take the test as a dress rehearsal; get up early on a Saturday, time it, use the answer sheets, and fill in the ovals. If you have competed this book, you will find that you are very well prepared. Correct and score the test, and review whatever you got wrong. Figure out which Mantras you could have used to get them right.

If you have some time, purchase *The Official SAT Study Guide*, published by the College Board. It contains eight practice tests. Take one practice test per week as a dress rehearsal. Take it when you are relaxed and focused. We want only your best work. Less than that will earn you a lower score than you are capable of and is bad for morale. Score each test and review whatever you got wrong. Figure out which Mantras you could have used to get them right.

Now, you are ready, you beautiful SAT monster. Go get 'em!

Posttest

This Posttest contains questions that correspond to our 50 Skills. Take the test. Then check your answers and review the Skills for any questions that were difficult.

> Each sentence below has one or two blanks, each blank indicating that something has been omitted. Beneath each sentence are five sets of words labeled A through E. Choose the word or set of words that, when inserted in the sentence, best fits the meaning of the sentence as a whole.

1 Even after she had scaled Mount Graylock, the highest mountain in the state, Clara felt that she needed to prove her ability and continued to _____ mountains.

(A) decline
(B) transfer
(C) ascend
(D) escalate
(E) allude

2 Although both on stage and behind the scenes Jim Edwards is known for selfish outbursts, at home, to his family, he is _____.

(A) egotistical
(B) theatrical
(C) thunderous
(D) giving
(E) ascetic

3 Since critics panned Selma's new novel for its _____, she has shortened several chapters and cut others entirely.

(A) span
(B) beauty
(C) creativity
(D) expertise
(E) hostility

4 The River Valley Market is a natural foods _____, which means that it is a grocery store owned jointly by its members.

(A) frugality
(B) cooperative
(C) claim
(D) definition
(E) request

5 The movie *Superbad* was successful for its _____ and _____; it presented with hilarity and insight the plight of teens in suburban areas.

(A) wit .. clarity
(B) presentation .. precision
(C) situation .. astuteness
(D) humor .. resolve
(E) charisma .. transmission

6 Ants have a reputation for treating other ant colonies with _____, though this is not always the case; sometimes they coexist peacefully.

(A) corruption
(B) magnificence
(C) flippancy
(D) belligerence
(E) sophistication

7 Milton believed that Theo had no _____ in him, and Milton hoped Theo would stay that way, _____ and free of hatred.

(A) anger .. livid
(B) disagreement .. denial
(C) disregard .. compelling
(D) evasion .. compassionate
(E) malice .. serene

8 Although it is not as _____ as New England, Arizona's _____ climate provided welcomed relief for Martha's allergies; she missed the four seasons, but enjoyed her increased health and Arizona's lack of humidity.

(A) varied . . arid
(B) beguiling . . tonifying
(C) florid . . ecological
(D) temperate . . sultry
(E) stunning . . scorched

9 Max is _____ and Sylvia is _____; while Max has concern for the sufferings of others, Sylvia can identify with and understand their suffering.

(A) passionate . . lithe
(B) compassionate . . empathetic
(C) heartful . . sophistic
(D) openhanded . . diminutive
(E) philanthropic . . divisive

10 Red Beard of South Salem is widely known for the rare quality of being a _____ pirate; _____ to friends and enemies alike.

(A) somber . . amiable
(B) just . . evenhanded
(C) staid . . vindictive
(D) versatile . . thwarting
(E) virtuous . . solitary

11 Since overeating and lack of exercise can have _____ health consequences, doctors recommend that their patients eat _____ and get ample physical activity.

(A) catastrophic . . heartily
(B) soporific . . reasonably
(C) propitious . . mindfully
(D) harmful . . plentifully
(E) deleterious . . moderately

The passages below are followed by questions based on their content; questions following a pair of related passages may also be based on the relationship between the paired passages. Answer the questions on the basis of what is <u>stated</u> or <u>implied</u> in the passages and in any introductory material that may be provided.

Note: Here is a passage you read earlier in Skill 13. Now, let's answer some questions about it.

The following passage was adapted from a 1998 essay written by a psychology graduate student exploring his heritage.

While my mother's parents spent their lives in New York, my paternal grandparents were born and raised in neighboring villages of Austria. My grandfather's father owned a liquor store
5　and was very religious. My grandfather was the academic of the family. He completed high school, college and graduate degrees. He worked as a teacher and principal, much more respected positions then than now. I connected
10　deeply with this grandfather, Herman. He and I are sensitive, loving, prone to worry, and innately talented teachers.

Though my grandparents and great-grandparents were born in Austria, I am not Austrian. This, I
15　believe, is the case for many Jews in the United States. Belonging to this religion is a cultural heritage as well as a faith. Though I rarely think of myself as Jewish and pay small heed to the holidays, Judaism is a large part of my identity.

⑫ The main purpose of the passage is to

(A) persuade
(B) inform
(C) apologize
(D) eulogize
(E) synchronize

⑬ The narrator does not consider himself Austrian (line 14) because

(A) his great grandparents were not born there
(B) he does not think of himself as Jewish

(C) his grandfather left at a young age
(D) his religion defines his heritage
(E) he is most connected to his grandfather

⑭ In line 2, the word "paternal" most nearly means

(A) great
(B) on my father's side
(C) on my mother's side
(D) adopted
(E) Austrian

⑮ The author gives all of the following as support for his grandfather being an "academic" (line 6) EXCEPT

(A) he was a talented teacher
(B) he completed graduate degrees
(C) he was prone to worry
(D) he worked as a principal
(E) he completed high school

⑯ What does the narrator imply in lines 18 and 19 by "pay small heed to the holidays"?

(A) The narrator contributes very little money to religious organizations.
(B) The narrator rarely observes Jewish holidays.
(C) Judaism is a large part of the narrator's identity.
(D) The narrator is not Jewish.
(E) The narrator does not enjoy the holidays.

140

This passage is from a 2007 scientific paper that explores the water resources of the town of Meadville.

The city of Meadville is particularly well blessed in terms of water resources. The town's two municipal aquifers, the Cussewago sandstone bedrock aquifer and the glacial outwash

5 aquifer, are capable of producing a more than sufficient yield for industry and residents. The outwash aquifers exist mainly in the valleys and produce far better yields, since the thick drifts of sand and gravel are far more

10 permeable.

The two most significant bedrock aquifers are found in Sharpsville Sandstone and in Cusswego Sandstone. The Meadville aquifers are recharged through precipitation. The

15 recharge zone for these aquifers is large, consisting of all ground areas within the groundwater divide of the French Creek valley watershed. Stream flow and groundwater levels are highest in early spring as snowmelt is

20 discharged, and lowest in late summer, when precipitation is low and evaporation high. Evaporation is particularly important since Woodcock Creek is influenced by the reservoir, and the water level of the reservoir changes

25 from evaporation in warmer weather. French Creek and its tributaries run through rural, subtropical terrain and, thusly, transpiration affects the hydrologic cycle significantly.

French Creek and the Meadville aquifer are

30 recharged through precipitation, as has been said before. But this isn't a simple process. Precipitation that falls anywhere within the French Creek valley, as long as it's on the correct side of the water divide, will end up in

35 French Creek or in an aquifer eventually (and *eventually* into the Atlantic Ocean). But how it gets there varies considerably. Some water will precipitate and enter the system promptly.

Some will precipitate in the form of snow,

40 and be released at a later time, usually in larger volume. Water traveling from higher, more distant locations takes longer to reach French Creek than does water closer to the discharge area.

17 From the italicized introductory material, the reader can assume that the primary tone of the passage as a whole will be

Ⓐ affectionate nostalgia

Ⓑ awe and fear

Ⓒ uncertainty and impatience

Ⓓ sadness and confusion

Ⓔ analytical detachment

18 The author's tone in the first sentence is best described as

Ⓐ joyous

Ⓑ contemptuous

Ⓒ diagnostic

Ⓓ mischievous

Ⓔ solemn

19 A major difference between paragraph 2 and paragraph 3 is

Ⓐ paragraph 3 explores a statement of paragraph 2 in greater detail

Ⓑ paragraph 2 describes events that happened before those of paragraph 3

Ⓒ paragraph 3 describes three types of aquifers

Ⓓ paragraph 3 is more emotive

Ⓔ paragraph 3 is fictional whereas paragraph 2 is expository

20 The final paragraph is primarily concerned with

Ⓐ the water supply shortage in Meadville

Ⓑ Meadville's European exchange program

Ⓒ Meadville's municipal budget

Ⓓ Meadville's geological foundation

Ⓔ how Meadville's water supply replenishes

21 The parentheses around "and eventually into the Atlantic Ocean" (lines 35 and 36) serve to

Ⓐ emphasize the vast size of the Atlantic Ocean

Ⓑ criticize Meadville's water politics

Ⓒ emphasize the limitations in a theory

Ⓓ demonstrate the geological significance of Meadville

Ⓔ indicate that the information is interesting but inessential

22 Which of the following is an example of "Some water will precipitate and enter the system promptly" described in lines 37 and 38?

Ⓐ Water treated in an adjacent plant

Ⓑ Rain that falls directly on the area

Ⓒ Snow that falls in the aquifer

Ⓓ Water that evaporated at high altitudes

Ⓔ Drinking water brought into the area

23 The passage is primarily

Ⓐ a reflection on a educational journey

Ⓑ a dispassionate plea for government funding to save an endangered aquifer

Ⓒ a report on a water system

Ⓓ a criticism of water resource management in Meadville

Ⓔ a scathing social commentary

The following sentences test your ability to recognize grammar and usage errors. Each sentence contains either a single error or no error at all. No sentence contains more than one error. The error, if there is one, is underlined and lettered. If the sentence contains an error, select the one underlined part that must be changed to make the sentence correct. If the sentence is correct, select choice E. In choosing answers, follow the requirements of standard written English.

24 Waking at six in the morning, Glen
    A   B
stretched for an hour and then works for
           C   D
three hours before heading to school.
No error.
E

25 Musical accompaniment by K. Roddly
has been enjoyed for years, but only this
    A   B   C
past year was his original songs been
         D
widely heard and enjoyed. No error
                          E

26 Sitting at her computer, writing a history
         A
paper on the Civil War, Tzipora listened to
                                  B
her mom singing before she ate
        C   D
breakfast. No error
          E

142

27. In high school Matthew was a
    $\underline{\text{A}}$
    nationally ranked swimmer, $\underline{\text{but}}$ in college
         $\underline{\text{B}}$ C
    he continued to swim and $\underline{\text{placed}}$ third in a
                                       D
    national competition. $\underline{\text{No error}}$
                                E

28. $\underline{\text{Before}}$ Gwen $\underline{\text{left}}$ to meet Kyle for
         A B
    rock climbing, $\underline{\text{she checked}}$ her helmet,
                          C
    shoes, ropes, and $\underline{\text{safety clips}}$.
                            D
    $\underline{\text{No error}}$
         E

29. Ivan often said that the themes,
                 $\underline{\text{A}}$
    characters, $\underline{\text{and gags}}$ in *Seinfeld*
                       B
    $\underline{\text{are not}}$ only hilarious but also
         C
    $\underline{\text{demonstrate keen insight}}$. $\underline{\text{No error}}$
                   D E

30. Professor Mils stated that $\underline{\text{the 1950s}}$,
                                      A
    $\underline{\text{contrasted to}}$ the 1970s, $\underline{\text{demonstrated}}$
         B C
    a significant change $\underline{\text{in social norms}}$.
                                D
    $\underline{\text{No error}}$
         E

31. Katie $\underline{\text{admired}}$ her geometric
             A
    artwork; the two hexagons $\underline{\text{were blue}}$
                                     B
    and sat $\underline{\text{proud}}$ $\underline{\text{on the page}}$. $\underline{\text{No error}}$
             C D E

32. Millie signed $\underline{\text{her name}}$ to the card
                        A
    $\underline{\text{which now was signed}}$ by Professor
         B C
    Chen, Kendra, Jamaal, $\underline{\text{and she}}$. $\underline{\text{No Error}}$
                                D E

33. The poems $\underline{\text{we are studying}}$ were
                     A
    written by Emily Dickinson, a poet
    $\underline{\text{which}}$ lived in Amherst, Massachusetts,
         B
    and $\underline{\text{wrote}}$ $\underline{\text{hundreds of poems}}$. $\underline{\text{No error}}$
         C D E

The following sentences test correctness and effectiveness of expression. Part of each sentence or the entire sentence is underlined; beneath each sentence are five ways of phrasing the underlined material. Choice A repeats the original phrasing; the other four choices are different. If you think the original phrasing produces a better sentence than any of the alternatives, select choice A; if not, select one of the other choices.

In making your selections, follow the requirements of standard written English; that is, pay attention to grammar, choice of words, sentence construction, and punctuation. Your selection should result in the most effective sentence—clear and precise, without awkwardness or ambiguity.

34. Being as she is the best on the team, Raquel was unanimously chosen to take the goal kick.

    (A) Being as she is the best on the team
    (B) She being the best on the team
    (C) With her as the best on the team
    (D) Being as good or better than everyone else
    (E) The best on the team

35 A great teacher, <u>writing books is now what Tolle does</u> to spread his teachings to a wider audience.

   (A) writing books is now what Tolle does
   (B) Tolle now writes books
   (C) book writing is now what Tolle does
   (D) writing is now what Tolle does with books
   (E) Tolle now does the writing of books

36 <u>Running to town went Nedly</u> to tell his friends about his new bicycle.

   (A) Running to town went Nedly
   (B) Nedly ran to town
   (C) Running to town is where Nedly went
   (D) To run to town Nedly went
   (E) Nedly went running to town

37 Which of the following is the best way to revise and combine the underlined portion of the sentences reproduced below?

   Tree frogs are typically <u>found in trees. They are also found in</u> other high-growing vegetation.

   (A) found in trees; also being found in
   (B) found in trees, since they are also found in
   (C) found in trees and
   (D) found in trees and also found in
   (E) found in trees, as well as typically in

38 Francis Stacey Smith, <u>who is from Canada, is sweet, kind, and intelligent.</u>

   (A) who is from Canada, is sweet, kind, and intelligent
   (B) who is from Canada, is sweet, kindly, and has intelligence
   (C) being Canada, is sweet, kind, and intelligent
   (D) which is Canadian, is sweet, kind, and intelligent
   (E) who is from Canada, she is sweet, kind, and intelligent

Skills 39 to 49: Essay
See Essay prompt on next page.

50 The morning of the test you should

   (A) eat as huge a breakfast as you can stuff into your face
   (B) eat a normal (healthy) breakfast
   (C) drink 4 Jolt colas for energy
   (D) wake up at 4:30 a.m., run 10 km, study until test center opens
   (E) leave your house without your ID, calculator, pencils, and admission slip

Essay

Time: 25 minutes

The essay gives you an opportunity to show how effectively you can develop and express ideas. You should, therefore, take care to develop your point of view, present your ideas logically and clearly, and use language precisely.

Your essay must be written on the lines provided on your answer sheet—you will receive no other paper on which to write. You will have enough space to write if you write on every line, avoid wide margins, and keep your handwriting to a reasonable size. Remember that people who are not familiar with your handwriting will read what you write. Try to write or print so that what you are writing is legible to those readers.

Important Reminders:

- **A pencil is required for the essay.** An essay written in ink will receive a score of zero.
- **Do not write your essay in your test book.** You will receive credit only for what you write on your answer sheet.
- **An off-topic essay will receive a score of zero**.

You have 25 minutes to write an essay on the topic assigned below.

Think carefully about the issue presented in the following excerpt and the assignment below.

> The old saying "No man is an island" is perhaps outdated, but its message is still true today. Though people work more independently and have lives more secluded from one another, advances such as the Internet keep people as connected as ever.

Assignment: Are people as connected with each other today as they have been at other times in history? Plan and write an essay in which you develop your point of view on this issue. Support your position with reasoning and examples taken from your reading, studies, experience, or observations.

Solutions

Skill 1 (page 15)

Don't Be Such a <u>Blank</u>

Note: Answers can vary, here are some suggestions.

1. Hardworkingness, reliability
2. Punctual, on time
3. Combination, range
4. Lively
5. Aggressive
6. Hilarious, effective
7. Not typical
8. Pressured
9. Close-knit
10. Arts

Skill 2 (page 17)

This Suit Is NOT Black

1. Not social
2. Does not like (dislikes)
3. Not the most adept
4. Not lying (honest)
5. Not spiteful
6. Not lazy (eager)
7. Do not hinder (increase)
8. Detrimental

Skill 3 (page 19)

Positive, Negative, or Neither

1. **A** We want a positive word to describe his family, specifically one that relates to "very close."

2. **B** If you don't know the word "patently," cross it out. Then think of a word to fill the blank. We want "betrayer." If you can't think of that, look for a negative word, and then choose the one that fits best. Notice that while they might have been angry and called him an "imbecile," it does not fit in the rest of the sentence as well as "deserter" does.

3. **C** If you do not know the word "incessant," cross it out. "Chloe receives _____ from angry critics," so it must be a negative word, and more specifically it must be something like "anger." Use the process of elimination; even if you didn't know what *tirades* meant, you can get it.

4. **A** If you don't know the word "didactic," cross it out. We want a negative word, more specifically a word meaning something like "bored" or related to the "slow-paced" lecture style. So we can eliminate "inspired" and "convinced." "Patronized" means "treated with kindness tinged with superiority."

5. **E** If you need to, you can cross out difficult words and still get this question correct. "Disempowering" and "problems" tell us that we want a negative word for the blank; and specifically, we want a word meaning "disempowering" or "problematic." So we can eliminate "affirming" and "invigorating." "Disenfranchising" means "disempowering."

6. **D** If you can see that we want a word for "observed rather than experienced," that's great; if not, just say that we want a word that is neither positive nor negative. Then use the process of elimination. Cross out any positive or negative choices, and choose the best of the "neither" words. "Vicarious" means "experienced through another."

Skill 4 (page 21)

SAT Crashers Rule #4:
Process of Elimination

1. **B** Choose a word that you'd like to see. People who are always on time are by definition <u>on time</u>.
Then use the process of elimination.
   - (A) ~~tardy~~—Nope, "tardy" means "late."
   - (B) punctual—Yup, "punctual" means "on time."
   - (C) ~~steadfast~~—Nope, "steadfast" means "steady."
   - (D) ~~dull~~—Nope.
   - (E) ~~leaders~~—Nope.

2. **D** Choose a word that you'd like to see. To properly represent its <u>divergent (varied)</u> forms, Manpriya included, in her paper on the history of Renaissance art, over 20 sections, each describing a divergent style.
The correct answer will fit with the meaning of the whole sentence.
   - (A) ~~simplest~~—Nope.
   - (B) ~~oldest~~—Nope.
   - (C) ~~singular~~—No way.
   - (D) diverse—Yes.
   - (E) ~~solitary~~—No.

3. **A** Choose a word you'd like to see, and cross out "sagacious" if you don't know it.
Friends often seek out Ben's <u>advice</u>: he is known for his ability to listen carefully and offer unbiased sagacious advice.
   - (A) counsel—Maybe, sounds advicy, as in a Guidance Counselor.
   - (B) concern—Kinda, but not really, leave it for now.
   - (C) ~~trouble~~—No.
   - (D) empathy—Maybe, a good listener is empathetic, but friends don't only seek his listening, they seek his advice, it doesn't quite fit.
   - (E) ululation—What? Who knows this word!? "Ululation" means "a howl."

The best answer is choice A. "Counsel" means "advice."

4. **B** Choose a word you'd like to see, and cross out "admonition" if you don't know it.
Zibby refused to believe her mom's admonition that the sweet and innocent-seeming demeanor of the salesman was a <u>fake</u> for gaining her trust and taking advantage of her.
   - (A) plea—Not really, but leave it for now.
   - (B) ruse—Yes, nice word, it means "trick."
   - (C) ~~denial~~—No.
   - (D) ~~mood~~—No.
   - (E) ~~challenge~~—No.

The best answer is choice B.

5. **D** Choose a word for the blank. Behavioral theory is <u>direct</u> in nature as it focuses on the observation and direct study of actions.
   - (A) ~~didactic~~—Nope, "didactic" means "preachy."
   - (B) ~~theoretical~~—Nope, "theoretical" is the opposite of "direct."
   - (C) ~~obtuse~~—Nope, "obtuse" means "dull-witted."
   - (D) empirical—Yes, "empirical" means "directly observed."
   - (E) ~~phlegmatic~~—Nope, "phlegmatic" means "slow to excite," interesting since it sounds like "phlegm," which is thick and slow-moving.

6. **E** Al Gore's movie *An Inconvenient Truth* helped bring environmentalism into the spotlight, raising public awareness and inspiring environmental <u>awareness</u>.
   - (A) ~~retraction~~—Nope, "retraction" means "taking back."
   - (B) blame—Not really, leave it for now.
   - (C) recrimination—Not really, "recrimination" means "blame," interesting since it sounds like the word "crime".
   - (D) stockpiling—Maybe, but not really.
   - (E) husbandry—yes, "husbandry" means "skillful management of resources."

The best answer is choice E. Remember, if you can eliminate even one choice, take an educated guess.

Skill 5 (page 23)

Two Blanks

1. **C** "Subsequent" means "later." So Reisner's work **set** the tone for later **leaders**.

2. **B** If you don't know "lucid," cross it out. He impressed them with "jokes" and "style," so they praised him for his "humor" and "clarity." Notice that the two words are in parallel structure—they are in the same order both times. The SAT always follows parallel structure.

3. **E** Use the process of elimination. The second blank must be something like "exhausting," and the first blank is the opposite, something like "not exhausting."

4. **A** For the second blank we want something like "superior." When you absolutely can't think of a word to fill the other blank, just try the choices.

5. **D** Use the process of elimination. The first blank must be a word for a person who challenges authority. Cross out any that are definitely wrong. The second blank must mean "authority and tradition." Cross out any that are definitely wrong. Then choose the best from the remaining choices.

Skill 6 (page 25)

Vocab I: Compliment or Insult

a. peevish—irritable
b. petulant—irritable
c. sophisticated—stylish
d. soporific—sleep-inducing
e. saccharine—sugary
f. bombastic—showy, pretentious, conceited
g. magnificent—wonderful
h. abased—belittled
i. astute—shrewd, perceptive

j. flippant—off-hand, jokey
k. enthralling—interesting, gripping
l. vapid—insipid, bland
m. diminutive—very small
n. salutary—helpful
o. magnanimous—generous
p. insipid—dull
q. sagacious—wise
r. baneful—destructive
s. dazzling—stunning
t. resolute—determined
u. pernicious—harmful
v. disingenuous—insincere, devious, dishonest
w. truculent—aggressive, obstreperous, hostile
x. diverting—diverting, fun
y. corrupt—crooked
z. charismatic—charming, appealing

1. **B** To avoid being not-amusing (dull) (a negative word), the teacher often includes jokes and amusing anecdotes in her lectures.
   - (A) amusing—Nope, "amusing" is the opposite of "dull."
   - (B) insipid—Yes, "insipid" means "dull."
   - (C) complex—No, "complex" is not related to dull.
   - (D) eccentric—Nope, "eccentric" means "odd."
   - (E) servile—Nope, "servile" sounds like servant and means "overly submissive."

2. **E** The miners of the gold rush dug so deeply into the mountain that any more excavation could have had very bad consequences, causing a cave-in or complete collapse.
   - (A) alienating—Nope, "alienating" is unrelated to "very bad."
   - (B) rigid—Nope, "rigid" means "stiff."
   - (C) moderate—Nope, "moderate" means "mild."
   - (D) worthy—Nope, "worthy" means "valuable."
   - (E) devastating—Totally, "devastating" means "very bad."

3. **A** You can get this one even if you do not know the word "discord." If you don't know it, just cross it out.

Despite the committee's efforts to <u>heal</u> the discord between the two factions, no progress was made and the two groups remain sworn enemies.

(A) assuage—Maybe, "assuage" means "soothe."

(B) ~~intensify~~—No, "intensify" means "increase."

(C) ~~exploit~~—No, "exploit" means "utilize."

(D) ~~excite~~—Nope, "excite" means "stimulate."

(E) ~~scour~~—No, "scour" means "make clean."

Choice A is the best answer.

4. **E** Just as a rhino's tough hide gives it both protection from predators and insulation from heat and cold, the exterior walls of old castles provided <u>protection</u> from attackers and <u>insulation</u> from the wind.

Do one column at a time. For the first blank, we want "protection." Remember, cross off only the choices that you are sure are wrong!

(A) ~~dispersion~~—Nope, "dispersion" means "spreading."

(B) ~~admission~~—Nope, "admission" means "admittance."

(C) safety—Yes, "safety" could mean "protection."

(D) fortification—Yes, "fortification" means "protection," like a military fort.

(E) asylum—Maybe, "asylum" means "refuge" or "protection."

Now we try only choices C, D, and E for the second blank. We want "insulation."

(C) ~~safety . . conduction~~—Nope, "conduction" means "transfer" and is the opposite of "insulation."

(D) ~~fortification . . transmission~~—Nope, "transmission" means "spread" and is the opposite of "insulation."

(E) asylum . . sanctuary—Yes, "sanctuary" means "protection."

Skill 7 (page 27)

Vocab II: Superbad Vocabulary

1. *Lord of the Rings: The Fellowship of the Ring* (New Line Cinema, 2001). "Malice" means "hatred."

2. *Three Amigos!* (HBO Films, 1986). "Plethora" means "a lot." The SAT also loves the words "surplus" and "surfeit," which also mean "a lot."

3. *Star Wars: Episode VI—Return of the Jedi* (20th Century Fox, Lucasfilm Ltd., 1983). "Imminent" means "about to happen, looming."

4. *Batman Begins* (Warner Bros., 2005). "Ramifications" means "results" or "effects."

5. *Superbad* (Columbia, 2007). "Supple" means "flexible," great SAT synonym: "lithe."

6. *Pirates of the Caribbean: The Curse of the Black Pearl* (Walt Disney, 2003). "Negotiate" means "discuss" or "parley." "Cessation" means "end" or "termination." "Hostilities" means "fighting" or "aggression." "Naught" means "not anything." "Humble" means "modest." "Disinclined" means "reluctant." "Acquiesce" means "give in" or "assent, comply, concede, or yield."

7. *The Shawshank Redemption* (Columbia, Warner Bros., 1994). "Meticulous" means "careful." The SAT also loves the related words: "scrupulous," "pedantic," "assiduous," "plodding," "diligent," and "punctilious."

8. *Wedding Crashers* (New Line Cinema, 2005). "Erroneous" means "incorrect."

9. *The Matrix Reloaded* (Warner Bros., 2003). "Altered" means "changed." "Irrevocably" means "irreversibly" or "permanently." "Ergo" means "therefore." "Concordantly" means "consistent" or "in agreement." "Pertinent" means "relevant" or "important." "Irrelevant" means "not relevant" or "not important."

10. *The Matrix Reloaded* (Warner Bros., 2003). "Affinity" means "attraction."

11. *The Simpsons Movie* (20th Century Fox, 2007). "Epiphany" means "a sudden breakthrough of understanding."

12. *Monty Python and the Holy Grail* (20th Century Fox, 1975). "Temperate" means "mild" or "moderate." The SAT loves to say that something tempered or temporizes something, meaning makes more mild.

13. *Pirates of the Caribbean: Curse of the Black Pearl* (Walt Disney, 2003). "Superfluous" means "not required." "Nigh" means "near."

14. *The Shawshank Redemption* (Columbia, Warner Bros., 1994). "Tenure" means "term." "Immutable" means "absolute" or "unchallengeable." The SAT also loves the word "incontrovertible," which means "unchallengeable."

15. *Star Wars: Episode IV—A New Hope* (20th Century Fox, Lucasfilm Ltd., 1977). "Protocol" means "etiquette" or "rules governing polite behavior."

16. *The Matrix Reloaded* (Warner Bros., 2003). "Inherent" means "inborn" or "naturally occurring." Great SAT synonyms: "intrinsic" and "innate." "Eventuality" means "possibility." "Anomaly" means "glitch" or "irregularity." "Assiduously" means "diligently" or "tirelessly." "Inexorably" means "inevitably" or "unavoidably."

17. *Monty Python and the Holy Grail* (20th Century Fox, 1975). "Exploiting" means "taking advantage of." "Imperialist" means "royal" or "imposing." "Dogma" means "system of belief," "canon," "tenets," or "creed." "Perpetuates" means "continues." "Inherent" means "natural," "in-built," or "intrinsic." "Repressed" means "subdued" or "put down."

18. *V for Vendetta* (Warner Bros., 2006). "Paradox" means "an inconsistency" or "a contradiction."

19. *Ferris Bueller's Day Off* (Paramount Pictures, 1986). "Socialism" is a political theory in which the people collectively own all property. "Fascist" means "an authoritative system of government." "Anarchist" means "revolutionary." "Condone" means "allow" or "pardon." "-Ism" means "a practice or philosophy."

20. *The Matrix Reloaded* (Warner Bros., 2003). "Terminated" means "ended." "Eradicated" is similar and means "erased," "exterminated" or "wiped out."

21. *V for Vendetta* (Warner Bros., 2006). "Auspicious" means "fortunate." Great SAT synonym: "propitious." "Sobriquet" means "nickname."

22. *Harry Potter and the Order of the Phoenix* (Warner Bros., 2007). "Implore" means "beg." Great synonyms: "beseech" and "entreat." "Incontrovertible" means "unquestionable." Great SAT synonyms: "irrefutable," "indubitable," "unassailable," "indisputable."

23. *Iron Man* (Paramount Pictures, 2008). "Incinerate" means "burn." "Nostalgic" means "wistful" or "remembering fondly."

24. *Harold & Kumar Escape from Guantanamo Bay* (Warner Bros., 2008). "Thwart" means "prevent."

Skill 8 (page 31)
Vocab III: Deodorant and Spanish Class

1. "Diverting" has Spanish word "divertir" which means "to entertain." That's perfect because in English "diverting" means "fun."

2. "Facile" sounds a lot like the Spanish for "easy." Great, 'cause in English it means "very easy."

3. "Luminance" sounds a lot like the French word "lumière" for light. Good, because in English it's a fancy word meaning "the condition of emitting or reflecting light."

4. "Clairvoyant" sounds like the French words "clair" meaning "clear" and "voyant" meaning "seeing." Does "clairvoyant" mean "clear-seeing"? Yep, pretty much, or at least enough to get a sentence completion question right. It means "someone who sees things beyond normal vision."

5. In French, "comportment" means "behavior," which is exactly what it means in English!

6. In French, "fille" means "daughter," which is a pretty good lead, since in English "filial" means "pertaining to a son or daughter."

7. "Arid" was actually another word on my SAT. I didn't know it, but I remembered a TV commercial jingle for the antiperspirant deodorant Arid Extra Dry. I thought, "If Arid is the name of a deodorant, there's no way it means 'smelly' or 'foul' or 'wet' or anything bad. It must mean 'smells good' or 'dry' or 'attractive,'" and that was enough to vibe the word and get the question correct. "Arid" means "very dry."

8. The Impervious Charm is the one that makes things repel substances like water, and "impervious" means "impermeable" or "resistant."

9. "Stupefy" is the Stunning Spell that stuns an opponent, and "stupefy" means "bewilder" or "stun."

10. In *Harry Potter*, "flagrate" causes a wand to leave fiery marks, and the word "conflagration" means "a fire."

11. "Sagacious" means "wise," like a sage.

12. If your intelligence is 16 or better, you might know that Sylvan is the language of the Elves. And "sylvan" is a great SAT word that means "pertaining to the forest."

13. I was psyched when this word showed up on the SAT; you know they game! When you need to get out fast, Expeditious Retreat is a cheap potion and an easy first-level wizard spell. "Expeditious" means "speedy."

Skill 9 (page 33)
Vocab IV: Splitting Words

1. sympathy—understanding
   empathy—compassion
   apathy—lack of concern
   pathos—grief
   pathetic—pitiable
   antipathy—bad feelings, hatred

   "path" means "feeling"
   "a" means "not" or "without"
   "anti" means "against"

2. philanthropy—love for humankind or generosity
   philosophy—love of knowledge or a system of thought
   technophile—a person who likes technology
   technophobe—a person who fears technology
   technology—the study of devices
   phobia—a fear

   "phil" means "love"
   "anthro" means "humans"
   "soph" means "knowledge"
   "tech" means "devices or tools"
   "phobe" means "fear"
   "ology" means "study of"

3. terrestrial—relating to the earth
   terrain—ground
   extraterrestrial—from beyond the earth
   extraordinary—beyond the ordinary

   "terr" means "earth"
   "extra" means "beyond"

4. homogeneous—having the same nature
   heterogeneous—having a different nature
   homologous—sharing the same structure or origin
   heterologous—differing in structure or origin
   homosexual—attracted to one's own gender
   heterosexual—attracted to opposite gender

   "homo" means "same"
   "hetero" means "different"
   "gen" means "kind" or "birth"

5. circumscribe—to draw around
   circumnavigate—to sail or fly around
   circumvent—to get around something

recirculate—to circulate again

postscript—something written at the end
  of something

transcribe—to translate

circumambulate—to walk around something

amble—walk

manuscript—something written by hand

manufacture—to make something (technically
  by hand)

transatlantic—across the Atlantic Ocean

"circum" means "around"

"post" means "after"

"scribe" means "write"

"man" means "hand"

"re" means "again"

"trans" means "across"

"amb" means "walk"

"dis" means "not," like distrust = not trust

"co" means "together," like cooperate = operate
  together

"sub" means "under," like submarine =
  underwater

Skill 10 (page 35)

Couples Counseling

1. **A** There is not enough information to choose
words for the blanks, so decide if the two
blanks are synonyms, opposites, or cause and
effect. In this sentence, the two blanks need to
be similar. So analyze each set of two words
and eliminate any that are not similar. Then
pick the pair that fits the sentence best.

   (A) distress . . harmful—Maybe, both are
   "negative" words and certainly related.

   (B) ~~injury . . acceptable~~—Nope, they are not
   synonyms.

   (C) ~~worry . . sympathetic~~—Nope, they are not
   directly related.

   (D) ~~calm . . agitating~~—No way, they are more
   like opposites.

   (E) ~~healing . . malicious~~—No sir, they are not
   similar.

2. **D** There is not enough information to choose
words for the blanks, so decide if the two
blanks are synonyms, opposites, or cause and
effect. In this sentence, the two blanks need to
be similar. So analyze each set of two words
and eliminate any that are not similar. Then
pick the pair that fits the sentence best.

   (A) ~~altered . . steadfast~~—Nope, they are
   opposites.

   (B) ~~maintained . . mercurial~~—Nope, they are
   opposites. If you don't know "mercurial,"
   which means "changing," leave it.

   (C) ~~condoned . . nostalgic~~—Nope, they are just
   unrelated.

   (D) changed . . irresolute—Sure, they are
   similar, both referring to "change".

   (E) ~~vacillated . . reliable~~—No, they are
   opposites.

3. **C** There is not enough information to choose
words for the blanks, so decide if the two
blanks are synonyms, opposites, or cause and
effect. In this sentence, the two blanks need to
be opposites. So analyze each set of two words
and eliminate any that are not opposites. Then
pick the pair that fits the sentence best.

   (A) ~~sympathetic . . selfless~~—Nope, they are
   sorta loosely related or unrelated, but not
   opposites.

   (B) ~~egotistical . . terrestrial~~—No way, totally
   unrelated.

   (C) whimsical . . staid—Yes, they are opposites,
   meaning "quirky" and "serious."

   (D) ~~nefarious . . malicious~~—No, they are
   similar, meaning "evil" and "mean."

   (E) ~~intense . . severe~~—No, they are synonyms,
   both meaning "intense."

4. **C** There is not enough information to choose
words for the blanks, so decide if the two
blanks are synonyms, opposites, or cause and
effect. In this sentence, the two blanks need to
be opposites. So analyze each set of two words
and eliminate any that are not opposites. Then
pick the pair that fits the sentence best.

(A) renovation .. rebuilt —No, not opposites, actually they are cause and effect.

(B) renaissance .. innovative —No, they are synonyms.

(C) collapse .. solvent—Yes, opposites, "solvent" means "having enough money."

(D) catastrophe .. bankrupt —No, they are not opposites.

(E) devastation .. complex —No, they are not related.

5. (A) There is not enough information to choose words for the blanks, so decide if the two blanks are synonyms, opposites, or cause and effect. In this sentence, the two blanks need to be similar. So analyze each set of two words and eliminate any that are not similar. Then pick the pair that fits the sentence best.

(A) revered .. adored—Perfect.

(B) amusing .. exploited —No, they are unrelated.

(C) moderate .. beloved —No, they are unrelated.

(D) sagacious .. dismissed —No, they are not synonyms.

(E) dazzling .. despised —No, they are not synonyms.

6. (D) There is not enough information to choose words for the blanks, so decide if the two blanks are synonyms, opposites, or cause and effect. In this sentence, the two blanks need to be cause and effect. So analyze each set of two words and eliminate any that are not cause and effect. Then pick the pair that fits the sentence best.

(A) flippant .. stockpile —Nope, they are unrelated.

(B) phlegmatic .. thrive —Nope, they are not cause and effect.

(C) industrious .. fail —No way, they are not cause and effect.

(D) assiduous .. succeed—Totally, if you are diligent, you will succeed.

(E) divisive .. be trusted —No, they are not cause and effect.

Skill 11 (page 37)

How to Be a Sentence Completion Master

1. (E) Matty is a multitalented athlete; he excels at baseball and football and even gives his brother Wilson a good game of squash.

(A) speedy —Nope, he may be fast, but that's not what the blank and the sentence are about.

(B) translucent —Nope, cool word though, "trans" means "across" and "luc" means "light," so "translucent" means "light can pass through."

(C) hearty —No, again he may be hearty, but that's not the point of the blank or the sentence.

(D) droll —Nope, "droll" means "funny in an odd way."

(E) versatile—Yes, perfect.

2. (D) Clair has a gift for collecting sea glass; from a distance she can spot beautiful pieces that other collectors miss.
Let's try the second blank first.

(A) hatred .. find —Nope, "find" is the opposite.

(B) penchant .. ward —Weird, but no, "ward" means "protect."

(C) distaste .. miss—Yes!

(D) knack .. overlook—Yes!

(E) gift .. stockpile —No, "stockpile" means "collect," so it is sorta opposite.

Now, we need to try the first blank only in choices C and D.

(C) distaste .. miss —No, "distaste" means "dislike" and does not mean "gift."

(D) knack .. overlook—Yes, "knack" means "gift" or "ability."

Since this questions is "easy," the correct answers are "easyish" words. If it were a "hard," the correct answers would probably have been the "harder" words such as "penchant" and "ward".

3. **B** Although opponents decry the tax code as inequitable, the government has kept it in place for decades and argues that the code is not inequitable (fair).

Remember if you don't know "decry," just cross it off.

(A) ~~antagonistic~~—Nope, "antagonistic" means "hostile."

(B) evenhanded—Yes sir, "evenhanded" means "fair."

(C) ~~sophisticated~~—No, someone might say that the code is sophisticated (complex), but that is not the point of the blank or of the sentence.

(D) ~~petulant~~—Nope, "petulant" means "irritable."

(E) shrewd—Maybe, "shrewd" means "smart," but that's not the point of the blank or the sentence. Choice B is better since it is the opposite of "inequitable" and therefore better fits the sentence as a whole.

4. **A** Certain types of squirrels are treeish, spending most of their time jumping from tree to tree.

(A) arboreal—Totally, "arboreal" means "pertaining to trees."

(B) ~~terrestrial~~—Close, but "terrestrial" means "pertaining to earth."

(C) ~~dramatic~~—Nope, "dramatic" means "theatrical."

(D) ~~homogeneous~~—Nope, "homogeneous" means "similar."

(E) ~~circumscribed~~—No way, "circumscribed" means "drawn around" or "confined."

5. **C** To reflect the variety of people's interests, the community art association commissioned the mural to depict 31 professions and 62 hobbies.

(A) uniqueness—Maybe, probably not, but leave it.

(B) ~~astuteness~~—No, "astuteness" means "smartness."

(C) heterogeneity—Yes! "Heterogeneity" means "variety."

(D) ~~transference~~—No, "transference" means "transfer."

(E) ~~passion~~—Not quite, "passion" means "fervor, ardor, or intensity," but that's not the point of the blank.

6. **D** There is not enough information to choose words for the blanks, so decide if the two blanks are synonyms, opposites, or cause and effect. In this sentence, the two blanks need to be similar. So analyze each set of two words and eliminate any that are not similar. Then pick the pair that fits the sentence best.

The candidate's supporters cite her _____ as her greatest asset, and claim that her opponent falls short with far less _____.

(A) ~~concordance . . pertinence~~—Nope, they are unrelated.

(B) ~~temperance . . peevishness~~—No, they are unrelated or sorta opposite.

(C) ~~experience . . naïveté~~—No, they are opposites.

(D) resolve . . tenacity—Perfect, they both mean "determination."

(E) ~~acumen . . ignorance~~—No, they are opposites.

Reading Comprehension

Skill 12 (page 41)

Italics

1. Both passages are about environmentalism and both are fairly recent. The second passage was written very recently and is about environmentalism of the 1970s. We pretty much know the main idea of both passages. Now we would just need to pay attention for the tone/attitude of each.

2. From a fairly recent novel; women are discussing relationships. Might not seem like much, but it's a big leg up toward knowing the main idea of the passage. With this info alone, I bet we could eliminate three choices on a main idea question.

3. A recent article that describes new medical technologies; written by a doctor. The passage might use science terms, but don't be intimidated. The SAT always defines any science terms in the passage.

4. Both passages are about *Roe v. Wade*, an important and controversial case that legalized abortion. Since both are about the topic, they probably take slightly different angles on it.

5. Written in 1820, so it's older and of a different time period, possibly more "proper." Mr. Peabody wants to date Mrs. Primberly's daughter, Josephine. This is quite a bit of info, probably enough to answer any main idea question.

6. Discusses changes brought about by CDs and MP3 players. Probably a fairly unbiased account since it's written by an historian.

Skill 13 (page 43)

The SAT Reading Meditation

1. Main idea: The author is describing his heritage.
   Point/tone: Author is giving insight into his heritage.

2. Notice that this passage does not begin with italics. Some short passages do not begin with italics. This is a great passage to practice with because many students are initially intimidated by its fancy language. But the beginning and end of the passage directly state the main idea. If you get intimidated when looking for the main idea, just keep reading and pay close attention to the beginning and end of the passage.
   Main idea: Law is not just a set of rules, but also the pursuit of justice and fairness.
   Point/tone: Author is **describing** information in a **neutral** way.

Skill 14 (page 45)

"Plethora" Most Nearly Means

1. **B** The author is using "flair" here as "appeal" or "style," but goes on to write about fire and light, so choices A and C seem like good choices. But choice B is correct, "panache" means "spirited style" or "flair." Another great SAT synonym for flair is "élan."

   If you are unsure, treat it like a sentence completion question. Choices A and C do not work because they do not fit the meaning of the sentence.

2. **C** Line 10 mentions that she fed their (referring to the public) adoration with her poems, so the "public" refers to her readers.

3. **E** The three words before "nature" are "charismatic," "headstrong," and "passionate," and these describe her personality. Use the process of elimination. The best fit is "spirit."

4. **A** The previous lines stated that the public adored her. She fed this adoration by writing her poems. "Adoration" means "love," and the closest answer is "respect."

5. **A** The next sentence tells that her father left the family, they were very poor, and her mom worked hard, so "bleak" must mean tough or harsh. "Austere" means "harsh." Great SAT synonyms for austere: "stark," "spartan," "ascetic." "Bland" is incorrect because we have no evidence in the passage that her childhood was dull.

6. **C** All of these choices have been mentioned in the passage, but in the context of the sentence, "the others" are her siblings of whom she is the oldest.

7. **B** The paragraph describes an austere (harsh) childhood. Use the process of elimination; remember, sometimes you find the best answer not because it jumps right out, but by eliminating the others.

(A) ~~twisted~~—No, its not warped, it's just tough.

(B) wan—If you don't know the word, leave it. "Wan" means "pale," so maybe.

(C) ~~evil~~—No, it was a tough childhood, but not evil.

(D) ~~virtuous~~—No, "virtuous" means "honorable," vibe it out with the word "virtue."

(E) ~~enigmatic~~—No, "enigmatic" means "mysterious."

Eliminate the ones that you can, and then pick the best of what's left. Even if you are not right every time, you will be right more than before and will gain points!

Skill 15 (page 47)
Direct Info

1. (E) The "three stages of life" refer to "three ways of being in the world." This is shown in the first sentence where the author states that the stages are not "youth, adulthood, and old age," but "three modes of relating to the world."

2. (B) When you answer a line number question, always read a little before and after. The answer to this question comes directly after the reference. The passage refers to "the first and third poems" as "internal" and the second poem as "external."

3. (B) Great question! The phrase "passing elegiacally over the lore of the land" seems tough. Many kids throw their hands up and move on, but it is clearly explained in the next line: "The dying poet is taking a nostalgic survey of his works." He is looking back and "taking stock." Easy if you stay with it and don't get thrown by tough language.

4. (A) The sentence referred to might seem confusing or unclear, but just read before and after and it's clear! The previous sentence states that he must "find the memories in which he was most alive" in order to "give his passing meaning," that is, leave his mark.

5. (C) This is directly from the poem. In line 17, the author refers to the poem as a ceremony.

Skill 16 (page 49)
What Are You Trying to Suggest?

1. (D) The "changes" help a person to successfully engage or run from a physical threat (material danger), not to deal with intellectual challenges, so choice D is best. This is nearly a "direct info" question.

2. (D) The problems listed are intellectual. We can infer that they, therefore, are not solved by the stress response, which only helps a person to fight or to flee. Choice B is incorrect because while the passage states that they can persist, it does not give that as a reason for the stress response not solving them.

3. (A) The last paragraph states that the goal of stress management is to experience the stress response **only** when relevant and helpful, implying that it is to be avoided when it cannot help.

4. (D) This "attitude" question is a specific type of "suggest" question that we will address more in Skill 18. We also predicted this question as we initially read the passage, reading for main idea and tone. The answer to an "attitude" question is usually moderate. Rarely, on the SAT, does the author hate or love. Let's take a look at the choices:

(A) ~~qualified disapproval~~—No, the author shows no disapproval.

(B) ~~resentment~~—No again, no resentment.

(C) ambivalence—Maybe, but the author does not seem wishy-washy.

(D) unbiased appreciation—Yes, the author seems to be presenting an unbiased account. Also, since we know from the italics that the passage is from a master's thesis, we can assume that it is scholarly and unbiased, not opinionated and biased.

(E) ~~moral indignation~~—Nope, way too strong, it is not full of "righteous anger."

Skill 17 (page 51)
ASS of U and ME

1. **B** In line 1, the author is making a generalization that assumes that "others" do not understand the complexity of polarity. To find the best answer, think of the answer you'd like to see and use the process of elimination. While choice B is not worded the way I would have put it, it is the best choice, and even the only choice that works. That's why elimination works so well. Choice C is tempting, but the passage states that people misunderstand, not that they are not interested.

2. **E** The author states that "in one of the greatest minds . . . one might expect a preference for knowledge over creativity, or hard work over play." He is stating that people might assume Einstein was all about hard work instead of intuition, creativity, and play. Using the process of elimination, you can get this question, even if you didn't know the fancy vocab word "assiduous." To review the word, see *The Architect*'s quote, Skill 7!

3. **E** Use the process of elimination. The paragraph is based on the assumption that science and religion are considered opposites. The whole point of the paragraph is to counter this assumption and demonstrate that they go hand in hand. So answer choice A might be the main idea of the paragraph, but choice E is the assumption.

4. **D** Reread the lines before and after any "line number" question. The answer is found after line 1, in line 4, "opposites." You can also treat it like a sentence completion and think of a word that you'd like to see and then use the process of elimination with the choices. Remember that the answer to this type of question will rarely be the most easy and obvious of the answer choices that you might choose without having read the passage.

Skill 18 (page 53)
Some Attitude

1. **A** The italics help a lot; the speaker is mourning the loss of Donny. If you are unsure, use the process of elimination and choose the best choice. Even if you don't know the word "eulogy," you can get it with elimination.

2. **A** The first line reads, "Donny was a good bowler, and a good man." The speaker relates the two and considers bowling very important. Then "He was one of us." He respects bowling. Remember to answer based on the passage, not your opinion of bowling!

3. **E** The speaker is upset (not "ambivalent," which means "unsure") that these men died before "their time," but he is not bitter. He is resigned which means "accepting." If you are not sure, use the process of elimination. And remember to answer based on this passage, not your opinion, and not based on Walter's body language as he delivers this in *The Big Lebowski,* if you've seen it! (Great movie that I highly recommend!)

4. **C** "Solemn" means "somber" or "serious." The speaker is serious and mournful. This was given away in the italics, since we knew from the start that he was scattering ashes. Don't be confused by "what we think your dying wishes might well have been." He is a doof, but he's primarily not confused. He's solemn.

5. **B** "Bright" could means any of the answer choices, but in the passage it describes Donny and the young men that the speaker mourns who died at the battles mentioned. Choice B is the best; they were intelligent "flowering young men." You can treat this like a sentence completion and think of a word that you'd like to see and then use the process of elimination with the choices. Remember that the answer to this type of question will rarely be the most easy and obvious of the answer choices that you might choose without having read the passage.

6. **D** Treat this like a sentence completion. Think of a word that you'd like to see, and then use the process of elimination with the choices. Remember that the answer to this type of question will rarely be the most easy and obvious of the answer choices that you might choose without having read the passage. "Comfort" is the only choice that works; they are scattering his ashes there for him to "rest in peace."

7. **D** The speaker is eulogizing his friend Donny as he scatters his ashes. In doing so, he remembers others that he has lost and digresses for a moment to them. The line suggests that he misses them as he misses Donny. Remember that the key to a "suggest" question is not to overthink it. You could convince yourself of any of the answers, but only choice D has evidence and makes sense in the passage.

Skill 19 (page 55)

Two Passages

Note: Notice that the passages in this Drill section were not introduced by italics. Sometimes passages, especially the shortest ones, are not proceeded by italics.

1. **E** Usually there are a few questions that ask about only the first passage. That's why you read just the first and answer those questions before you even read the second passage. In this case, that eliminates choices C and D which are not even mentioned in Passage 1. The other choices are mentioned in the passage, but only pharmaceuticals is cited as an example of a biochemical medicine. This is a "direct info" type of question. Just find the proof. If you do, you can't go wrong!

2. **E** This is a classic "two-passage" question. After you read the first passage, jot down or circle a word or two that identify both the main idea and tone; and after you read the second passage, do the same. This helps keep their differences and similarities clear. The author of

Passage 1 mentions three systems and details the biochemical system. The author of Passage 2 describes the Indian system of Ayurveda as a natural and holistic medical system that considers a "whole substance." The biochemical model is described as isolating an active ingredient, so Ayurveda is not biochemical and the author of Passage 1 would consider it either bioenergetic or biospiritual.

3. **B** Use the process of elimination. The only choice that is encouraged in both passages is the consideration of the whole effect of medicines on the body. Passage 1 describes biochemical medicine and states that a drawback of isolated active ingredients can be unanticipated side effects. Passage 2 discusses Ayurveda, which considers the whole effect of a medicine on a person. Don't overthink and choose choice C. Perhaps Passage 1 very lightly alludes to medical reform, but Passage 2 never mentions it at all.

4. **A** As you read the second passage, you can pretty much predict all of these questions. You are watching for what is the same and what is different. We know they'll ask these questions. Use the process of elimination. I like this type of question. It is like a two-blank sentence completion; we can eliminate a choice if either is wrong. Here we can eliminate the choice if it is incorrect about either passage. Choice A is correct since the main idea of the first is the three-system model and the second passage is only about one system.

5. **D** This is a very literal question. Just use the process of elimination and check each choice to see if the author used it or not. Choice D is correct since only Passage 2 cites an authority.

Skill 20 (page 57)

Main Idea

1. **B** Most of the choices are mentioned in the passage, but the main idea, the primary purpose of the passage, is to demonstrate Olmsted's vision. Let's find evidence: it is

demonstrated by the words "foresaw," "anticipated," and "see into the future."

2. **C** Interesting, all are possible at first glance. But only choice C is correct. Here's the evidence:

   (A) ~~depict an era~~ —Nope, it does not depict an era, just a particular situation.

   (B) ~~justify an expenditure~~ —Nope, the author cites Gustave's justification, but that is not the author's point.

   (C) give an historical account—Yes, it is the account of Parisians' response to the building of the Eiffel Tower.

   (D) ~~defend a decision~~ —No, the author cites Gustave defending his decision, but that is not the author's point.

   (E) ~~criticize an architectural work~~ —Nope, the Parisians were criticizing, but the author is just telling the story.

3. **C** Find the evidence: It seems the author is recollecting, but "If we had this tree . . ." proves that it is actually a fantasy.

Skill 21 (page 59)

Gretchen Is "Such" a Good Friend

1. **A** The misspelled words simulate the narrator's accent. This is a cool "don't overthink it" question. Use the process of elimination. There is no evidence for choice B "indicate his disapproval of the accepted spellings" or choices C, D, or E.

2. **B** Use the process of elimination. We have evidence only for choice B. When the author writes, "there's a name no man would self-apply," he is reiterating his opinion of the unusualness of the name. Remember that quotes around a word on the SAT that are not used to simply cite a source usually indicate that the word is meant in an unusual way.

3. **E** Use the process of elimination. No other answer makes any sense with the passage.

The repetition of the lines is used to demonstrate the narrator losing focus.

4. **C** Treat this type of question very literally.

   (A) ~~a hypothesis and supporting details~~ —Nope, no hypothesis and no support for it.

   (B) ~~a common argument following by counterexamples to disprove it~~ —No, nothing being disproved.

   (C) description interspersed with tangential remarks—Yes, lots of description and lots of tangential (unrelated) remarks.

   (D) ~~several sides to a single issue~~ —No, not several sides.

   (E) ~~explication of an unusual belief~~ —No, unusual name, but no unusual beliefs.

5. **D** Treat this like a sentence completion question. Reread the lines around it and think of a word to fill the blank. Then use the process of elimination. In this case, "handle" refers to "name" in the previous line, so "title" is the best answer. Remember that the answer is not usually the word that you would pick without having read the passage, such as "handle" meaning "grip."

6. **C** This is a "direct info" question. The phrase explains the one before it, "See, they call Los Angeles the 'City of Angels.'" So he is saying that even though it's called "City of Angels," he didn't exactly meet "angels."

Skill 22 (page 63)

Parallel

1. **A** The lines say that the media makes people think they have to be fit and wealthy and to own things. Use the process of elimination. Choice A fits this situation best.

2. **C** The passage describes a situation that the writer finds unacceptable. He or she riles up readers and ends with an alternative. Likely, next the writer will give more info about the alternative. You can also use the process of elimination; certain other answer choices use

words from the passage, but they do not fit the nature of the passage.

3. **B** Use the process of elimination and remember that you are looking for the one that **least** undermines the assertion that 2.5 hours of TV per day is not making people happy and that it confuses people by skewing their expectations of life. What would detract least? Basically, an example that supports that idea, rather than refutes it. Anything opposite would disprove or detract and not be the answer. So the best answer is choice B. Choice B supports the idea that people believe the messages they see on TV. All other answers do not support the assertion and therefore detract more from it.

4. **E** The tone of a passage is expressed in the words and punctuation. This passage is pointing out problems with media and television in society. The author is angry, but controls the anger in expressing his or her point. You can also use the process of elimination. None of the other choices work. The author is not laughing, confused, relieved, or begrudging.

Skill 23 (page 69)

How to Be a Reading Ninja

1. Main idea question (Skill 20). D. As the first and last lines of the paragraphs ("pursuing a dream," "pursue what they love") clearly demonstrate, choice D ("follow their hearts") is the best answer—the other choices do show up in the passage, but only choice D is the **main point** of the passage. We can use several Skills here. Since this is a "main idea" question; it's not a bad idea to skip it and come back after you've done the line number questions; by then you'll know the passage even better. When you answer it, you can also reread the italics and the first and last lines of each paragraph for clues to the main idea. Then come up with a main idea you'd like to see and use the process of elimination. Also avoid the careless error of choosing an answer based on

only a few words; make sure the whole answer makes sense.

2. "Such" a good friend question (Skill 21). A. This type of question asks why the author chose quote marks, parentheses, or a certain word or sentence to accomplish something. Use the process of elimination.
   - (A) to indicate a side comment to the reader— Sure, that makes sense.
   - (B) ~~to indicate that it is unimportant~~—Nope, if unimportant, it would be left out.
   - (C) ~~to indicate a humorous tone~~—No, it's not funny!
   - (D) ~~to indicate a shift in meaning~~—No, no change in meaning.
   - (E) ~~to indicate a change in tone~~—No, there's no big change in tone.

3. "Direct info" question (Skill 15). E. Go back and read a few sentences before and after. The answer comes several times and most clearly a few lines before. Trident dislikes Eric solely because he is human—a different species. You can also use the process of elimination. No other answer makes sense.

4. "Parallel" question (Skill 22). C. The question asks which of the answers best illustrates the assertion "Disney movies encourage children to question preconceived ideas that we may have against a certain group." Use the process of elimination. Only choice C describes a plot line that clearly involves someone questioning preconceived ideas, she is **overcoming** her fear of snakes. You could try to overthink this one and argue that one of the other answers might set the stage for overcoming previously held beliefs, but only choice C directly states it. This type of question often throws kids when there are choices that they do not recognize from the passage. Remember, a "parallel" question usually provides choices that are not from the passage, and you need to decide which one would illustrate the point from the passage.

5. "Suggests' question (Skill 16). B. Reread a few sentences before and after the line. Look for evidence. She screams, "So much for true love" victoriously. "Victoriously" indicates that she considers beating "true love" a victory, so we have evidence for choice B, she is mocking "true love." Don't overthink it and go for choice A, C, D, or E. We have no evidence for these. Choice B is closest to the evidence in the passage—it is the most literal interpretation. Remember that a "suggests" question will often have an answer worded slightly differently than the wording in the passage, but the meaning should be the same. In fact, beware of choices with wording directly from the passage—they are not always wrong, but double-check them.

6. "Most nearly means" question (Skill 14). C. Choice C is best since Eric did not "love," "succeed," "squash," or "vanish" Ursula; he "bested" or "defeated" her. Treat this like a sentence completion question. Think of a word that you'd like to see replace "vanquishing" in the sentence. Then use the process of elimination on the choices. Eliminate only if you are sure a choice does not fit. Then choose the best answer. If you can't think of a word that you'd like to see, you can try each choice for "vanquishing" and see which one works.

7. "Attitude" question (Skill 18). D. Attitude is expressed in words and punctuation. The author repeatedly expresses respect for the valuable lessons that Disney gives children in *The Little Mermaid*. You can also use the process of elimination.
   - (A) ~~frustration~~—Nope, no frustration.
   - (B) ~~stoicism~~—Nope, the author is not "stoical" or "unemotional."
   - (C) ~~ambivalence~~—No, the author is not uncertain.
   - (D) respect—Yes, the author respects Disney's lessons.
   - (E) wonder—Maybe.

   Don't be fooled by choice E. "Wonder" is associated with Disney's movies, but that is definitely not the author's point or attitude. Remember to answer questions based on the passage, not your own opinions.

Writing Multiple-Choice

Skill 24 (page 73)
Subject/Verb Agreement

1. **D** Trust your ear on easy and medium questions. "Practices" should be "practiced."

2. **E** No error. All the underlined words work. Trust your ear; if an easy question sounds correct, then it is.

3. **A** Cool question. Organizations like "the school association" or "the high school," or "the fire department" are singular. Even though they are comprised of many people, the organization itself is one group and is singular. So since the subject of the underlined verb "are" is a singular subject, "are" should be "is." Trust your ear; and if in doubt, identify the subject of the underlined verb.

4. **C** "Lives" should be "living" to fit the rest of the phrase "and the other *living* in caves."

5. **A** "Is" should be "was" to match "voted."

6. **A** "Vote" is the subject of the underlined verb "indicate," and since "vote" is singular, "indicate" should be "indicates."

7. **C** The subject of "taunt" is "who," so "taunt" should be "taunts."

8. **A** I included this question because "had swam" appeared on an SAT and so many kids got it wrong. "Had swam" should be "swam" because the "after" implies that the swimming is done. This is a tough rule for a "medium," but the question is considered medium, because your ear can tell that "had swam" is wrong. Moral of the story: Listen to your ear!

Skill 25 (page 75)

Subject/Verb Agreement Tricks

1. Stephen ~~for two more weeks~~ **is** single.

2. Margarita ~~with her sisters~~ currently **runs** a marketing firm.

3. Tricky! Running from the bulls **is** Jimmy ~~with his friends~~. ("Jimmy" is the subject.)

4. The way ~~of samurais~~ **is** a strict path.

5. Tricky! Around the corner **are** a dog and a cat. ("Dog and cat" is a compound subject.)

6. The PTA ~~through generous donations~~ **is** building a new school building.

7. The boys ~~with their dog Alfred~~ **walk** to school.

1. **A** The subject of the verb "has" is "craftsmanship," so "has" is correct. When a verb is underlined, identify the subject.

2. **E** This is a reminder that sometimes you will get a "No error." In fact, on the SAT about 20% of writing questions have no error. Usually, but not always, if one of these subject/verb tricks shows up in a "medium," then it is not the error; and if it shows up in a "hard," then it is the error. So here "has" is the verb of the subject "music" and is correct.

3. **C** When you see a verb underlined, ask yourself, What is the subject? Cross off prepositional phrases and notice what is doing the action of the verb. In this case, what is doing the "is-ing," not the office, but the trophies. The subject "trophies" came after the verb "is," which is a trick we know to look for. The verb should be "are." I love these, they are tricky, but we know they are coming!

4. **B** "Number" is the subject and "of milligrams" and "of various minerals" are prepositional phrases, so "demonstrate" should be "demonstrates." The cool thing about writing multiple-choice and our strategies is that once

you find something that is definitely wrong, you know that it's the answer and no matter how strange other answer choices seem, there can be only one error.

Skill 26 (page 77)

Pronoun Clarity and Agreement

1. **B** "A doctor" is wrong because it should match "Bill and Edward" and be the plural "doctors."

2. **C** How true! Except for the error. "It is" refers to "Brian's SAT prep books" and should be "they are."

3. **A** The plural pronoun "those" clearly refers to and matches her "accomplishments." Don't forget that sometimes sentences are already written correctly and choice A is the answer. Skill preview: This sentence demonstrates proper parallel structure, which we will discuss in Skill 29.

4. **B** First, organizations like "the school association" or "the high school," or "the fire department" are singular. Even though they are comprised of many people, the organization itself is one group and is singular. So "they" should be "it," but that's not all. Even as "it," the pronoun is unclear. Borat might think that "they" refers to the organization or the newsletter or even the paper, so it needs to be clarified. Of course, for this type of question, you don't need to correct the error, just to identify it. Again, trust your ear on "easies" and "mediums." I bet "they" sounded a little funny to you.

5. **D** Even though we are smart and can figure out that the pronoun "it" refers to "first songs," technically it is unclear. Usually, a pronoun refers to the nearest important noun, which here would be "singers." Ask yourself, What would Borat think if he translated this sentence? He would think that "it" refers to "singers," so we must replace it with something more clear. This question is a "hard" because

no one likes the wording of choice D and most kids skip this question or get it wrong. But by using the process of elimination, choice D is the only choice without a direct grammar violation. On a hard, look for violations and eliminate them. That actually works better than looking for correct answers. Choice D is the best of the choices; it could be smoother, but it's the best of what we are offered.

6. **(A)** Another great "hard" that becomes easy with our skills. When you see a pronoun underlined, identify the noun it refers to. "It" refers to "petroleum products" and should be the plural "they." Nice!

Skill 27 (page 79)

Correct Transition Word

1. **(C)** Classic transition word question. As it's written, the sentence doesn't make sense. The fact that Iron Man would lose to Superman is surprising considering he is hearty, so the two parts of the sentence are in opposition and we need an opposition word, like "though." Notice what is wrong with the sentence and then use the process of elimination. All of the other choices sound slangy or indirect (Skill 34).

2. **(C)** For an easy or medium question, trust your ear. You can also analyze each underlined word to see which skill it applies to. "Since" the doubles team has won so much, they will represent the school, not "but." They are picked because they are so good, so it should be a direct cause-and-effect word, not an opposition word.

3. **(E)** Identify the problem. Then shop around— use the process of elimination. Only choices D and E correct the opposition word to a direct cause-and-effect word. I included this question because the SAT does this a lot; the only difference between D and E is the semicolon (;) versus comma (,) Use the ";" or ", and" when separating two sentence parts that could stand alone; and use a "," when separating two sentence parts that could not stand alone.

In this case, choice E is correct since the last part of the sentence could not stand alone.

4. **(E)** "So" is a direct cause-and-effect word and works perfectly here; it's because of the first part of the sentence that people say the second part. Trust your ear.

5. **(C)** "Nevertheless" is a mouthful, that's for sure, and here it should be a direct cause-and-effect word, not an opposition word. Because he invented the style, he'll be remembered. A few other words might seem a little wonky here, but if you can prove one word wrong with one of our Skills, then it is the answer.

Skill 28 (page 81)

Brave, Honest, and Relaxed

1. **(E)** The list must match: "uprooting saplings, leveling huts, and . . . ." So "disturbing animals' homes" is the best match.

2. **(C)** The list must match. Kathy feels "healthy, grounded, and . . . ." So "is ready" should just be "ready."

3. **(C)** The list must match: "had been interesting, informative, and . . . ." The first two members of the list are adjectives, so the third must be too. You don't need to think of it this way; your ear can hear which one works. If it doesn't, doing these drills will train it to hear. So the answer is "had been interesting, informative, and eye-opening." The verb "had been" is shared by all three. Either each new member has a verb, or none do; it's like bringing cupcakes to school in third grade—either you have enough for everyone or don't you bring 'em!

4. **(C)** Good lesson here. At workshops, kids often ask me about this. Don't flip out if you get three or more C's or A's or whatever in a row. Sometimes it happens! Anyway, the list must match. The second part has no verb, so the third should not either. The guard checks "Billy's key, then his ID card, and then his

tattoo." The verb "checks" is shared by all three.

5. **D** The list must match: "guitarist, vocalist, drummer, and . . . ." Since each of these members of the list does not have a verb, the last should not either.

6. **E** The list must match: "guitarist, vocalist, drummer, and . . . ." Since each of these members of the list does not have a verb, the last should not either. Instead, it should just be the noun "soundman" to match.

Skill 29 (page 83)

Comparison

1. **A** Don't forget that 20% of the time there is no error, which is represented in this type of question by choice A. The words that are being compared must match, and they do: "Anyone who has **extra time** or **great interest** . . . ."

2. **B** Words that are being compared must match: ". . . paint **for fun**, rather than **for profiting** . . . ." So "profiting" should just be "profit."

3. **D** Words that are being compared must match: ". . . will be known not only **as an honored graduate** . . ., but also **he writes** . . . ." So "he writes" should be "as an author" to match "as a graduate."

4. **B** Words that are being compared must match: "**Taking the bus** is one way . . . **to bike** is another." So "to bike" should be "biking."

5. **E** Many kids just skip this one because it's a little convoluted and weird to understand. But it's just a comparison question. Words that are being compared must match: ". . . more on **consumer spending** than **do they rely on government subsidies** . . . ." So "than do they rely on government subsidies" should be "than on government subsidies." The verb "rely" is used by both "consumer spending" and "government subsidies," and there is no need to repeat it before "government subsidies."

6. **D** Words that are being compared must match: "**The novel** . . . . than **Karl Marx**." We can't compare a novel to a person. We can compare a novel to a novel or a person to a person. So "Karl Marx" should be "(a novel) by Karl Marx." This seems a small obscure specific thing, but for some reason nearly every SAT has one of these on it. So expect it, and you'll get it right!

Skill 30 (page 85)

Correct Preposition

1. **D** "For the true enjoyment" sounds strange; it should be "of the true enjoyment."

2. **B** "In the catching of" sounds weird; it should be "to catch."

3. **E** "A major threat **of** both travelers and Americans" sounds weird; it should be "a major threat **to** both travelers and Americans."

4. **A** This is another reminder, that sometimes there is no error, represented in this type of question as choice A. "Pride in his education" sounds fine and makes sense. Choice B, "pride in his schooling;" sounds fine also, but the semicolon does not work. The second part of the sentence could not stand alone, so a semicolon does not work; we need the comma.

5. **D** "Love for the music" sounds fine and makes sense. "Dedication **on** technique" should be "dedication **to** technique." Literally they are dedicated **to**, not **on**, technique.

6. **E** This is another reminder that sometimes there is no error, represented in this type of question as choice E. (Approximately 20% of writing questions have no error.) This is a "hard" because choices B, C, and D sound somewhat weird. Something that sounds weird in an "easy" or "medium" question is probably wrong, but for a "hard" you need to use Skills to prove it wrong. I have noticed that on a "hard" question, if several choices sound weird, the answer is usually E, "no error." And, if on a "hard" nothing sounds weird, definitely something is wrong, or else it would not be a "hard"!

Skill 31 (page 87)

Adverbs End in 'ly"

1. **B** Easy, if you know to watch for it! It should be "understanding this article **correctly**."

2. **A** The trucks "passed **constantly**," not "**constant**."

3. **E** His feet brought him places "**slowly**" not "**slow**." The other answer choices violate parallel structure and obscure the meaning of the sentence.

4. **E** No error. "**Quickly**" sounds correct and is correct.

5. **D** The tourist is trying "**desperately**," not "**desperate**," to communicate. Other choices either sound terrible or obscure the meaning of the sentence.

6. **B** "Promotes healing more **quick**" should be "promotes healing more **quickly**."

Skill 32 (page 89)

I vs. Me

1. **B** To test if "him" is correct, just drop "the other runners." Then it reads "**him** quickly ran" which sounds terrible. It should be "The other runners and **he** quickly ran." This is a great skill!

2. **A** To test if "I" is correct, just drop "Josh and" so it reads "Quincy passed the ball to **I**," which sounds weird. Instead, "Quincy passed the ball to **me**" sounds great.

3. **E** To test if "us" is correct, just drop "kids." "For us, concerns about . . ." sounds good, whereas "For we, concerns about . . ." sounds strange.

4. **B** When there is no one to drop or swap, try plugging in "I vs. me" instead of the "who versus whom" and trust your ear. "This is being mailed to I" sounds weird, and "This is being mailed to me" sounds fine. Since "I" corresponds to "who" and "me" corresponds to "whom," it should read "This is being mailed to

whom." Choice D does not work because a semicolon would imply that the words after it could stand alone as a sentence, which they can't.

5. **C** Since the "no one" and "me" are being compared, we can swap them. "Me is happier" sounds terrible, and "I am happier" sounds good. Skill 34 preview: Choices A and B are wrong since "more happier" is redundant and should just be "happier." You are either happier or not, you can't be more happier.

Skill 33 (page 91)

A Few More Rules

1. **C** "Either" is followed by "or," not by "and."

2. **B** The part of the sentence beginning with "who have been" describes the books, and should be "which have" instead of "who have."

3. **E** Since we are comparing **two** candidates, we use "more" instead of "most."

4. **E** There is no error. "Whose" works since Sam is a person, not a thing. Skill review: "fully" works since they did not leave off the "ly."

5. **C** "Not only" should be followed by "but also." And since "honored" comes before the "not only," it applies to both parts of the sentence and does not need to be repeated.

6. **D** "Neither" is followed by "nor."

Skill 34 (page 93)

Direct, to the Point, Not Redundant

1. **E** Choice E is the most clear, concise, and nonredundant.

2. **A** The original sentence is grammatically correct and the most clear and concise. The process of elimination works well on these questions; cross off choices that are wordy, unclear, redundant, or weird.

3. **B** Choice B is grammatically correct and most clear, concise, and nonredundant. There is no need to say "a total of" three years; "three years" implies "a total of."

4. **D** No need to say "these days" after also saying "currently." It's redundant.

5. **C** Use the process of elimination. Choice C makes most sense and is most clear and direct. Skill 29 review: "Protested" matches "asked."

6. **C** Choice C is the most clear, concise, direct, and nonredundant. Many kids get this one wrong, I think because it seems to change the meaning of the underlined phrase. But it does not; it just takes out the wordiness and redundancy.

Skill 35 (page 95)

Misplaced Phrases

1. **B** The sentence makes it sound like "running" was "pressed for time," which makes no sense. "Pressed for time" should be as close to "Devon" as possible, since it is describing her. Don't be fooled by choice C, which puts it next to "Devon's running" not "Devon." This sentence also uses Skill 34 (Direct, to the Point, Not Redundant) and is a great preview of Skill 36 (Jedi Master Yoda).

2. **E** The sentence makes it seem that "Seth's search" was carrying the tiramisu, when of course it was "Seth." So "Seth" needs to be next to the descriptive phrase "Carrying the tiramisu." Seem like a picky thing? I guess it sorta is, but at least we know to watch for it and we can catch it every time. If there were a million of these picky things, that'd be tough, but there are only a few.

3. **D** The sentence makes it unclear to anyone not quite so intelligent as you and I to whom the descriptive phrase "Having played third base for four years" applies. It applies, of course, to Abigail, so it should be as close to her as possible. Don't be confused by choices

B and C, which put the phrase next to "Abigail's upset" instead of "Abigail"!

4. **E** The sentence makes it seem that "the town" is "returning to Northampton" which makes no sense. Choice E is the best correction. You can get this one by the process of elimination. Even though it's a "hard," once you notice that the original sentence violates Skill 35, most of the other choices are crazy and only choice E makes any sense.

Skill 36 (page 97)

Jedi Master Yoda

1. **E** "Passing . . . is what Juana did" is passive and wordy. Choice E, "Juana passed," is active and direct.

2. **C** The whole sentence is wordy, indirect, passive, and confusing. Choice C is more active and direct. To make this "hard" question easier, use the process of elimination. Most of the choices are crazy and confusing. Trust your ear. If you can't even understand what a sentence is saying, then it's not written well— eliminate it as a choice!

3. **B** "Learning . . . is the reason that" is passive and wordy. Choice B is more direct and clear. To make this "hard" question easier, use the process of elimination. Most of the choices are crazy and confusing. Trust your ear. If you can't even understand what a sentence is saying, then it's not written well—eliminate it as a choice!

4. **D** "Five is the number he counted to" is passive and wordy. (Bad grammar, Brother Maynard!) Choice D is direct and clear. To make this "hard" question easier, use the process of elimination.

Skill 37 (page 99)

Editing Paragraphs

1. **D** Choice D is the most clear, direct, and concise revision.

2. **A** "The book has many interesting characters" is a nice transition into the next two paragraphs which look at specific characters.

3. **C** "Next, there's Harry Potter" introduces the third paragraph which is primarily about Harry Potter.

4. **A** A concluding sentence for the essay should sum up the whole essay—its main idea. Several of the sentences are interesting, but choice A best sums up the main idea of the passage.

Skill 38 (page 102)

How to Think Like a Grammar Genius

1. **D** Skill 34, Direct, to the Point, Not Redundant. The sentence in the question is way too wordy. We can make it more direct. Use the process of elimination, looking for a more direct choice. Most choices sound terrible or are less direct than choice D.

2. **B** Skill 27, Transition Word. "However" does not quite fit the sentence. It's not "however" he asked repeatedly, it's "after" he asked repeatedly.

3. **E** Skill 28, Brave, Honest, and Relaxed. The words in the list must match: "addition, multiplication, and **subtraction**."

4. **D** Skill 35, Misplaced Phrases. This question is rated "hard" because it sounds pretty good as is. But if you were Borat reading this, you'd think that the critics are soon to be a famous artist. The descriptive clause "Soon to be a famous artist" must be clearly associated (usually next to) the thing that it modifies, "Colette." This question is rated "hard," but you know what to watch for and then it's easy!

5. **B** Skill 24, Subject/Verb Agreement. Your ear can definitely hear that choice B sounds bad. Trust your ear on the easy and medium questions. Trust your ear on the hard ones too, but use the Skills to prove your answer.

6. **C** Skill 33, A Few More Rules. "Either" must always be followed by "or," not "and." If there were a billion things like this to watch for, that'd be tough; but there are only 15 and we know them and predict them, so they're easy!

7. **E** Skill 29, Comparison. There is no error. Things being compared must match. "Pausch's book" should be compared to another book, not to people. So "other books" is correct. This seems like a strange thing to test, but the SAT loves it and it shows up on almost every SAT.

8. **B** Skill 30, Correct Preposition. When a preposition is underlined, ask yourself if it is the correct preposition. If you weren't looking, it'd be easy to miss this. But if you stop and question it, you can hear that "knowledge **for** the subject" is wrong and should be "knowledge **of** their subjects."

9. **E** There is no error. Use our Mantras to analyze each blank. If it's a verb, identify the subject, etc.

10. **C** Skill 25, Subject/Verb Agreement Tricks. When a verb is underlined, identify its subject and cross out any prepositional phrases between the two. The prepositional phrase "of enriching and prolonging peoples' lives" makes it seem that "were" is correct. But the subject of "were" is "Ayurveda," so the verb should be the singular "was." Of course, you don't need to correct it here, just to identify that choice C is wrong. Again, if you didn't know to look for this trick, it'd be tough to catch, but we expect it and it's easy!

11. **C** Skill 26, Pronoun Clarity and Agreement. This question is rated "hard" because choice C sounds correct to many students, but Miller High School is considered singular not plural. Sure, there are hundreds of people who comprise the school, but as an institution it is one institution and singular, so "their" should be "its." Other institutions that seem plural but are singular include the labor union, the corporation, the United States, the congregation, the family, anyone, everyone, either, no one.

Essay

Skill 39 (page 107)

Brainstorm

Answers will vary, but we want specifics, not generalizations. We want names, dates, places, numbers, statistics, etc. Coming up with specifics at this stage will definitely improve the essay. The more specific the details, the more powerful the argument, and the higher your score.

Here's an example with specific details: Dr. Martin Luther King, Jr., challenged the status quo, wanted an end to racial segregation and discrimination, 1960s, he used nonviolent methods such as civil disobedience, received Nobel Peace Prize in 1964, inspired millions.

Skill 40 (page 109)

Brainfreeze Help

Answers vary. Use specific details from your papers. Use the Internet to fact-check if you need to.

Here's an example with specific details: Salem witch trials, hearings before local magistrates, prosecute people accused of witchcraft in Essex, Suffolk, and Middlesex counties of colonial Massachusetts, February 1692 to May 1693, over 150 people were arrested and imprisoned, courts convicted 29 people of the capital felony of witchcraft.

Skill 41 (page 111)

Outline

Answers vary. Circle or jot down the best details. These will be the focus of the body paragraphs.

Skill 42 (page 113)

Write Your Intro

Answers vary. Use opener, link, and thesis. And within that framework let your own particular brilliance, interests, and style shine.

Here's a great example that one of my students, Kyle, used for the second question to get a perfect 12:

Our American culture pivots on our materialistic values. The "modern" society that we see daily is saturated with unecessay and wastful objects. The Amerian idealism that we hold so dear, as our identity, is slowly decaying admist a storm of consumption and over production. Perhaps Aristotle was right when he said that the best life is the most simple life. Modern society is much too concerned with amassing material wealth, that materialism has blinded our vision and blocked our paths to becoming a truly productive American society.

Notice that it's not perfect. But graders don't expect a perfect essay in 25 minutes, and they loved his vocabulary, use of Aristotle, and structure. You need not be perfect to score high!

Skill 43 (page 115)

Transition Sentences

Answers vary. Does your transition sentence accomplish one or more of the following? Introduce the main idea of the paragraph, link to the previous paragraph, and remind us of your thesis.

Here's Kyle's transition sentence for his first body paragraph: "The average american life is fraught with consumption." Great link from the intro to the body, and he sets up the topic of the paragraph—consumption.

Skill 44 (page 117)

Body Paragraph I

Answers vary. Is your body paragraph written around a single main idea? Is it jam packed with specific details?

Here is Kyle's body paragraph:

The average american life is fraught with consumption. Part of our identity that makes us so different is our extravigant and excessive lifestyles. However over the years of our frivolous wasting, we have aquired a feeling of hubris, and eminency when we should be ashamed and remorseful. America's modern mass-producing society will inevitably collapse if our materialistic values are not tamed. Our great country will inevitably fail if our American instinct emerges victorious over our inteligence and understanding. Our current battle against the monster of materialism resembles the 1920's conflicts. A time of flappers, bootleggers, flagpole sitters, and speakeasies was a short lived period of progressivisim and materialism. The collide between rural, traditional values and America's new defiant generation resulted in violence and ultimately The Great Depression. Our history shows what can potentialy happen when we remain naïve and let our encumbering burden of production weigh us down. We will be crippled!!

Again, it's not perfect. It can't be in 25 minutes and graders know that. But he blew them away with vocab, details, and depth. The paragraph centers around consumption and uses the 1920s, with great specifics, as an example of the risks of this kind of materialism.

Skill 45 (page 119)

Body Paragraph II

Answers vary. Does your next body paragraph (or two) finish demonstrating your thesis? Is it focused on a specific example that demonstrates your thesis? Does it begin with a transition sentence that smoothly links it to the previous body paragraph? Are the body paragraphs connected in some way (set scene and demonstrate thesis, same period or literary work, chronological)?

Here's Kyle's other body paragraph:

> However, perhaps there are some positive aspects of the quest to material affluence. The fourth republic of nigeria, established by president Obasanjo in 1999 has created a economy based on mass production and consumption rather than its one scarce commodity, oil. Nigeria's culturaly fragmented interior, that is infamous for extreme tribal violence, has been calmed. A history of military coups, ethnic riots, and civil warfare as been forgotten with the newly established, progressive attitude of materialism. In 1989, after the death of conservative dictator Sani Abach, Nigeria presented a united front between all ethnic groups (Iboo, Yoruba, Hausa-fulani), on the basis of increased economic production. Perhaps materialism isn't always a curse, but a cure.

If you can bring that many specific details into an essay, you're guaranteed a 12! But how do you do it? Here's the catch. Kyle is the guy I mentioned earlier. He always uses the Fourth Republic of Nigeria. He has the details prepared! Yes, Kyle is brilliant and has a great mind for details, but you can do it too; these drills teach you to do what he did!

Skill 46 (page 121)

Conclusion

Answers vary. Does your conclusion restate thesis, link, and end with a bang? Remember, I'm not telling you to be boring or predictable. Use this as a framework and build your own masterpiece around it.

Here's Kyle's conclusion:

> However, there are obvious differences between Nigeria's fragil economic situation and the U.S.A.'s. But it is undeniable that without some measures to increase stringency on modern society, we will inevitable cripple. Perhaps Aristotle was on to something.

Kyle was running out of time, so he threw down a few sentences, and made a few spelling and grammar errors. But the sentences accomplish the task. (Most importantly, there must be a conclusion of some kind to get full credit.) His conclusion wraps up the essay and brings us full circle back to his thesis (that modern society is too materialistic). He ends by alluding back to his Aristotle quote in the intro. Graders loved that.

Skill 47 (page 123)

Other Stuff That Matters

1. "Immutable" means "unchanging" or "indisputable."
   Example: Death and taxes are immutable truths.

   "Eradicated" means "erased completely."
   Example: Vaccines have nearly eradicated polio.

   "Auspicious" means "fortunate" or "lucky."
   Example: The French interest in a Northern victory proved auspicious for Lincoln.

"Superfluous" means "unneeded" or inessential."
Example: Critics state that the government overspends on superfluous items.

"Affinity" means "liking" or "inclination."
Example: Gatsby was known for his large parties, yet he had an affinity for privacy.

"Concordant" means "in agreement."
Example: The ideas expressed in Lincoln's speech were concordant with his earlier declarations.

"Pertinent" means "relevant."
Example: Gandhi's way of life is pertinent if we want to understand his politics.

"Thwart" means "to prevent."
Example: The storm thwarted the thief's plan.

"Ramification" means "effect."
Example : There were many ramifications of the Civil War.

2. Answers vary. In your paragraph, did you get deep, write a fair bit, use some impressive vocab, vary your sentences, write readably, and avoid basic grammar and spelling errors?

Skill 48 (page 125)

Proofread

Answers vary. Proofread for omitted words, misspellings, and punctuation errors, and to make sure that you indented new paragraphs when you meant to and wrote details correctly.

Skill 49 (page 127)

How to Be a Writing Monster

Did you use the Skills? Check your essay, item by item, with this checklist. If you don't feel confident checking your own essay, ask a parent or teacher to use the list. Check off items that you mastered, and circle items that need improvement.

1. Brainstorm for specific details, not generalizations.

2. If something else brilliant occurs to you, of course use that; but if not, use whichever of your planned examples applies best.

3. Jot down or circle the best details from your brainstorm. These details form the outline for the body paragraphs of the essay.

4. Your intro paragraph should be 3 to 4 sentences: an opener, a link, and a thesis.

5. Use transition sentences to begin each paragraph, link it to the previous paragraph, and remind the reader of your thesis.

6. Each "body" paragraph begins with a link to the previous paragraph and is written around a single main idea.

7. The second or third body paragraph should finish demonstrating your thesis. It should be organized around a specific example of your thesis. Ideally, it smoothly links to your previous body paragraph(s).

8. Structure your conclusion by restating your thesis, linking, and ending with a bang.

9. Get deep, write at least 1.5 pages, use some impressive vocab, vary your sentences, write readably, and avoid basic grammar and spelling errors.

10. Leave a few minutes to proofread your essay for omitted words, misspellings, and punctuation errors, and to make sure that you indented new paragraphs when you meant to and wrote details accurately.

Generally, an organized essay will earn at least an 8. Details, depth of analysis, and cool vocab will earn you a 9 to 12. The more details, depth of analysis, and cool vocab, the higher your score will be.

Skill 50 (page 131)

Brian's Friday Night Spiel: Recommendations for the Days Preceding the Test

Practice this relaxation technique every day.

Posttest (page 138)

1. **C** Read the question and think of a word you'd like to see fill the blank.
Choose a word right from the sentence when possible; we can use "scale."
   - (A) decline —No.
   - (B) transfer —No.
   - (C) ascend—Yes.
   - (D) escalate—Maybe.
   - (E) allude —No.

   Choice C is the best choice. "Ascend" means "climb," whereas "escalate" means "to become greater or more intense."

2. **D** Watch for key words ("but," "however," "though," . . .) that tell you to look for an opposite.
"Although" tells us that the second part of the sentence might be opposite the first, so at home he is "not selfish:"
   - (A) egotistical —No.
   - (B) theatrical —No, don't be tricked by this answer. "Theatrical" relates to the sentence, but not the blank. That's why we think of a word we'd like to see before we look at the choices.
   - (C) thunderous —No.
   - (D) giving—Yes.
   - (E) ascetic —No, "ascetic" means "austere" or "frugal."

3. **A** If there is a word you don't know in the question, cross it out! You can get this question even if you don't know "panned," which means "criticized." To fill the blank, we want a word meaning "length."
   - (A) span—Maybe.
   - (B) beauty —No.
   - (C) creativity —No.
   - (D) expertise —No.
   - (E) hostility —No.

   Cool question. Even though I didn't love "span" as a choice, by using the process of elimination, it is the only one that works!

4. **B** This is a classic sentence completion setup; the blank is defined by the phrase that follows it. We want a word meaning "store owned jointly by its members." Who the heck knows a word for this? We can use the process of elimination. Cross out answer choices that are **definitely** wrong, and choose the best from what's left. The correct answer should make sense with all the parts of the sentence.
   - (A) frugality —No, "frugality" means "stinginess."
   - (B) cooperative—Yes, sounds like "owning something jointly."
   - (C) claim —No.
   - (D) definition —No.
   - (E) request —No.

   Lots of students skip this question, thinking that they can't come up with a word for the blank. But if you just use "store owned jointly by its members" and the process of elimination, it's easy!

5. **A** When you see two blanks, answer one blank at a time, using the process of elimination.
If you can't come up with a word to fill a blank, just decide if it should be +, −, or neither. Usually we begin with the second blank, but in this case, the first might be easier. For the first blank, we want a word meaning "hilarity."
   - (A) wit . . clarity—Maybe.
   - (B) presentation . . precision —No.
   - (C) situation . . astuteness —No.
   - (D) humor . . resolve—Yes.
   - (E) charisma . . transmission—Maybe.

   Then think of a word for the other blank and use the process of elimination. We want a word meaning "insight." We do not need to try choices that we eliminated already.
   - (A) wit . . clarity—Maybe.
   - (D) humor . . resolve—Probably not.
   - (E) charisma . . transmission —No.

If you have a few choices left, pick the best choice. You can test them in the sentence and see which makes the most sense. Choice A is better than choice D because "resolve" means "firmness," not "insight."

6. **D** Notice the key word "though" tells that the two parts of the sentence are opposites. To fill the blank, we want a word meaning "not peacefully," a negative word. If you don't know the meaning of a word in the choices, determine if it sounds positive, negative, or neither.

Ⓐ corruption—Maybe, it is a negative word.

Ⓑ ~~magnificence~~—No.

Ⓒ flippancy—Maybe.

Ⓓ belligerence—Yes, "belligerence" means "hostility."

Ⓔ ~~sophistication~~—No.

Then choose the best of what's left. Choice D is best; it is most clearly opposite "peaceful."

7. **E** Let's begin with the second blank. Think of a word that you'd like to see, maybe "free of hatred."

Ⓐ ~~anger .. livid~~—No, "livid" means "very angry."

Ⓑ ~~disagreement .. denial~~—No.

Ⓒ ~~disregard .. compelling~~—No.

Ⓓ evasion .. compassionate—Yes.

Ⓔ malice .. serene—Yes, "serene" means peaceful.

For the first blank we want a word that means "hate."

Ⓓ ~~evasion .. compassionate~~—No, "evasion" means "avoidance."

Ⓔ malice .. serene—Yes, remember from Skill 7 movie quotes (*Lord of the Rings*) that "malice" means "hatred."

8. **A** For the second blank, we want a word meaning "lack of humidity."

Ⓐ varied .. arid—Yes, "arid" means "dry."

Ⓑ ~~beguiling .. tonifying~~—No, "tonifying" means "strengthening."

Ⓒ ~~florid .. ecological~~—No.

Ⓓ ~~temperate .. sultry~~—No, "sultry" means "hot and damp."

Ⓔ stunning .. scorched—Yes, "scorched" means "very dry."

Remember that sentence completions always use parallel structure, so for the first blank we want a word meaning something to do with "having four seasons."

Ⓐ varied .. arid—Yes, "varied" could imply "having four seasons."

Ⓔ ~~stunning .. scorched~~—No.

You may think that New England is stunning, but "stunning" does not fit the blank, and "varied" does.

9. **B** For the second blank we want a word meaning "able to identify with others' suffering." If you don't know the meaning of a choice, see if it has parts that you can dissect.

Ⓐ ~~passionate .. lithe~~—Nope, "lithe" means "flexible."

Ⓑ compassionate .. empathetic—totally, "pathos" means "grief."

Ⓒ ~~heartful .. sophistic~~—No, "soph" means "knowledge."

Ⓓ ~~openhanded .. diminutive~~—No, "diminutive" means "small."

Ⓔ ~~philanthropic .. divisive~~—No, "divisive" means "troublesome."

10. **B** When there is not enough info to determine the words for two blanks, decide if the two words should be synonyms, opposites, or cause and effect. If you can't tell, put a positive word in the first blank and see if the second blank should then be positive also or negative. The words in this sentence should be synonyms.

Ⓐ ~~somber .. amiable~~—No, they are sorta opposites.

Ⓑ just .. evenhanded—Yes, synonyms, and probably rare qualities for a pirate.

Ⓒ ~~staid .. vindictive~~—No, they are not related.

Ⓓ ~~versatile .. thwarting~~—No, unrelated.

Ⓔ ~~virtuous .. solitary~~—No, unrelated.

11. **(E)** Usually it's easier to think of a word to fit the second blank. Here's an example where the first blank might be easier. For the first blank, we want a word meaning "bad."

(A) catastrophic . . heartily—Maybe.

(B) ~~soporific . . reasonably~~—No, "soporific" means "causing sleep."

(C) ~~propitious . . mindfully~~—No, "propitious" means "favorable."

(D) harmful . . plentifully—Yes.

(E) deleterious . . moderately—Yes, "deleterious" means "harmful."

For the second blank we want a word meaning "not overeating" or "moderately."

(A) ~~catastrophic . . heartily~~—No.

(D) ~~harmful . . plentifully~~—No.

(E) deleterious . . moderately—Yes.

This is a great question. Some of these words are tough, like "soporific" and "deleterious", so some kids skip this one. But by using the process of elimination, you can get it!

12. **(B)** Always begin a reading passage by reading the italics; in the passage the author is "exploring his heritage." This is confirmed throughout the passage. So, let's use the process of elimination, looking for "exploring his heritage."

(A) ~~persuade~~—No, she or he is not persuading us.

(B) inform—Yes.

(C) ~~apologize~~—No.

(D) ~~eulogize~~—No, he respects his grandparents, but it's not a eulogy.

(E) ~~synchronize~~—No.

This is a great example of why the process of elimination is so great. I might not have looked for the answer "inform," but it is certainly the best of the choices and the correct answer.

13. **(D)** The answer should be in the lines referred to or soon after them. In this case, the answer comes in the next two sentences; the author

considers Judaism, rather than being Austrian, his or her heritage. Choice D is the best answer.

14. **(B)** To answer a "most nearly means" question, reread a few lines before and a few lines after. "**While** my mother's . . ., my paternal . . . " indicates that "paternal" is the opposite of "mother's", so it is "father's." The word "while" indicates that the two parts of the sentence are in opposition.

15. **(C)** The answers are in the sentences following the line referred to. The sentences tell us that "he completed high school, college, and graduate degrees . . . worked as a principal . . . was a talented teacher." Choice C "prone to worry" is mentioned in the passage but not as a reason for being an "academic."

For a "direct info" question, always read before and after a line and find proof. Sometimes you need to read even more for an EXCEPT question; so if you are pressed for time, you can skip and come back to an EXCEPT question. Sometimes they're easy, and at other-times they're like four questions in one and you have to search the whole passage for info.

16. **(B)** The answer comes in the previous part of the sentence. Even though Judaism is a large part of the narrator's identity, she or he rarely thinks of it and does not observe holidays. Be careful of choice C which is mentioned, but has nothing to do with the question. The answer to a "suggest" question is often a rewording of something in the passage, and rarely a direct quote, like choice C. For "suggest" questions look for the answer that is hinted at in the passage. Though it might have different language, it should be pretty close to what is actually said.

17. **(E)** Since the italics state that the passage is from a scientific paper that explores water resources, we can assume that it will be scientific, in other words, that it will be unbiased, detached, and analytical.

18. **C** The author's tone in the first sentence is reflected by the language, "The city of Meadville is particularly well blessed in terms of water resources." The tone is analytical and almost enthusiastic. Use the process of elimination. It is not choice B or D, "contemptuous" (disapproving) or "mischievous." Choice A, "joyous," is too extreme. And even though the writer uses the phrase "well blessed," the tone is not solemn (somber). Choice C, "diagnostic," is best.

19. **A** We definitely want to use the process of elimination here. It might be initially tough to come up with a difference between the two paragraphs, but going through the choices shows that only choice A even remotely makes sense. The third paragraph tells about precipitation, which is only briefly mentioned in the second paragraph. The other choices do not work because there is no time order, no emotion, and no fiction. Remember, don't get intimidated. Stay with it and give it a try, and sometimes, like on this question, you get one right that you thought you had no chance on!

20. **E** If you need help with the main idea, reread the first and last lines of the paragraph. The final paragraph explores precipitation **replenishing** the water supply. This is demonstrated clearly in the first and last lines of the paragraph.

This question is another great reminder to read the whole answer and not just pick a choice based on the first few words. For example, the first few words of choice A look great, but the last few are clearly not related to the paragraph—there was no mention of a shortage.
Answering questions based on the first few words alone is the most common careless error I see on the reading section.

21. **E** Generally parentheses are used to include information that is interesting but inessential or to indicate a side comment to the reader. Choice E describes this best.

22. **B** For a "parallel" question, don't get thrown if the choices are not from the passage. Stay relaxed and focused, and look for the choice that proves or disproves the statement. In this case, the question asks which choice will enter the system promptly. Rain falling on the area will enter fastest. Even for a "parallel" question, we want proof in the passage, and choice B has the most proof. Choice C will enter, but later, as mentioned in the next line of the passage.

23. **C** The passage is primarily an unemotional account of the water system.

24. **D** When something trips up your tongue or you can't get its meaning, it's probably wrong. Listen to your ear, and when in doubt, identify the subject of an underlined verb. The verb "works" should be "worked" to match "stretched."

25. **D** When something trips up your tongue or you can't get its meaning, it's probably wrong. Choice D sounds weird because the verb "was" does not match its plural subject, "his songs." So "was" should be "have." Listen to your ear, and when in doubt, identify the subject of an underlined verb. Also watch for this SAT subject/verb agreement trick—the subject coming **after** the verb. Just ask yourself, What is doing the action of this verb?

26. **D** When a pronoun is underlined, we must be totally sure what noun it is referring to. If it is unclear in any way, it is incorrect. The underlined pronoun must also match (singular or plural) the noun that it refers to. The pronoun "she" is unclear. Does it refer to Tzipora or her mom? Also, this question is a great reminder that sometimes you'll get several answers of the same letter in a row. Don't panic, it happens!

27. **C** If a transition word (such as "although," "since," "but," "therefore," or "however") is underlined see if it works in the sentence. "But" would indicate that the two parts of the

sentence are in opposition and does not make sense, since the second part of the sentence results from the first, and does not oppose it.

28. **E** When words in a list are underlined, make sure they match. "Safety clips" matches the other words in the list.

29. **D** When words being compared are underlined, make sure they match. "Demonstrate keen insight" does not match "hilarious." It should be "keenly insightful."

30. **B** When a preposition is underlined, ask if it is the right preposition to use. "Contrasted **to**" should be "contrasted **with**." As long as you know to watch for this, your ear can pick it up.

31. **C** Make sure to read the sentence as it is. Don't correct it in your head; that is, watch for a missing "ly." "Proud" should be "proudly." As long as you know to watch for this, your ear can pick it up.

32. **D** To test if "she" is correct, use the same rule as you use for I versus Me. Try putting the "she" first or drop the other person and trust your ear. ". . . Was signed by she" sounds weird. ". . . Was signed by her" sounds good, so the sentence should say "her" instead of "she."

33. **B** "Who" is used for people, and "which" is used for things. So in this sentence "which" should be "who," since it is describing the poet Emily Dickinson.

34. **E** The correct answer on a "sentence correction" question will always be the most clear, direct, non redundant choice. "Being as she is the best on the team" is wordy. "The best on the team" expresses the same idea much more concisely. The SAT loves concise.

35. **B** Descriptive phrases on the SAT must be clearly associated with (usually placed right next to) the noun they describe. Tolle is the great teacher described in the sentence, so the phrase "A great teacher" must be as close as possible to "Tolle." That leaves choices B and E. Choice B is more clear and concise.

36. **B** On an SAT writing question, always choose active over passive voice. Choice B is the most clear, direct, active choice. Some students choose E because it corrects the sentence into active voice and looks more like the original, but choice B still keeps the meaning of the sentence and is more direct.

37. **C** Use the process of elimination. Look at each choice for errors, and eliminate it when you find one. For example, choice B is incorrect since the first part does not result from the second part of the sentence, which the "since" would indicate. Choice C is the most clear and concise.

38. **A** Analyze the underlined portion of the sentence, using the Skills. There are no errors. Choice B does not follow parallel structure, and choices C, D, and E are wordy.

39–49. Did you use the Skills? Check your essay, item by item, with this checklist.

If you don't feel confident checking your own essay, ask a friend, parent, or teacher to use the list. Check off items that you mastered, and circle items that need improvement.

1. Brainstorm for specific details, not generalizations.

2. If something else brilliant occurs to you, of course use that; but if not, use whichever of your planned examples applies best.

3. Jot down or circle the best details from your brainstorm. These details form the outline for the body paragraphs of the essay.

4. Your intro paragraph should be 3 to 4 sentences: an opener, a link, and a thesis.

5. Use transition sentences to begin each paragraph, link it to the previous paragraph, and remind the reader of your thesis.

6. Each "body" paragraph begins with a link to the previous paragraph and is written around a single main idea.

7. The second or third body paragraph should finish demonstrating your thesis. It should be organized around a specific example of your thesis. Ideally, it smoothly links to your previous body paragraph(s).

8. Structure your conclusion by restating your thesis, linking, and ending with a bang.

9. Get deep, write at least 1.5 pages, use some impressive vocab, vary your sentences, write readably, and avoid basic grammar and spelling errors.

10. Leave a few minutes to proofread your essay for omitted words, misspellings, and punctuation errors, and to make sure that you indented new paragraphs when you meant to and wrote details accurately.

Generally, an organized essay will earn at least an 8. Details, depth of analysis, and cool vocab will earn you a 9 to 12. The more details, depth of analysis, and cool vocab, the higher your score will be.

50. **Ⓑ**

Patronize

McGraw-Hill's Top 50 Skills for a Top Score: SAT Critical Reading and Writing by Brian Leaf

Tardy

McGraw-Hill's Top 50 Skills for a Top Score: SAT Critical Reading and Writing by Brian Leaf

Punctual

McGraw-Hill's Top 50 Skills for a Top Score: SAT Critical Reading and Writing by Brian Leaf

Steadfast

McGraw-Hill's Top 50 Skills for a Top Score: SAT Critical Reading and Writing by Brian Leaf

Counsel

McGraw-Hill's Top 50 Skills for a Top Score: SAT Critical Reading and Writing by Brian Leaf

Didactic

McGraw-Hill's Top 50 Skills for a Top Score: SAT Critical Reading and Writing by Brian Leaf

Obtuse

McGraw-Hill's Top 50 Skills for a Top Score: SAT Critical Reading and Writing by Brian Leaf

Empirical

McGraw-Hill's Top 50 Skills for a Top Score: SAT Critical Reading and Writing by Brian Leaf

Retraction

McGraw-Hill's Top 50 Skills for a Top Score: SAT Critical Reading and Writing by Brian Leaf

Phlegmatic

McGraw-Hill's Top 50 Skills for a Top Score: SAT Critical Reading and Writing by Brian Leaf

Recrimination

McGraw-Hill's Top 50 Skills for a Top Score: SAT Critical Reading and Writing by Brian Leaf

Husbandry

McGraw-Hill's Top 50 Skills for a Top Score: SAT Critical Reading and Writing by Brian Leaf

Subsequent

McGraw-Hill's Top 50 Skills for a Top Score: SAT Critical Reading and Writing by Brian Leaf

Peevish

McGraw-Hill's Top 50 Skills for a Top Score: SAT Critical Reading and Writing by Brian Leaf

Petulant

McGraw-Hill's Top 50 Skills for a Top Score: SAT Critical Reading and Writing by Brian Leaf

(adj.) on time	(v.) late	(v.) treat with kindness tinged with superiority
(adj.) preachy	(n.) advice	(adj.) steady
(n.) taking back	(adj.) directly observed	(adj.) dull-witted
(n.) skillful management of resources	(n.) blame	(adj.) slow to excite
(adj.) irritable	(adj.) irritable	(adv.) later

Sophisticated

McGraw-Hill's Top 50 Skills for a Top Score: SAT Critical Reading and Writing by Brian Leaf

Soporific

McGraw-Hill's Top 50 Skills for a Top Score: SAT Critical Reading and Writing by Brian Leaf

Saccharine

McGraw-Hill's Top 50 Skills for a Top Score: SAT Critical Reading and Writing by Brian Leaf

Bombastic

McGraw-Hill's Top 50 Skills for a Top Score: SAT Critical Reading and Writing by Brian Leaf

Magnificent

McGraw-Hill's Top 50 Skills for a Top Score: SAT Critical Reading and Writing by Brian Leaf

Abase

McGraw-Hill's Top 50 Skills for a Top Score: SAT Critical Reading and Writing by Brian Leaf

Astute

McGraw-Hill's Top 50 Skills for a Top Score: SAT Critical Reading and Writing by Brian Leaf

Flippant

McGraw-Hill's Top 50 Skills for a Top Score: SAT Critical Reading and Writing by Brian Leaf

Enthralling

McGraw-Hill's Top 50 Skills for a Top Score: SAT Critical Reading and Writing by Brian Leaf

Vapid

McGraw-Hill's Top 50 Skills for a Top Score: SAT Critical Reading and Writing by Brian Leaf

Diminutive

McGraw-Hill's Top 50 Skills for a Top Score: SAT Critical Reading and Writing by Brian Leaf

Salutary

McGraw-Hill's Top 50 Skills for a Top Score: SAT Critical Reading and Writing by Brian Leaf

Magnanimous

McGraw-Hill's Top 50 Skills for a Top Score: SAT Critical Reading and Writing by Brian Leaf

Insipid

McGraw-Hill's Top 50 Skills for a Top Score: SAT Critical Reading and Writing by Brian Leaf

Sagacious

McGraw-Hill's Top 50 Skills for a Top Score: SAT Critical Reading and Writing by Brian Leaf

(adj.) sugary	(adj.) sleep-inducing	(adj.) stylish
(v.) belittle	(adj.) wonderful	(adj.) pretentious, conceited
(adj.) gripping	(adj.) off-hand, jokey	(adj.) shrewd, perceptive
(adj.) helpful	(adj.) very small	(adj.) insipid, bland
(adj.) wise	(adj.) dull, bland	(adj.) generous

Baneful

McGraw-Hill's Top 50 Skills for a Top Score: SAT Critical Reading and Writing by Brian Leaf

Dazzling

McGraw-Hill's Top 50 Skills for a Top Score: SAT Critical Reading and Writing by Brian Leaf

Resolute

McGraw-Hill's Top 50 Skills for a Top Score: SAT Critical Reading and Writing by Brian Leaf

Pernicious

McGraw-Hill's Top 50 Skills for a Top Score: SAT Critical Reading and Writing by Brian Leaf

Disingenuous

McGraw-Hill's Top 50 Skills for a Top Score: SAT Critical Reading and Writing by Brian Leaf

Truculent

McGraw-Hill's Top 50 Skills for a Top Score: SAT Critical Reading and Writing by Brian Leaf

Diverting

McGraw-Hill's Top 50 Skills for a Top Score: SAT Critical Reading and Writing by Brian Leaf

Corrupt

McGraw-Hill's Top 50 Skills for a Top Score: SAT Critical Reading and Writing by Brian Leaf

Charismatic

McGraw-Hill's Top 50 Skills for a Top Score: SAT Critical Reading and Writing by Brian Leaf

Eccentric

McGraw-Hill's Top 50 Skills for a Top Score: SAT Critical Reading and Writing by Brian Leaf

Servile

McGraw-Hill's Top 50 Skills for a Top Score: SAT Critical Reading and Writing by Brian Leaf

Moderate

McGraw-Hill's Top 50 Skills for a Top Score: SAT Critical Reading and Writing by Brian Leaf

Worthy

McGraw-Hill's Top 50 Skills for a Top Score: SAT Critical Reading and Writing by Brian Leaf

Devastating

McGraw-Hill's Top 50 Skills for a Top Score: SAT Critical Reading and Writing by Brian Leaf

Assuage

McGraw-Hill's Top 50 Skills for a Top Score: SAT Critical Reading and Writing by Brian Leaf

(adj.) determined	(adj.) stunning	(adj.) destructive
(adj.) obstreperous, hostile	(adj.) insincere, devious, dishonest	(adj.) harmful
(adj.) charming, appealing	(adj.) crooked observed	(adj.) fun
(adj.) mild	(adj.) overly submissive	(adj.) odd
(v.) soothe	(adj.) very bad	(adv.) valuable

Escalate

McGraw-Hill's Top 50 Skills for a Top Score: SAT Critical Reading and Writing by Brian Leaf

Exploit

McGraw-Hill's Top 50 Skills for a Top Score: SAT Critical Reading and Writing by Brian Leaf

Squelch

McGraw-Hill's Top 50 Skills for a Top Score: SAT Critical Reading and Writing by Brian Leaf

Scour

McGraw-Hill's Top 50 Skills for a Top Score: SAT Critical Reading and Writing by Brian Leaf

Dispersion

McGraw-Hill's Top 50 Skills for a Top Score: SAT Critical Reading and Writing by Brian Leaf

Opportune

McGraw-Hill's Top 50 Skills for a Top Score: SAT Critical Reading and Writing by Brian Leaf

Conduction

McGraw-Hill's Top 50 Skills for a Top Score: SAT Critical Reading and Writing by Brian Leaf

Fortification

McGraw-Hill's Top 50 Skills for a Top Score: SAT Critical Reading and Writing by Brian Leaf

Asylum

McGraw-Hill's Top 50 Skills for a Top Score: SAT Critical Reading and Writing by Brian Leaf

Malice

McGraw-Hill's Top 50 Skills for a Top Score: SAT Critical Reading and Writing by Brian Leaf

Etiquette

McGraw-Hill's Top 50 Skills for a Top Score: SAT Critical Reading and Writing by Brian Leaf

Plethora

McGraw-Hill's Top 50 Skills for a Top Score: SAT Critical Reading and Writing by Brian Leaf

Imminent

McGraw-Hill's Top 50 Skills for a Top Score: SAT Critical Reading and Writing by Brian Leaf

Negotiate

McGraw-Hill's Top 50 Skills for a Top Score: SAT Critical Reading and Writing by Brian Leaf

Cessation

McGraw-Hill's Top 50 Skills for a Top Score: SAT Critical Reading and Writing by Brian Leaf

(v.) quiet	(v.) utilize	(v.) intensify
(adj.) appropriate	(n.) spreading	(v.) make clean
(n.) refuge	(n.) protection	(n.) transmission
(n.) a lot	(n.) the rules governing polite behavior	(n.) hatred
(n.) end	(v.) discuss	(adj.) looming

Hostility

McGraw-Hill's Top 50 Skills for a Top Score: SAT Critical Reading and Writing by Brian Leaf

Temperate

McGraw-Hill's Top 50 Skills for a Top Score: SAT Critical Reading and Writing by Brian Leaf

Disinclined

McGraw-Hill's Top 50 Skills for a Top Score: SAT Critical Reading and Writing by Brian Leaf

Flash Cards
Flash Cards
Flash Cards
Flash Cards
Flash Cards
Flash Cards

Acquiesce

McGraw-Hill's Top 50 Skills for a Top Score: SAT Critical Reading and Writing by Brian Leaf

Supple

McGraw-Hill's Top 50 Skills for a Top Score: SAT Critical Reading and Writing by Brian Leaf

Symmetrical

McGraw-Hill's Top 50 Skills for a Top Score: SAT Critical Reading and Writing by Brian Leaf

Flash Cards
Flash Cards
Flash Cards
Flash Cards
Flash Cards
Flash Cards

Meticulous

McGraw-Hill's Top 50 Skills for a Top Score: SAT Critical Reading and Writing by Brian Leaf

Alter

McGraw-Hill's Top 50 Skills for a Top Score: SAT Critical Reading and Writing by Brian Leaf

Irrevocably

McGraw-Hill's Top 50 Skills for a Top Score: SAT Critical Reading and Writing by Brian Leaf

Flash Cards
Flash Cards
Flash Cards
Flash Cards
Flash Cards
Flash Cards

Ergo

McGraw-Hill's Top 50 Skills for a Top Score: SAT Critical Reading and Writing by Brian Leaf

Concordantly

McGraw-Hill's Top 50 Skills for a Top Score: SAT Critical Reading and Writing by Brian Leaf

Irrelevant

McGraw-Hill's Top 50 Skills for a Top Score: SAT Critical Reading and Writing by Brian Leaf

Flash Cards
Flash Cards
Flash Cards
Flash Cards
Flash Cards
Flash Cards

Affinity

McGraw-Hill's Top 50 Skills for a Top Score: SAT Critical Reading and Writing by Brian Leaf

Erroneous

McGraw-Hill's Top 50 Skills for a Top Score: SAT Critical Reading and Writing by Brian Leaf

Epiphany

McGraw-Hill's Top 50 Skills for a Top Score: SAT Critical Reading and Writing by Brian Leaf

(adj.) reluctant	(adj.) mild or moderate	(n.) aggression
(adj.) balanced	(adj.) flexible	(v.) give in to, comply with
(adv.) irreversibly	(adj.) change	(adj.) careful
(adj.) not important	(adv.) in agreement	(adv.) therefore
(n.) a sudden breakthrough of understanding	(adj.) incorrect	(n.) attraction

Pertinent

McGraw-Hill's Top 50 Skills for a Top Score: SAT Critical Reading and Writing by Brian Leaf

Superfluous

McGraw-Hill's Top 50 Skills for a Top Score: SAT Critical Reading and Writing by Brian Leaf

Indignation

McGraw-Hill's Top 50 Skills for a Top Score: SAT Critical Reading and Writing by Brian Leaf

Flash Cards

Flash Cards

Flash Cards

Flash Cards

Flash Cards

Flash Cards

Tenure

McGraw-Hill's Top 50 Skills for a Top Score: SAT Critical Reading and Writing by Brian Leaf

Immutable

McGraw-Hill's Top 50 Skills for a Top Score: SAT Critical Reading and Writing by Brian Leaf

Incontrovertible

McGraw-Hill's Top 50 Skills for a Top Score: SAT Critical Reading and Writing by Brian Leaf

Flash Cards

Flash Cards

Flash Cards

Flash Cards

Flash Cards

Flash Cards

Protocol

McGraw-Hill's Top 50 Skills for a Top Score: SAT Critical Reading and Writing by Brian Leaf

Inherent

McGraw-Hill's Top 50 Skills for a Top Score: SAT Critical Reading and Writing by Brian Leaf

Eventuality

McGraw-Hill's Top 50 Skills for a Top Score: SAT Critical Reading and Writing by Brian Leaf

Flash Cards

Flash Cards

Flash Cards

Flash Cards

Flash Cards

Flash Cards

Anomaly

McGraw-Hill's Top 50 Skills for a Top Score: SAT Critical Reading and Writing by Brian Leaf

Assiduously

McGraw-Hill's Top 50 Skills for a Top Score: SAT Critical Reading and Writing by Brian Leaf

Inexorably

McGraw-Hill's Top 50 Skills for a Top Score: SAT Critical Reading and Writing by Brian Leaf

Flash Cards

Flash Cards

Flash Cards

Flash Cards

Flash Cards

Flash Cards

Imperious

McGraw-Hill's Top 50 Skills for a Top Score: SAT Critical Reading and Writing by Brian Leaf

Dogma

McGraw-Hill's Top 50 Skills for a Top Score: SAT Critical Reading and Writing by Brian Leaf

Perpetuate

McGraw-Hill's Top 50 Skills for a Top Score: SAT Critical Reading and Writing by Brian Leaf

(n.) anger	(adj.) not required	(adj.) relevant or important
(adj.) unchallengeable	(adj.) absolute or unchallengeable	(n.) term
(n.) possible event	(adj.) inborn or naturally occurring	(n.) etiquette or the rules governing polite behavior
(adv.) inevitably or unavoidably	(adv.) diligently or tirelessly	(n.) glitch or irregularity
(v.) make something continue	(n.) system of beliefs, canons, tenets, or creeds	(adj.) royal or imposing

Incinerate

McGraw-Hill's Top 50 Skills for a Top Score: SAT Critical Reading and Writing by Brian Leaf

Repressed

McGraw-Hill's Top 50 Skills for a Top Score: SAT Critical Reading and Writing by Brian Leaf

Paradox

McGraw-Hill's Top 50 Skills for a Top Score: SAT Critic Reading and Writing by Brian Leaf

Metaphor

McGraw-Hill's Top 50 Skills for a Top Score: SAT Critical Reading and Writing by Brian Leaf

Condone

McGraw-Hill's Top 50 Skills for a Top Score: SAT Critical Reading and Writing by Brian Leaf

Terminated

McGraw-Hill's Top 50 Skills for a Top Score: SAT Critic Reading and Writing by Brian Leaf

Eradicated

McGraw-Hill's Top 50 Skills for a Top Score: SAT Critical Reading and Writing by Brian Leaf

Auspicious

McGraw-Hill's Top 50 Skills for a Top Score: SAT Critical Reading and Writing by Brian Leaf

Sobriquet

McGraw-Hill's Top 50 Skills for a Top Score: SAT Critic Reading and Writing by Brian Leaf

Animosity

McGraw-Hill's Top 50 Skills for a Top Score: SAT Critical Reading and Writing by Brian Leaf

Implore

McGraw-Hill's Top 50 Skills for a Top Score: SAT Critical Reading and Writing by Brian Leaf

Irrefutable

McGraw-Hill's Top 50 Skills for a Top Score: SAT Criti Reading and Writing by Brian Leaf

Indubitable

McGraw-Hill's Top 50 Skills for a Top Score: SAT Critical Reading and Writing by Brian Leaf

Unassailable

McGraw-Hill's Top 50 Skills for a Top Score: SAT Critical Reading and Writing by Brian Leaf

Indisputable

McGraw-Hill's Top 50 Skills for a Top Score: SAT Criti Reading and Writing by Brian Leaf

n.) an inconsistency or contradiction	(adj.) subdued or put down	(v.) burn
(adj.) ended	(v.) allow or pardon	(n.) a symbolic representation of one thing for another
(n.) nickname	(adj.) fortunate	(adj.) exterminated or wiped out
(adj.) unquestionable	(v.) beg	(n.) strong hostility, hatred
(adj.) unquestionable	(adj.) unquestionable	(adj.) unquestionable

Flash Cards

Nostalgic

McGraw-Hill's Top 50 Skills for a Top Score: SAT Critical Reading and Writing by Brian Leaf

Flash Cards

Flash Cards

Ramifications

McGraw-Hill's Top 50 Skills for a Top Score: SAT Critical Reading and Writing by Brian Leaf

Flash Cards

Flash Cards

Thwart

McGraw-Hill's Top 50 Skills for a Top Score: SAT Critical Reading and Writing by Brian Leaf

Flash Card

Flash Cards

Egotistical

McGraw-Hill's Top 50 Skills for a Top Score: SAT Critical Reading and Writing by Brian Leaf

Flash Cards

Flash Cards

Facile

McGraw-Hill's Top 50 Skills for a Top Score: SAT Critical Reading and Writing by Brian Leaf

Flash Cards

Flash Cards

Arid

McGraw-Hill's Top 50 Skills for a Top Score: SAT Critical Reading and Writing by Brian Leaf

Flash Card

Flash Cards

Impervious

McGraw-Hill's Top 50 Skills for a Top Score: SAT Critical Reading and Writing by Brian Leaf

Flash Cards

Flash Cards

Stupefy

McGraw-Hill's Top 50 Skills for a Top Score: SAT Critical Reading and Writing by Brian Leaf

Flash Cards

Flash Cards

Antipathy

McGraw-Hill's Top 50 Skills for a Top Score: SAT Critical Reading and Writing by Brian Leaf

Flash Card

Flash Cards

Sylvan

McGraw-Hill's Top 50 Skills for a Top Score: SAT Critical Reading and Writing by Brian Leaf

Flash Cards

Flash Cards

Expeditious

McGraw-Hill's Top 50 Skills for a Top Score: SAT Critical Reading and Writing by Brian Leaf

Flash Cards

Flash Cards

Homogeneous

McGraw-Hill's Top 50 Skills for a Top Score: SAT Critical Reading and Writing by Brian Leaf

Flash Card

Flash Cards

Consummate

McGraw-Hill's Top 50 Skills for a Top Score: SAT Critical Reading and Writing by Brian Leaf

Flash Cards

Flash Cards

Polarized

McGraw-Hill's Top 50 Skills for a Top Score: SAT Critical Reading and Writing by Brian Leaf

Flash Cards

Flash Cards

Philanthropy

McGraw-Hill's Top 50 Skills for a Top Score: SAT Critical Reading and Writing by Brian Leaf

Flash Card

(v.) prevent	(n. pl.) results or effects	(adj.) wistful or remembering fondly
(v.) very dry	(adj.) very easy	(adj.) selfish
(n.) bad feelings or hatred	(v.) bewilder or stun	(adj.) impermeable or resistant
(adj.) having the same nature	(adj.) speedy	(adj.) pertaining to the forest
.) love of humankind or generosity	(adj.) divided	(adj.) perfect (v.) to begin

Circumscribed

McGraw-Hill's Top 50 Skills for a Top Score: SAT Critical Reading and Writing by Brian Leaf

Amble

McGraw-Hill's Top 50 Skills for a Top Score: SAT Critical Reading and Writing by Brian Leaf

Mercurial

McGraw-Hill's Top 50 Skills for a Top Score: SAT Critical Reading and Writing by Brian Leaf

Whimsical

McGraw-Hill's Top 50 Skills for a Top Score: SAT Critical Reading and Writing by Brian Leaf

Staid

McGraw-Hill's Top 50 Skills for a Top Score: SAT Critical Reading and Writing by Brian Leaf

Nefarious

McGraw-Hill's Top 50 Skills for a Top Score: SAT Critical Reading and Writing by Brian Leaf

Enigmatic

McGraw-Hill's Top 50 Skills for a Top Score: SAT Critical Reading and Writing by Brian Leaf

Solvent

McGraw-Hill's Top 50 Skills for a Top Score: SAT Critical Reading and Writing by Brian Leaf

Panache

McGraw-Hill's Top 50 Skills for a Top Score: SAT Critical Reading and Writing by Brian Leaf

Inimitability

McGraw-Hill's Top 50 Skills for a Top Score: SAT Critical Reading and Writing by Brian Leaf

Élan

McGraw-Hill's Top 50 Skills for a Top Score: SAT Critical Reading and Writing by Brian Leaf

Austere

McGraw-Hill's Top 50 Skills for a Top Score: SAT Critical Reading and Writing by Brian Leaf

Spartan

McGraw-Hill's Top 50 Skills for a Top Score: SAT Critical Reading and Writing by Brian Leaf

Ascetic

McGraw-Hill's Top 50 Skills for a Top Score: SAT Critical Reading and Writing by Brian Leaf

Wan

McGraw-Hill's Top 50 Skills for a Top Score: SAT Critical Reading and Writing by Brian Leaf

(adj.) changing	(v.) walk	(adj.) restrained
(adj.) evil	(adj.) serious	(adj.) fanciful or capricious
(n.) flair, style	(adj.) having enough money	(adj.) mysterious
(adj.) harsh	(n.) style	(n.) unique style
(adj.) pale	(adj.) harsh	(adv.) frugal

Solemn

McGraw-Hill's Top 50 Skills for a Top Score: SAT Critical Reading and Writing by Brian Leaf

Stoicism

McGraw-Hill's Top 50 Skills for a Top Score: SAT Critical Reading and Writing by Brian Leaf

Ambivalence

McGraw-Hill's Top 50 Skills for a Top Score: SAT Critical Reading and Writing by Brian Leaf

Qualified

McGraw-Hill's Top 50 Skills for a Top Score: SAT Critical Reading and Writing by Brian Leaf

Lackluster

McGraw-Hill's Top 50 Skills for a Top Score: SAT Critical Reading and Writing by Brian Leaf

Undermine

McGraw-Hill's Top 50 Skills for a Top Score: SAT Critical Reading and Writing by Brian Leaf

Assent

McGraw-Hill's Top 50 Skills for a Top Score: SAT Critical Reading and Writing by Brian Leaf

Comply

McGraw-Hill's Top 50 Skills for a Top Score: SAT Critical Reading and Writing by Brian Leaf

Beseech

McGraw-Hill's Top 50 Skills for a Top Score: SAT Critical Reading and Writing by Brian Leaf

Convoluted

McGraw-Hill's Top 50 Skills for a Top Score: SAT Critical Reading and Writing by Brian Leaf

Devious

McGraw-Hill's Top 50 Skills for a Top Score: SAT Critical Reading and Writing by Brian Leaf

Decry

McGraw-Hill's Top 50 Skills for a Top Score: SAT Critical Reading and Writing by Brian Leaf

Eulogy

McGraw-Hill's Top 50 Skills for a Top Score: SAT Critical Reading and Writing by Brian Leaf

Lithe

McGraw-Hill's Top 50 Skills for a Top Score: SAT Critical Reading and Writing by Brian Leaf

Ineffable

McGraw-Hill's Top 50 Skills for a Top Score: SAT Critical Reading and Writing by Brian Leaf

(n.) uncertainness	(n.) endurance of hardship without complaint	(adj.) somber or serious
(v.) to damage or weaken	(adj.) lacking in force	(adj.) made less
(v.) to beg	(v.) obey	(n.) agreement
(v.) criticize, condemn	(n.) deceitful	(adj.) complicated, complex
(adj.) too great to describe	(adj.) supple	(n.) a speech or piece of writing that praises